# German Catholics and Hitler's Wars

# German Catholics and Hitler's Wars

*A STUDY IN SOCIAL CONTROL*

## by Gordon C. Zahn

SHEED AND WARD - NEW YORK

# Contents

vi    Contents

**PART 3**

# German Catholics and Hitler's Wars

**Part 1**

# History and Methodology of the Study

WHEN THE WRITER left for Germany it was his intention to discover, if possible, what had happened to the German Catholic peace movement and its participants during the years of Nazi domination and, of course, during World War II. Such a movement had been formed shortly after the conclusion of the First World War and by the time Hitler came to power had achieved a remarkable degree of strength and standing. Under the leadership of the *Friedensbund deutscher Katholiken* (German Catholic Peace Union) and its principal founder and theorist, Franziskus Stratmann, O.P., the movement's impact led Catholics in other nations as well to begin giving new and serious consideration to the pacifist implications of their Faith. True, the German movement was not the sole source of such interest and concern; the horrors of World War I and its aftermath of almost complete disillusionment had inspired many similar movements, non-Catholic as well as Catholic, in other European nations. But few could claim the membership attained by the *Friedensbund* or the "official" tone given to it by its participation in the annual *Katholikentag* gatherings.

In a letter to the writer, Father Stratmann recalled that the *Friedensbund* had 40,000 members at one point in its history. This figure approximates the 41,000 quoted in the 1932 volume of a liberal Catholic periodical, *vom frohen Leben*. Both estimates included as "corporate members" the membership of Kolping Society groups which had affiliated with the *Friedensbund*.*

Of greater importance than its actual membership totals is the standing of the movement as reflected in the official encouragement and support it received from prominent members of the German Catholic hierarchy. Here, too, exact figures are not available; but one informant claimed that thirteen bishops were active members of the *Friedensbund* or had associated themselves with its program. A Berlin pastor, another of the organization's founders, named Cardinals Bertram (Breslau) and Faulhaber (Munich) and Bishops Schreiber (Berlin) and Sproll (Rottenburg) as prominent patrons. The writer's own research added Bishop Gröber (then of Meissen) to his list and sample.

The existence of so strong and respected a Catholic peace movement led to the formulation of the original research problem, which can be expressed in two questions: Was it possible for the movement to continue its work for peace after Hitler came to power? Was it, or were its adherents, able to keep alive any remnant of its pacifist and war-resisting activities once Nazi Germany embarked upon its military adventures?

As was expected, both questions were answered in the negative. But the negative was so complete and so immediately accomplished that it was obviously quite pointless to continue the type of research inquiry originally planned. In point of fact, the *Friedensbund* earned the distinction of being one of the very first organizations singled out to suffer the full brunt of Nazi oppression.** Several of

* It is interesting to note that the journal of the Kolping Society reported as early as 1940 that one third of its readers were under arms and that 32 members of the Society had already lost their lives in battle. (*Münchener Katholische Kirchenzeitung*, Jan. 14, 1940, p. 8.)

** Even after its suppression, the Catholic peace movement remained on the list of recognized enemies of the Third Reich. Applicants for government jobs were required to sign statements certifying nonmembership in Masonic lodges, organizations similar to such lodges, or membership in *ersatz* organizations like the *Schlaraffia* or the *Friedensbund deutscher Kath-*

the former *Friedensbund* leaders furnished the writer with the story of the dramatic events of those days. The organization was officially dissolved by the Nazis on July 1, 1933, and one informant described how 36 men suddenly descended upon the Frankfurt central office of the *Friedensbund* and carried off great packing cases filled with records and other materials. Another informant told of a frantic afternoon spent in burning all possibly incriminating *Friedensbund* literature and letters in his possession. Several of the leaders were arrested and later subjected to showcase trials (on charges of profiteering in international currency transactions, a favorite charge employed by the Nazis against the Catholic Church and its affiliated organizations). Many, including its cofounder and spiritual leader, Father Stratmann, spent part or all of the Nazi war years in exile or in hiding. At any rate, with its leadership scattered or imprisoned, its records confiscated or destroyed, the movement disappeared leaving no traces other than those recorded in the memories of individuals who had been associated with it. Yet the very fact of its total disappearance raised the new and even more challenging sociological problem: How could a movement be so strong and boast of such extensive and respected support one year, only to be effectively annihilated the next? Still more, how can we explain the fact that its dedicated opposition to war on grounds of Christian morality could be so completely stilled that even its leaders were unable to report any definite instances known to them of members openly refusing to serve in Hitler's wars of aggression?

Ideally, of course, this new problem should have been limited to those individuals who had formally associated themselves with the Catholic peace movement; but the destruction of all membership records (not to mention the technical impossibility of interviewing a sufficient sample of such members had the records been available) eliminated this as a research approach. It was necessary, therefore, to broaden the scope of analysis in order to consider the

---

*oliken!* The fact that this organization was considered worthy of being one of the two specifically named "subversive" groups may be taken as a tribute to its energetic work for peace in the pre-Hitler years.

behavior of German Catholics in general and the evidence that their almost total conformity to the war demands of the Nazi regime gave of an effectively operating system of social controls, and of the selection between the competing values of Catholicism and Nazism. And, although the value-selection dimension loses some of its clarity in the more general application to the Catholic population, it assumes heightened significance when the traditional Catholic teachings concerning the "just war" are considered in the specific context of the wars initiated by the Third Reich.

At this point it is advisable to describe some of the methodological procedures employed and the problems encountered in this study so that the reader may make his own evaluation of the sources used and the manner in which they were used.

In the original phase of the research project—that is, while the post-1933 history of the Catholic peace movement was still the contemplated focus of study—the approach to the problem depended mainly upon interviews with individuals who had been associated with the *Friedensbund deutscher Katholiken* or who were likely to possess some significant information concerning that organization, its membership, and its activities. In all, approximately one hundred persons in various parts of West Germany (including Berlin) were interviewed, and these included pacifists and nonpacifists from many walks of life—government officials and political leaders; professors and research scientists; bishops, theologians, and pastors; journalists, editors and publishers; social workers and many others. The interview usually took the form of a social visit preceded by a written request in which the purpose of the study was outlined in most general terms. The social aspect of the visit was achieved at the expense of surrendering any attempt to structure the interview, although a few set questions touching upon the extent of support a would-be Catholic conscientious objector to military service in the German army might have expected from his spiritual leaders and fellow communicants were included along with specific requests for the names and other information concerning Catholics who might actually have taken such a stand.

For the most part, however, the principal purpose behind even such set questions was to provide an initial area of discussion upon which the informant could then focus his personal reminiscences and projections.*

The selection of people to be interviewed was based, for the most part, upon direct requests for suggestions and the probing of leads presented in the course of the earlier interviews. American friends who had had some previous familiarity with the movement had furnished the researcher with a preliminary list of former *Friedensbund* members and officials, and the selection of informants spread out from this central core. An illustration of how this worked in actual practice is offered by one of the most profitable interview-sequences to develop during the months of research. The first informant, a former *Friedensbund* official, gave the researcher the name and address of Josef Fleischer, the only known conscientious objector to survive the war, as well as some of this man's published writings. One of Fleischer's articles contained charges that a high-ranking official of the Catholic chaplains' corps of the new German army had attempted to force him to drop his refusal to serve in the military forces of the Third Reich. These charges prompted the researcher to visit and interview the priest in question who, after categorically denying the charges, suggested that another priest in a nearby town would be a valuable informant because he had been the prison chaplain who had personally attended two Austrian Catholics before their execution for refusing to serve in the German army during the war. Actually, this officer of the *Friedensbund* furnished information and suggestions which opened the way for seven subsequent interviews leading to highly important

* For obvious reasons—including the social nature of the visit, the informality of the questioning and discussion, and the range and frankness of some of the opinions and evaluations expressed by the informants—the writer will refrain from identifying his informants lest they be subjected to some embarrassment by the potentially controversial character of some of his findings. Some oblique identification has been introduced where it promises to have a direct bearing upon the significance of the material treated; but, here too, a sincere attempt has been made to protect the anonymity of the informant.

information about three men (none of whom, incidentally, had been *Friedensbund* members) who had been conscientious objectors.

Such a pattern of accidental sampling leaves much to be desired; on the other hand, given the nature of the research problem, it is doubtful if any other sampling technique was possible. Every interview conducted in this admittedly insufficiently controlled fashion did provide some valuable and significant insights bearing upon the two dimensions mentioned above. Though the writer frankly admits that the unsystematic manner of selection and the unstructured form of the interview itself preclude any claim of random representativeness or statistical significance, he would insist that the insights gained from the admittedly impressionistic quality of the responses and the understanding of the situation such impressions offer the sensitive hearer and reader are more than sufficient justification for the research project.

In a sense, the standards and measurements more suited to the advocate of pure empiricism in sociological research are excluded by the very nature of the topic chosen. The story of any form of opposition to the Nazi Third Reich must necessarily be a construct of just such "scientifically inadequate" material as described above. This may even apply, more than is generally recognized, to other aspects of German history of the period covered here. Official documentation is not often complete and it is much too often unreliable —a result in part of the loss of records through the war's devastation, in part of intentional destruction by the last custodians of the Nazi state, and in part of the fact that many actions of crucial significance were undertaken in unrecorded secrecy or camouflaged by the responsible officials. The same considerations apply with even greater force to the representatives of what has been called "the other Germany"; anyone who would oppose either the Hitler regime or World War II found it necessary to operate in strictest secrecy and with a minimum of potentially incriminating records. This means that the social historian or sociologist who wishes to study this critical aspect of life under Hitler, and hopes to do so on the firm basis of a systematic analysis of empirical data and contemporary documentation, is doomed to much disappointment. The principal source of information for any such study is to be found in the usually inconsistent and often conflicting personal recollections of the individuals who lived through those trying years—distorted as those recollections undoubtedly are by such psychological states as emotional involvement in a time of terror, wishful reconstruction and unconscious selection of facts to suit the informant's ego needs, or nothing more sinister than the passage of time and the fallibility of human memory in its efforts to reach back across the span of a quarter century. The social scientist in particular can never be fully satisfied by such data; he will always be teased by the intriguing, but unanswerable, question of how these same events might have been "remembered" by his informants had they been looking back upon a German victory instead of the total defeat of the Third Reich.

As the interviews progressed, however, one significant note did recur with remarkable consistency. This was the flat assurance voiced by almost every informant that any Catholic who decided to refuse military service would have received no support whatsoever from his spiritual leaders. Of informants who were in favor of or who were sympathetic toward the peace movement, some tended to state this opinion in a tone of disappointment or even bitter disillusionment, while others accused these religious leaders of having failed in their responsibility. Informants not so emotionally involved usually coupled these opinions with the explanation that prudence demanded such a course, since any purported conscientious objector might, in reality, prove to be a Gestapo agent seeking to trap the unwary priest or bishop into a punishable act of "treason" or "defeatism" and thereby open the way to new assaults upon the Catholic Church in Germany.

It was just such a trick which did lead to the arrest and ultimately to the execution of Father Metzger (see below, pp. 55 n., 134 ff.). A Gestapo agent won his confidence and promised to deliver Metzger's personal appeal for moderate peace terms, following the anticipated defeat of Germany, to the Scandinavian prelate for whom it had been intended. Several of the priest-informants stressed the fact that not even the confessional was safe in this respect: Gestapo spies, they reminded me, might have appealed for counsel relative to anti-Nazi feelings or activities, or possible opposition to the war effort, only to arrest the confessor were he to give even the slightest indication of sympathy for such sentiments.

So broad an area of agreement—and on an issue so crucial to the research problem—led the researcher to seek more specific validation. An effort was made to locate and check whatever published sources might be available to serve as a documentary record of the official stand taken by the Church with regard to Germany's involvement in World War II. Such a source was found in the Catholic periodicals of general circulation and in official diocesan journals containing the texts of episcopal statements and pastoral letters. Once again, however, the survey of Catholic periodicals was necessarily somewhat incomplete, since it depended upon the availability of such materials in university, or, occasionally, chancery libraries. Some of the collections were incomplete, lacking occasional issues or even whole volumes. The absence of individual issues was frequently explained as the result of official suppression; the missing volumes, more often, as the result of destruction through aerial bombardment.

In working with the publications which did come into his hands, the researcher did not attempt any detailed analysis of the total contents. Only statements bearing directly upon the issue of support for the war were recorded, and, again, no effort was made to apply the quantitative or proportional measurement techniques used for more systematic content analysis. This reflects a methodological value judgment on the writer's part which holds that *any* statement by a Catholic spokesman in support of the German war effort (and this is especially true if that spokesman were a bishop)* constituted in itself significant evidence in deciding whether there was in fact a

---

* A discussion of this point is to be found in the writer's article, "The German Catholic Press and Hitler's Wars," *Cross Currents,* Vol. X, No. 4 (Fall 1960), pp. 337-51.

Church-mediated social control operating to induce the individual German Catholic to conform to the nation's demands. In any event, every such statement is to be viewed as at least a partial explanation of why German Catholics found it possible to give their support to Hitler's wars. In examining the material found in the publications, a sharp eye was maintained for any content which would have encouraged or even supported a refusal to help in waging the war. No such content was encountered—a fact which testifies to the validity of the judgment expressed by the writer's informants.

One thing more should be said lest this summary of the methodology employed in this study seem to strike too apologetic a note. Occasionally one encounters problems in social science which require a level of methodological improvisation not entirely suited to the neat formulations and procedures available to more carefully circumscribed areas of research. The only alternative to such improvisation is the abandonment of the attempt to analyze or understand the problem itself. The nature of Hitler's wars and the extent of the support they received from German Catholics is such a problem. This problem and its implications are much too serious and far-reaching to justify its abandonment under any circumstances.

# CHAPTER 2

# The Social-Control Dimension

THE SOCIOLOGIST must always be prepared to encounter some resistance when he begins to talk in terms of a "social-control" dimension to human behavior. There is a tendency to regard such a concept as somehow deflating or demeaning human dignity by making man a less "free" or "deliberate" or "responsible" being. But one need not deny that man is a free being, that he has the power to deliberate and to make responsible decisions concerning alternative possibilities of action—or choose not to act at all—if we nevertheless recognize that the decision he does make will involve a rational assessment of the total situation and thereby reflect the direct and indirect social pressures to which he is subjected as a member of society. The everyday experience of each of us offers evidence enough. Many a time we do something we would prefer not doing, or avoid doing something we should like to do, simply in response to social controls.

Our problem here is to identify and describe the means that were employed to influence and direct the individual German Catholic. Most immediately obvious, of course, are the formal controls exercised by the totalitarian regime; and here much of the work has already been done, there being a wealth of literature available describing the laws, edicts, and administrative directives which were used to control the behavior of the German citizen (or, failing this, to populate the prisons and concentration camps of the Third Reich). Thus, full compliance with the laws and directives aimed at waging the war and bringing it to a successful conclusion was a universal requirement in Nazi Germany. Refusal to comply—or even failure to show sufficient enthusiasm—carried the severest of sanctions, culminating in the death penalty. The fact that one Catholic who did openly refuse to serve in what he believed to be an unjust war did escape the executioner's axe certainly does not disprove the general effectiveness of these social controls.

The informal social controls were similarly mobilized to induce full participation in all phases of the war and may well have been even more effective an influence upon the individual's behavior. In times of national emergency, the full force of public opinion is employed to reward the man who does his part (or, preferably, even more than his part) and to punish the man who would seek to evade or refuse to bear what is socially defined as his share of the common burdens. The man who would have refused to take part in Nazi Germany's military undertakings not only risked certain death but also knew that, except for those nearest and dearest to him (and often enough even this exception might not hold), such a death would earn him only public dishonor and disgrace in the eyes of all who chanced to take note of it. The former *Friedensbund* official already referred to[1] stressed the point that men who might otherwise have made such a refusal to serve were deterred by the knowledge that the true grounds for the execution might never be known, that they would most probably be tried, convicted, and executed under some general charge of "treason" or "defeatism"—or, worse still, under a fabricated charge of homosexuality or some similar morals offense. The utter hopelessness of the situation, the complete inability to make one's protest known, accounted in great part, he felt, for the collapse of the German peace movement and the total absence of any effective pacifist opposition to Hitler's wars. His analysis is extremely pertinent, but one may go beyond it. For even if the actual grounds for the execution *were* made known, the man who refused to do his "duty" would have still been viewed as an object of public scorn and disapproval.*

The unwillingness to suffer a *shame* that would live on after one's death, or the emotional state of *despair* arising from a sense of the utter hopelessness of making an effective individual stand against the totally mobilized Nazi state, shows the operation of internal controls. Other psychological states acting as internal controls would include *fear* (for oneself or for those dependent upon oneself, or both), *anger* (provoked by the enemy air raids against Germany or the enemy's insistence upon unconditional surrender), *pride* (in the past greatness of Germany and her military accomplishments) together with some *resentment* arising from the memory of defeat and its consequences. Involved in the latter three are what might be termed "the myths men kill by." In this context the word "myth" is not used in the customary literary sense but rather in the sociological sense; as employed by MacIver, it refers to "the value-impregnated beliefs and notions that men hold, that they live by or for."[2] Among such myths would be included the following: *Volk, Vaterland, Heimat, Heldentod,* and a great number of other terms, the mere mention of which would provoke an emotional response in the individual. These myths form major components of the total complex of patriotic and nationalistic values underlying the commitment to the war which will be discussed in Chapter 3 in connection with the value-selection frame of reference. Here it is enough to note that they would constitute powerful internal controls upon the individual for whom they held such value-impregnated meaning.

The major function of the external controls is to trigger the internal controls into effective operation. For this purpose all the media of communication, education, and entertainment are put to the service of the war-making authority. There is, therefore, no

* In a letter to the writer, the widow of Franz Jägerstätter, the Austrian peasant executed for conscientious objection to military service (see below, p. 78 n.), wrote that many of the people living in the rural village from which he came still resented the fact that her husband had not been a soldier. It is significant that this attitude persists in an *Austrian,* not German, village almost twenty years after his execution as a conscientious objector to Hitler's wars.

doubt that the Nazi rulers were able to exploit their highly organized and thoroughly effective propaganda machine in such a way as to surround the German citizen with constant and inescapable reminders of the part he had to play in the war. The posters, the massed flags, the military songs and parades—even so effective a touch as Hitler's melodramatic appearance in his old army coat and his vow not to cease wearing it until the war was won—in short, every mechanism and appeal suited to the task were brought to bear upon the German citizen in such a way that they were certain to stimulate the intended patterns of response which he would then experience as the manifestation of an inner imperative.

Before proceeding further, it must be stated that this whole complex of social controls has a much more general application. War could not be successfully waged in the modern world, either by a democratic or a totalitarian regime, unless the full range of social controls was utilized to insure the most effective and extensive support for the war. Americans, too, can look back upon the pressures and appeals to which they were subjected during the war years. Formal legislation and official government programs demanded various degrees of active participation and punished those who failed to comply or sought to interfere with the compliance of others. Even the recognition given in the Selective Service Act of 1940 to the draft-eligible man with conscientious objections to military service was accompanied by the manifest injustice of penalizing those who chose to exercise their rights under that provision by requiring them to do "work of national importance" without compensation for such alternative service. On the level of the informal controls, voluntary community activities welded the forces of public opinion into one vast we're-all-in-this-thing-together mentality so that the man who was not in uniform or the housewife who did not contribute her tin cans and waste fats to the war effort was made to feel out of step with neighbors and associates. The internal controls of nationalistic pride and patriotic sentiments were stirred by the challenge to "Remember Pearl Harbor" as a "day of infamy" and by the boast that "we did it before and we can do it again." And Americans, like their German coun-

terparts, were always and everywhere surrounded by external reminders of the war and their duty, whether these reminders took
the form of the playing of the national anthem before every concert
and sports event, the billboard which told the selfish motorist that
there was "a Jap in every empty seat," or the flag hanging in the
front window of almost every house, its blue or gold stars at once
a proud boast for the householder and a challenge to the observer.
The present study focuses its attention upon the social controls
which produced conformity to the demands of the Hitler war effort
in Germany, but the same analytical framework could be employed
with respect to American participation in World War II and to that
of all the nations involved in that conflict.

But the controls were more efficiently organized in the totalitarian state. Certainly, with its unlimited recourse to terror and reprisal, the formal social controls and their supporting elements
were more extensive than could be true in non-totalitarian settings.
Imperfect though the American conscription program might have
been, it did make some legal provision for conscientious objection,
in contrast to the practice of making it a capital crime as was the
case in Nazi Germany. The informal controls, too, may have had
greater effectiveness in the totalitarian setting than they could have
attained in a nation which allowed some room, however slight, for
legal opposition to the government and its war-making policies.
By the same token, the military history and traditions incorporated
into and supporting the myths and emotions constituting the principal internal controls may have boasted an intensity greater for
the German than for some of his opponents. For example, the
American culture does indeed give special reverence to its soldier
dead; but one rarely, if ever, encounters anything resembling the
virtually unquestioned assumption that the German youth who puts
on the soldier's uniform marches off to battle in a kind of consecration to a hero's death—a note that will be encountered repeatedly
throughout the statements examined in this study. And, finally,
with its complete control over all communication and propaganda
agencies, the totalitarian state was the more successful in organiz-

ing and manipulating the external social controls over the behavior of the individual citizen.

But the German *Catholic* citizen was a member of two great societies, the Nazi Third Reich and the Roman Catholic Church, each having its own system of values and its own set of social controls to induce its members to behave according to the patterns set by those values. So far we have been concerned with social controls influencing all German citizens, whether Catholic or not. We must now consider the pattern of behavior encouraged or required under the controls operated by the religious community.

In briefest statement, the pattern was the same as that encouraged and required by the secular community. The similarity may be traced to certain elements of the Catholic value system which will be dealt with shortly. Suffice it to say, however, that these values have the effect of prejudicing the issue in favor of the secular authority, making it almost inevitable that the Church will find itself reinforcing and augmenting the controls of the secular ruler. And thus it did happen that the German Catholic who looked to his religious superiors for spiritual guidance and direction regarding service in Hitler's wars received virtually the same answers he would have received from the Nazi ruler himself.

In terms of formal social controls operating within the religious community, the official statements of his bishops placed him under a moral obligation to fulfill faithfully whatever duties might be required of him. No support of any consequence would have been furnished him had he refused to serve. Indeed, there were at least two instances in which men awaiting execution for such refusal were actually denied access to the sacraments for a time because the prison chaplain interpreted their action as a violation of their Christian duty.*

* Kreuzberg reports that Father Reinisch (see note on p. 55 n. below) was denied Holy Communion by the priest whom he, Kreuzberg, succeeded as chaplain at the Tegel prison. He points out that the chaplain had intended to limit this denial to his first visit (though it was not revoked until Kreuzberg assumed his duties) and that he did this to make the prisoner fully aware of what the chaplain considered his Christian duty to take the mili-

The contents of the Catholic diocesan press, to the extent that it was still in existence, clearly reflect the informal controls operating in support of the war effort within the Catholic community. Letters from soldiers at the front or bereaved mothers were published frequently as models of inspiration to assure the home-front unity of the parish and its members with the nation's cause. Men in service were honored in the parishes and community prayer meetings were scheduled in their behalf. Catholics were encouraged *as Catholics* to participate in the various collections organized to meet the emergency needs of the war economy and to take special pride in the patriotism and loyalty demonstrated by the religious community in these contributions and sacrifices.

The influence of the internal controls has already been anticipated in the statement that faithful performance of duty was made a *moral obligation,* certainly the most powerful internal control that could be brought to bear upon the behavior of a member of the religious community. The external controls—the special prayers and prayer services, the parish honor rolls, the patriotic jingles in the diocesan papers, and so on—assumed significance, not only in terms of the additional stimuli for war-supporting action they presented, but, more importantly perhaps, to the extent that they could invest these actions with the halo of moral righteousness.

---

tary oath of allegiance to Hitler. Cf. Heinrich Kreuzberg, *Franz Reinisch: Ein Martyrer unserer Zeit* (Limburg: Lahn Verlag, 1953), p. 86.

Similarly, in the course of an interview with a member of the *Christ-königsgesellschaft,* he reported that Brother Maurus of that community had also been told by his prison chaplain that the stand he had taken against the war was completely contrary to the teachings of the Church. He, too, was then denied the sacraments until just before he went to his execution.

*NOTES*

1. See above, p. 7.

2. Robert M. MacIver, *The Web of Government* (New York: Macmillan, 1947), p. 4.

# CHAPTER 3

# The Value-Selection Dimension

THE IDENTIFICATION of a value-selection dimension to the specific behavior under study implies that the individual was confronted by, or committed to, two or more systems of values which carried with them conflicting behavioral consequences. Certainly one such set of values—and one which will have but peripheral or contributory significance in the present context—is that which centers upon personal well-being and physical survival. Both the secular or national value system, with its emphasis upon a willingness to sacrifice one's life for the good of the political community, and the spiritual value system, which would call for a similar sacrifice if the only alternative were sin, would go counter to the personal-survival value which would incline the individual toward an avoidance of danger and preservation of his life in any way possible.

But we are concerned with competition between the value systems affecting the individual as a citizen of the political community and as a communicant of the Roman Catholic Church. Each of these institutions imposes or demands his active and wholehearted identification with its immediate interests. Of course, in the Good Society of the philosopher in which "right order" obtains, one would expect to encounter no difficulty in reconciling the demands of Church and State. When we turn to the real world and actual historical situations, unfortunately the individual often, if not usually, finds himself forced to resolve a conflict between his political and religious identities and their associated roles. And to the extent that one or the other community is, or fancies itself to be, facing a crisis, the demands will become more insistent, the controls more binding, and the sanctions more severe.

This was certainly the case for the Catholic citizen of Nazi Germany during World War II. The secular rulers had determined that military action had become necessary and unavoidable if their goals were to be achieved, and they had brought the full weight of their total authority to the support of this decision. In their eyes, every citizen, regardless of his station in life, was immediately obliged to make whatever contribution to the war effort they might demand. Any question of justice, if it occurred to them at all, was easily settled in terms of the nation's needs and objectives as interpreted by the secular rulers. No provision was made for releasing an individual citizen from his defined duty on grounds of conscientious objection simply because no right was granted him or anyone else to judge or even call into question the decisions made by Hitler and his subordinates.

The value-selection dimension, then, can be summarized as follows. On the one hand, the state claimed sole competence to determine and judge its own actions and objectives, holding that the individual citizen had no alternative but to render loyal and obedient service even to the point of offering his life in battle. In opposition to this, the Church in its "just war/unjust war" distinction[1] at least *implied* a right and duty, first, to evaluate these actions and objectives according to a rather specific formulation of moral conditions, and, second, to refuse to serve in any war which did not meet these conditions. The heart of the whole selection problem lay in the fact that both state and Church claimed ultimate jurisdiction over the individual's behavior. In Nazi ideology, the state held final and absolute rights which the citizen had to respect regardless of how they might conflict with other personal or institutional values. The moral teachings of the Church, however, would resolve such conflicts in terms of the principle which has earned so many of her followers the martyr's reward: It is better to serve God than man.

In the light of this basic difference in its more general application, the more specific content of the secular and religious value systems as they relate to military service and conscientious objection must be considered. The underlying and uniting rationale of the secular system stresses the dependence of the individual citizen upon the civil order and the corollary that he must, therefore, be prepared at all times to contribute whatever may be necessary for the preservation of that order and to do so in a spirit of loyal dedication and patriotic resolve. This rationale gives rise to and is maintained by the complex of myths referred to briefly in connection with the discussion of internal social controls. Every secular value system embraces its own set of these myths which it invests with a kind of "sacredness"; for the German, the most sacred of all are those designated by the terms *Volk, Vaterland,* and *Heimat.*

All three defy any attempt at adequate translation. *Vaterland* is closest in meaning to its English counterpart, "fatherland"; but the linguistic equivalence is weakened by underlying differences in the status and role of the father in the German and American families. To the degree that the German conception of the father/child relationship involves a greater measure of arbitrary authority exercised by the former and a more binding sense of unquestioning and submissive obedience on the part of the latter,* it is clear that the

* Lewin offers support for this interpretation in the following passage: "To the one who comes from Germany, the degree of freedom and independence of children and adolescents in the United States is very impressive. Especially the lack of servility of the young child towards adults or of the student to the professor is striking. The adults, too, treat the child much more on an equal footing, whereas in Germany it seems to be the natural right of the adult to rule and the duty of the child to obey. The natural relation of adult and child is in the United States not considered that of a superior *(Herr)* to a subordinate *(Untergebener)* but that of two individuals with the same right in principle. . . . They [the American parents] will let the child feel that he is doing them a favor in a situation in which the German parent is much more likely to give short orders. . . ." Kurt Lewin, *Resolving Social Conflicts* (New York: Harper & Bros., 1948), pp. 6-7.

relationship between the citizen (i.e., the "child") and the "father"-land will carry the same overtones. This is borne out by the frequent use of the term *Untertan* (subject, underling) in designating the status of the citizen and the same term in its adjectival form to describe the role of the citizen. Some writers have gone so far as to suggest that this note of rigid subordination has become something of a "principle"* governing the German approach to political (and social) relationships and responsibilities. This somewhat sardonic bit of humor had its real and deadly serious parallel in the *Führer Prinzip* (leadership principle), upon which Hitler's New Order was to be based. The frightful extent to which this principle did win acceptance and the results it produced in the pyramiding of authority until full power rested in the hands of a *Führer* who then assumed the role of the all-competent, all-deciding "father" and disciplinarian for the entire nation—these are indelibly recorded in some of the most tragic pages of human history.

*Volk* presents a far more difficult challenge to the translator. None of the English terms usually employed, such as "people," "folk," "nationality," and so on, carries with it the essential note of blood unity and common destiny suggested by the German word. They have nothing of that distinctly mystical quality which infuses this particular myth with a compelling force reaching far beyond any mere reference to a large and territorially identifiable category of human beings. The *Volk* is much more than a category or a national classification; it is an organism, a kind of "mystical body" in the secular order. For a full-dimensional presentation of this myth, one need only turn to Hitler's own description of the *Volksstaat* in *Mein Kampf*. If, however, such a source would seem to prejudice the thesis to be developed here, it would do just as well to refer to Archbishop Gröber's formulation[2] or to Military Bishop Rarkowski's grateful acknowledgment that Hitler had restored this term (and other related myths) to its proper place in the German hierarchy of values.[3]

---

* The so-called *"Fahrrad"* (bicycle) *Prinzip: oben bücken, unten treten* (bow to those above; tread upon those below).

The third crucial myth is that of the *Heimat,* and this is the most difficult of all to explain. The usual English translations are "homeland" or "native province," but, again, these words offer no real equivalence of meaning. If anything, there is an even deeper mystique to the *Heimat* than that noted for *Volk.* The same dominant note of a blood tie, a sacred unity of past and future generations with that of the present, is stressed; but *Heimat* refers to a much more specific and often quite restricted locality where the *Blut und Boden* work together to produce distinctive regional character types and customs—in some instances, this applies even to separate villages, hills, and valleys within the same region. Perhaps the sociologist's concept of the "habitat" represents the best approximation of this myth-concept; and, if so, it would be no accident that this term is most frequently encountered in those areas of study relating to human ecology, with its strong dependence upon the biological sciences. But even "habitat," with all of its implications of an intimate and symbiotic relationship between man and land over the generations, catches none of the emotional fervor which is so much and so essential a part of *Heimat* as myth. No eyes would mist over references to the lakes and meadows and the sounds and sights of one's habitat; nor would so cold a term be adequate to describe the great body of traditions and associated imagery that keeps the sense and memory of the *Heimat* and its ties forever alive.*

From the critical core of the values represented by the *Volk-Vaterland-Heimat* myths there arises a set of secondary, or derived,

* The hypothesis might be advanced that the absence of a comparable awareness of such a mystical unity of blood and region in American culture may be explained by the greater mobility and proverbial rootlessness of the American. Certainly we have no true parallel to the *Heimat* film, which has tremendous popularity in Germany. In these movies simple villagers in traditional costume pursue their quiet lives while the camera pauses lovingly to record the comic doings of wild animals, the flight of birds in craggy mountain settings, and so on. Nor does one find here a special category of *Heimat* songs intended to stir the soul and evoke tears of pride and longing in the one who has been separated from the *Heimat.* Perhaps the closest approximations furnished by American culture are the plantation-and-pickaninny Old South, the romantic lore of the Frontier West, and the exaggerated provincialism of the professional Texan.

values which have a more immediate relevance to the behavior of the individual citizen. Among values of this kind are such attitudes as the willingness to sacrifice personal well-being for the greater good of the whole community (*Opferbereitschaft*), a dedicated sense of loyalty (*Treue*) owed to that community and its rulers, a readiness to obey those rulers and whatever commands they may issue (*Gehorsam*) as a binding duty (*Pflicht*), the performance of which involved and enhanced one's personal honor (*Ehre*). These values, let it be said at once, are in no sense specific to the German culture patterns alone; indeed, they have universal application in the sense that every national community regards these expected attitudes and actions as values that must be inculcated in all of its members. If in the German setting they appear to be more highly romanticized, this is undoubtedly another reflection of the qualitative difference noted in the discussion of the central myths.

All of these good-citizenship values take on much greater intensity when they are converted into the soldierly virtues applying to men called into military service. They are still the same values of self-sacrifice, loyalty, obedience, duty, and honor; but the soldier's sacrifice is always set in terms of blood and the loss of life itself, his obedience is expected to be unquestioning in nature and unlimited in scope, and the preservation of his (and the nation's) honor in the loyal performance of duty becomes his very *raison d'être*. This elevation of the customary civic virtues into something hallowed is, again, not to be viewed as something peculiar to the German culture. Nevertheless, it is quite proper to suggest that there may be a difference in degree arising from a more rigorous commitment to traditions associated with the "Prussian" heritage from Germany's Bismarckian and Wilhelmian past. All nations hallow the profession of arms, but not all do so with the enthusiasm shown by the Germans (and, among others, the French).

The popular stereotype of the American soldier, for instance, is that of the "good Joe" who makes the best of an unwanted situation; who certainly is not interested in developing a professional attitude toward his task but, instead, is out "to beat the system" as long and as completely as he can get away with doing so; who, if he does decide "to stick his neck out," does so not for the glory of it all but only because he suddenly encounters something that has to be done and he is there to do it. At present it is only in the officer formed in the West Point tradition that we find anything similar to the German *Ehrentod* (death with honor) and *Heldentod* (hero death) concepts. It is, perhaps, an oversimplification to take these differences at their face value; nevertheless, the tone of the battle-front letters written by German soldiers clearly reveals a definite commitment of a very personal nature to these ideals and values. It should be noted that these suggested differences in degree are offered more as observations than as conclusions, although they are based in large part upon the interviews and documentation which form the basis of the present study.

So much, then, for the value system presented and upheld by the secular community. Let us turn now to the value system presented and upheld by the religious community of the Roman Catholic Church as that system relates to the same areas of human behavior.

While it is true that there has always been what might be described as a pacifist tradition in the Roman Catholic Church reaching back to the earliest days of its existence, this has usually been a minority tradition—most certainly so since the granting of toleration to Christianity under Constantine. To speak, then, of a conflict between secular and religious value systems forcing an act of selection on the part of the individual who is both the citizen of a state and communicant in the Church does not imply, in the present instance at least, that the lines of division are clearly drawn in some formally defined dogmatic formula. For, unlike the so-called "peace churches"—the Society of Friends (Quakers), the Mennonites, and so on—the Catholic Church in its traditional moral teachings concerning war makes a distinction between the "just war" in which its members' participation is permitted or, under some interpretations, required, and the "unjust war" in which participation would be forbidden under pain of sin.

However much this teaching of the just war complicates the

issue, a real problem of value selection remains. For the individual must now concern himself, not with the permissibility of supporting war in general, but with the much more involved question of whether the particular war in which he is ordered to serve is just or unjust. A summary presentation of the conditions which must prevail for a war to be just will be reserved for later in this chapter. At this point, the rationale of the value-selection problem facing the Catholic in a time of war requires some elaboration.

As a sociologist, the writer examines the behavior of the individual as an empirical manifestation of the values motivating him at the moment of action. In this light one can, by familiarizing himself with the values supposedly subscribed to by an individual, set forth an expected or predicted pattern of behavior for him. And when we know the values supposedly subscribed to by a group, we should be able to state the same kind of expected or predicted behavior patterns to be manifested by individual members of that group. Thus, knowing the abstinence requirements of the Catholic Church, one could predict a drop in the consumption of meat on Fridays in a community containing a sizable Catholic population; indeed, a survey of restaurant menus for any week will offer illustration enough that this kind of prediction is made all of the time in the practical world of commercial affairs. Demographers will take note of the Church's value directives in formulating expected religious differentials in birth rates and in interpreting divorce-remarriage patterns. It should follow, then, that one ought to be able to predict a pattern of Catholic refusal to conform to the demands of a war which does not meet the theological conditions set for the definition of the just war.

The objection will undoubtedly be raised that this places too great an emphasis upon individual judgment and responsibility. Indeed, as will be seen, it does conflict rather sharply with some of the theological opinions to be cited in the course of this study. But the present writer will hold to the following formulation: all members of the Catholic religious community subscribe to a value system which requires them to refuse to co-operate with evil knowingly and willingly; since an unjust war would constitute such a moral evil, members of the Catholic religious community may be expected to refuse to contribute to or support such a war. In this context there would be no value-selection problem for the German Catholic who believed the Third Reich was conducting a just war; he would be permitted (or obliged) to take part in it. Such Catholics, we might then predict, would evidence patterns of support. But the German Catholic who believed the war was not a just war would be obliged to refuse to serve—even were such a refusal to mean the martyr's death.

In many respects the two systems are not only highly compatible, but, to a very significant degree, the religious value system specifically and intentionally supports the secular value system. This is quite in keeping with St. Paul's instruction to the early Christians to be subject to the powers placed over them, and to the Gospel narrative of Christ and the tribute coin bearing Caesar's image. Thus the Catholic Church—both in its theological formulations and its acceptance of the natural law philosophy with its fundamental concern for the *bonum commune*—has generally and in a very real sense baptized the secular myths and the subsidiary values derived from them. Examples of this point are the teachings in the catechism which include civil obligations under the obedience required by the Fourth Commandment. The writer once encountered such an application in an American parochial school textbook in which assurances were offered that the soldier who dies on the battlefield earns immediate entry into heaven. Other illustrations of this relationship will be offered in the main part of this study in episcopal reference to the Catholic Church as a *"Volks* church in the most exalted sense," or to Catholics as making the best and most loyal soldiers because they are performing "not only a patriotic but also a religious obligation." Even the grossness of the children's textbook exaggeration is not too far removed from the more sophisticated formulation, offered by one of the prominent bishops whose statements will be discussed in the body of this study, that "in God's eyes, the death for the *Vaterland* . . . atones for much and . . . erases whatever remains of sin and guilt on the soul."

In order that the preceding discussion would not seem to eliminate the value-selection dimension as a meaningful aspect of our research problem, it is necessary to return to the just war/unjust war distinction mentioned earlier. For in the last analysis all of the values promoted and supported by the Church must ultimately relate to  its institutional function: the salvation of the individual soul and the redemption of the world. Anything which contributes to the salvation of the individual soul—and being the virtuous man, the good citizen, and so on, is defined as such a contribution—is taken over or approved by the Church and its leaders. Anything which interferes with the salvation of the individual soul is anathematized and forbidden. By implication, conscious and willing participation in an unjust war—actually, a form of murder—would constitute such an interference. In the light of the ultimate good or values of the religious community, loyal and obedient performance of a state-prescribed duty would be neither virtuous nor even permissible behavior for the Christian in such an unjust war. For the value-selection frame of reference to assume its full meaning for our study, we must address ourselves to the question of whether or not Hitler's wars were unjust wars and could be identified as such.

This obviously introduces the need for at least a cursory summary of the traditional Catholic thought on the morality of war. To avoid becoming involved in an extended theological discussion for which the writer would not be qualified, he will rely primarily upon a pamphlet published in 1941, which was prepared and released under the auspices of the Ethics Committee of the Catholic Association for International Peace, an agency of the National Catholic Welfare Conference of America. This source, it is believed, is particularly well suited to this discussion because it represents an *officially sponsored* instruction intended for the guidance of Catholics who were subject to military service and relates directly to the morality of conscientious objection. The fact that this is an American publication does not reduce its relevance to this analysis of German behavior; to Catholics, the moral principles upon which the Cyprian Emanuel discussion is based are both universal and unchanging. The contents of the pamphlet, issued at a time when a war-preparatory conscription program was in effect, suggest that one of its purposes was to eliminate possible misconceptions of the more peace-oriented Christian teachings and thereby *to restrict, not participation in the war but, instead, conscientious objection.* For these reasons, the document serves the purposes set for the present study far better than would a more intricately formulated discussion intended for specialists at a much higher level of sophistication. According to Cyprian Emanuel,

The morality of the counsels of perfection and conscientious objection to war may be epitomized in the following three statements:

(a) If the necessary conditions are verified and the war is in every way a just war, if I fall within the military age, and if my country actually needs my services, and, especially if I am now conscripted for military service, I am *forbidden* to be a conscientious objector. My refusal to give my services, far from being the more perfect—"the better part"—would undoubtedly be a direct violation of the natural law and, hence, positively sinful. Naturally, under these conditions, there can be *no question of either right or duty* to object conscientiously [italics in published text].

Having thus disposed of what has been termed the "perfectionist" opposition to military service,* he continues:

(b) If the war, or certain practices of war, are certainly unjust and immoral, I am *commanded* to be a conscientious objector, not, however, because of the counsels, but by the natural law. Under these conditions, I have *both the right and the duty* to object conscientiously.

(c) If the war is a just war, if conscription is not in force but my country is recruiting its military forces from volunteers, and if citizens are volunteering in sufficient numbers to assure my country's safety, then, and only then, can the questions of the counsels rightly enter. Since I am now bound neither to refrain from military service nor to

---

* As the writer's study of American Catholic conscientious objection to World War II reveals, a number of Catholic CO's would have taken strong exception to Cyprian Emanuel's analysis because they did base their opposition to World War II upon the perfectionist argument. See Gordon C. Zahn, *A Study of the Social Backgrounds of Catholic Conscientious Objectors in Civilian Public Service During World War II,* unpublished M. A. thesis, The Catholic University of America, 1950.

enter it, I am free to choose the former out of love and reverence for the life of Gospel perfection, and thus I *may become* a conscientious objector (i.e., in the loose sense of the term; it is evident, one who refrains from war, whatever be one's motive, when there is no obligation one way or the other, cannot be styled a conscientious objector in the strict sense). Under these conditions, I have *the right, but not the duty,* to refuse military service [italics in published text].[4]

To clarify his reference to "necessary conditions," the pamphlet's author quotes from an earlier [1932] pamphlet published by the Ethics Committee:

The conditions required by the natural law before a war can be considered justified, are generally enumerated as follows: (1) Defensive warfare alone is justifiable; (2) it may be undertaken solely in vindication of a strict right; (3) there must be adequate proportion between the violated right and the evils of war; (4) recourse may be had to war only after all less drastic measures have proved unavailing; (5) there must be a reasonable hope of victory; (6) war may be initiated by public authority only; and (7) the right intention must be had on the part of the combatants.[5]

A final set of requirements concerns the manner in which the war may be conducted:

The natural law demands, not only that a war be justly initiated but also that it be rightly conducted. The following points are commonly enumerated as the demands of the natural law in this matter: (1) international agreements must be observed; (2) malicious and slanderous propaganda is immoral; (3) excessive violence to combatants is unjustifiable; (4) violence to non-combatants is unjustifiable; (5) prisoners of war must be treated humanly and humanely; (6) indiscriminate air raids and sinking of merchant vessels is morally wrong; and (7) excessive reprisals are immoral.[6]

If Cyprian Emanuel's summary of the traditional Catholic morality of war is valid and accurate, both sets of conditions make it difficult to see how the German Catholic could have escaped being forced into a selection between the secular values as defined by the

Nazi rulers and the religious values requiring a judgment concerning the justice of the war. One might interpret the virtual unanimity of Catholic support for Hitler's wars as prima-facie evidence that Catholics were convinced that these were just wars. This conclusion, however, is not supported by information obtained in a series of interviews conducted among knowledgeable and highly respected German Catholics. Not one of these informants claimed that Germany's war had been the "just war" defined above. Even more significant, all agreed that few German Catholics considered it such even while World War II was in progress. The most favorable judgment encountered—and this in only a few cases—held that both sides could claim some justice for their cause and both sides incorporated some injustice. But virtually all agreed in 1957 that the war had been an unjust war and that German Catholics and especially their spiritual leaders, the bishops, were aware of its injustice.

Some informants offered a more elaborate analysis. A Frankfurt theologian, an advocate of the "mixed-justice" evaluation, readily granted that the German aggressions against France and Belgium (and presumably, though he did not so specify, Poland) were unjust; and he interpreted the lack of Catholic enthusiasm for the war against these nations as evidence of a general awareness of this injustice. There was a difference, he felt, in the attitude toward Britain and the United States (which nations had not been subjected to direct assault) and the Soviet Union (itself the purveyor of an aggressive political doctrine). Also, once the war was fully under way, the Allies, by resorting to questionable means (e.g., the terror bombing of German civilian areas) and declaring an unjust war aim (unconditional surrender with its threatened consequence that Germany would cease to exist as a nation) lost their claim to the status of victims of aggression. When this happened, he felt, the war became an unjust war for all participants.

The mixed-justice position might seem to present some difficulty for the value-selection frame of reference employed here. It will be recalled that Cyprian Emanuel's formulation was based on the condition that the war be *"in every way a just war"* [emphasis added]. It would seem that this is a necessary condition. Since the taking of human life in a just war is one of the three exceptions* to the otherwise general proscription stated in the Fifth Commandment, it would seem consistent to hold that a war which does not meet all the specified conditions would be forbidden. This is the position taken in 1939 by the Rt. Rev. Barry O'Toole, then professor of philosophy at The Catholic University of America. Basing his position on an application of the principle *bonum ex integra causa, malum ex quocumque defectu,* O'Toole concludes that

compliance with only one or the other condition [of the just war] is not enough, they must all be complied with under pain of the war's becoming immoral and sinful . . . Hence . . . if but one of these conditions is wanting, the war is thereby vitiated and the men who participate in it commit, at least, material (i.e., unconscious) sin.[7]

In the interests of clarifying the value-selection dimension, O'Toole's position, supplemented as it clearly is by Cyprian Emanuel's condition, will be utilized here. Actually, however, the point may be a moot one: the same theologian who advanced the mixed-justice formulation went on to admit that, as far as most German Catholics were concerned, questions as to the over-all justice or injustice of Hitler's wars simply did not present themselves. To the extent that such was the case, the mixed-justice distinction holds little or no behavioral relevance for the present analysis.

Thus we have (a) a series of wars which, the writer's informants

---

* If one uses the preferred version of the Fifth Commandment reading "Thou shalt not kill the innocent," the term "exception" does not apply to the just war or to the other two instances of permitted killing (capital punishment and emergency last-resort self-defense). This is not to deny, of course, that there are other theological interpretations which insist upon a thoroughly literal compliance with the Fifth Commandment in the more familiar "Thou shalt not kill" form. Under such interpretations there are no exceptions whatsoever to the total and universal prohibition against the taking of human life.

agreed, were not regarded as "just" wars by Germany's Catholics, and (b) a theological value system which would have obliged Catholics to refrain from serving in any but a just war. In the face of the direct conflict of values this situation implied, we find a pattern of near total conformity to the demands of the Hitler war effort. Allowance must be made for the fact that many German Catholics did not serve in Hitler's armed forces. Some escaped into exile, and others managed to evade participation by hiding from the Nazis or exploiting (in some cases, even feigning) physical disabilities. Still others adopted a rationale whereby they intentionally limited their participation to what they believed was the absolutely unavoidable minimum—a minimum, however, which frequently involved work in war industry or noncombatant service in military units.

In some cases, even *combatant* service was interpreted as being a limitation of participation in the war. That this attitude may have been widespread is illustrated by the writer's interview with a professor of theology. This informant—not a pacifist, incidentally—described in some detail his personal solution to the wartime dilemma facing every Catholic who tried to apply the traditional morality of war to Hitler's wars. He declared that he had been convinced of the war's injustice and would personally have refused to serve had he been subject to call—which, as a priest of some standing, he was not. At the same time, he did not feel that he had a right to "require martyrdom" of others by placing them under an obligation openly to refuse to serve. He made it clear to those students who were particularly close to him that they would have his full respect in the performance of the military service required of them; but he also made it clear that any of them who would return bearing the Iron Cross or some other evidence of service beyond the minimum expectations of required duty (except in situations where the extra service involved saving their own lives or the lives of comrades) would find his door closed to them. If a distinguished moral theologian found it possible to reach such a personal compromise with an immoral situation, one should not be too surprised to find a roughly similar pattern revealed in the behavior of the "ordinary" German Catholics—even including that of another informant who described his own service in the *Luftwaffe* as a "limitation" of his participation in the war effort.

As we have seen, few, almost no one, openly refused all degrees of participation in and support for a war effort which—if the writer's informants are correct—they recognized as being unjust.

This study has proceeded on the heuristic assumption that a value-selection problem was actually present, that according to the traditional Catholic teachings concerning the morality of war, World War II did in fact represent a series of objectively unjust wars as initiated and conducted by Hitler's Third Reich. Indeed, as one of the theologian-informants suggested, these wars may have offered the classic example of the unjust war.*

Two qualifications must be introduced at once. First, even if the heuristic assumption is valid, it must not be interpreted to imply that the nations ranged against the Third Reich were necessarily fighting a just war. It could be quite possible that the war was, as the Frankfurt theologian suggested, unjust from both sides. However, it can be maintained, nonetheless, that the injustice of the Nazi wars was more clearly evident, if only because these wars were *aggressive* wars. If, indeed, we are dealing here with the classic example of the unjust war, the scholarly value of an analysis of Catholic participation in and support of that war in terms of social controls and their impact upon the individual Catholic and his value selection is obviously enhanced.

The second qualification is implied in this latter statement in that it emphasizes once more the sociological focus of this study. All that is sought is some understanding or explanation of that

* This informant, it should be noted, made his observation in the course of an interview with the writer. To the writer's knowledge, neither this man nor any other nonpacifist German theologian then or since has publicly declared that Hitler's wars were unjust wars. Only those few theologians who, even before the war, tended toward pacifist interpretations of the Catholic morality of war have publicly stated such judgments of Hitler's wars and the support given them by German Catholics.

behavior. Questions relating to moral justification or condemnation of that behavior is not directly involved in the analysis. Where the moral theologian would be inclined to evaluate Catholic support for Hitler's wars in terms of at least material sin, the sociologist must limit his concern to the evidence it offers of the operation of social controls and their effectiveness in governing the outcome of a value-selection situation.

The separate considerations of the social-control and value-selection dimensions now converge. If it is true that, for most German Catholics, the question as to the over-all justice or injustice of the war did not arise, this would mean that there was no value-selection situation at all; it would mean that German Catholics stood united in support of the national cause because no one had suggested that there was any possible alternative course to be followed or, indeed, considered. But we cannot leave it at this if we are willing to grant that the war might have been or actually was an unjust war. We must seek some explanation of why the question was not raised and the value-selection situation defined for the individual. The explanation most frequently encountered in the course of the researcher's inquiries was a simple one: there was nothing else one could do. In the context of the present analysis, this is an explanation in terms of the array of social controls operating upon the individual Catholic and the spiritual leaders who might have been expected to define his value-selection problem for him.

For the most part, this explanation stressed what have been referred to as formal and external social controls. Two or three informants, including one bishop, dismissed the issue merely by reminding the interviewer that the law included no provision for conscientious objection or any other legitimate basis for a refusal to perform one's military duty. Since the conscription program was so universally inclusive, the conclusion was immediately drawn that (a) there was no conscientious objection on the part of German Catholics, and (b) there could have been none—a conclusion contradicted by the fact that a few Catholics did refuse to serve and were executed for their refusal. This implication that a moral duty (i.e., to refuse to take part in an unjust war) could rest upon the provisions of a formally enacted law was actually strengthened by the assurance that followed in each case that now, under the new conscription law which *does* make provision for conscientious objection, things would be quite different.

Of course, this legalistic explanation may merely reflect the more realistic explanation offered by the majority of the writer's informants, the frank admission that an open refusal to serve would have demanded an exceptional level of heroism. This assertion was sometimes voiced in the context of the humble acknowledgment that "we were no heroes"; sometimes in the context of an appeal to practicality which led one theologian to declare that an individual had *no right* to place his life in jeopardy in so hopeless a situation.\*
And these basic premises were unquestionably true: the total power of the Nazi state was mobilized behind the war; every means at its disposal, legitimate or not, would be employed to support it; the individual who would dare to challenge that power did, in effect, sign his own death warrant. Any interpretation of these facts and their effect demands a certain measure of humility on the part of the would-be interpreter; for he who has not experienced the full pressure of the social controls exerted by the unscrupulous rulers of a totalitarian state is in no position to pass moral judgment upon the degree of heroism, or lack of it, evidenced by others who were subjected to such a test.

But the external and formal secular controls do not tell the whole story. *Every* social control was employed to wage the war effectively. The informal controls of public opinion were undoubtedly operative, and there is evidence that these controls varied in intensity and effectiveness throughout the war. One journalist recalled that the outbreak of war was marked by an astonishing lack of enthusiasm on the part of the general population; then, as the

---

\* This theologian identified himself as a close friend and associate of Father Metzger (see below, pp. 134 ff.); surprisingly enough, he categorized the latter's choice of apparent martyrdom as "folly."

victories mounted in Poland and France, there was a belated surge
of enthusiasm; later, as the war was prolonged and events turned
progressively worse for Germany, this morale born of enthusiasm
was gradually replaced by a morale born of the fatalistic acceptance
that there was nothing left for the individual but to bear his share
of the sorrows of the suffering *Volk*. Certainly, as the Allied air
attacks increased in frequency, intensity, and destructiveness, the
individual German Catholic who would have refused to do his
share, for whatever reason, would have run afoul of all the unor-
ganized and informal controls just as surely as he would have
placed his head on the executioner's block.

This analysis would not be complete without including some
consideration of the internal controls consisting of socially and cul-
turally induced values. Once Nazi Germany was involved in actual
warfare, however questionable the justice of her cause, the internal
forces of patriotic and nationalistic sentiments became fully operative. That hypothetical German who refused to do what others
defined as his share would have learned that such refusal carried
with it an oppressive burden of deeply troubling doubts and guilt
feelings. The Catholic in particular, continually under pressure
during the Hitler years to prove that he was as good a German as
anyone else, was highly sensitive to such feelings. And when we
realize that these internal pressures to conform by faithfully and
loyally fulfilling whatever duties were placed upon him received
public reinforcement and emphasis from the religious superiors to
whom he would be expected to turn for moral guidance, these
internal social controls take on new significance for the explanation
of the near unanimity of German Catholic support for Hitler's wars.

The Frankfurt theologian who advanced the mixed-justice thesis
discussed above offered a similarly elaborated analysis of Catholic
support for the war effort. He classified individuals according to a
set of three carefully reasoned categories:

(1) Men who believed the war was unjust but who were willing
to fight in the belief that, since they merely followed orders, all moral

responsibility lay with the leaders and superiors who issued those orders. [This position, the informant added, was morally wrong.]

(2) Men who admitted the German cause was unjust but who believed that, since injustice was present on both sides, it was permissible to obey commands that were not in themselves unjust while refusing to obey specific commands that were unjust. In actual battle, this theologian suggested, such men would feel no qualms about destroying enemy property (since such property would rank lower in the scale of values than would the soldier's own life) but would shoot into the air or otherwise avoid killing persons who were victims of Hitler's unjust aggressions. [The informant was convinced that a great number of ex-soldiers would be included in this category—men who would proudly claim that they served through the entire war without killing an enemy.]

(3) Men who admitted the German cause was unjust but who felt that the Allied cause was also unjust; since they did not have access to all the facts to permit them to reach a more exact moral judgment, they believed themselves privileged (or even obliged) to give the benefit of the doubt to their own leaders and responsible authorities.

This classification was presented as the informant's personal analysis; few men, he added, consciously formulated these considerations and distinctions under the stress of the wartime situation.

These classifications, however, do introduce the problem of the Catholic in doubt, the man who did not believe the war was just and yet was not convinced in conscience that it was unjust. The traditional theological answer is that such a Catholic is obliged to give the presumption of justice to his legitimate authority. Thus, this problem is quite easily resolved in terms of the two dimensions set for this study. In brief, the individual in doubt was one whose value selection had not been completed or who had not yet reached the point at which a selection could be made. His decision, then, to act in support of the war out of the obedience recommended by the presumption-of-justice teaching finds its complete explanation in terms of the effective operation of social controls.

But in such a case the controls involved are neither solely nor even primarily those of the secular order. Instead we must recognize that a new determinant has entered into the equation: the fact that the Catholic Church in Germany itself represented a major force for assuring conformity to the demands of the national war effort on the part of the individual German Catholic; and, in assuming this role, it employed the full range of the institutional controls at its command.

*NOTES*

1. See below, p. 28 ff.
2. See below, pp. 126-127.
3. See below, p. 160.
4. Cyprian Emanuel, O.F.M., *The Morality of Conscientious Objection to War*, (Washington: Catholic Association for International Peace, 1941), pp. 26-27.
5. *The Ethics of War*, quoted in Emanuel, *op. cit.*, p. 17 n.
6. *Ibid.*, p. 19 n.
7. *The Catholic Worker*, Vol. 7, No. 9 (June 1940), p. 2.

CHAPTER 4

# A Question of Judgment

THE CATHOLIC SCHOLAR who would engage in research having the potential for controversy involved in the study to be presented in the forthcoming pages is forced to address himself at the very outset to a critical question. The question was clearly expressed by Yves Congar, O.P., in a recent issue of *Perspectives:*[1]

Can we, without imprudence, expose evils and abuses in the history of the Church and publish works of self-criticism and self-accusation? In researches and avowals of this kind is there not some risk of disturbing the confidence of the faithful and, in fact, of promoting a kind of religious indifferentism which is the very vestibule of neo-paganism?

This study does not set out to "expose evils and abuses"; it will, however, reveal some grievous mistakes in judgment and action, and perhaps some rather critical inadequacies in certain prevailing theological formulations. The question, therefore, is pertinent. Congar's answer is pertinent, too. As he points out, the workings of the Holy Spirit within us begin with what he terms "His first act— to convince us of sin." Thus what many may choose to dismiss or denounce as a public washing of dirty linen may also be viewed as a probing search for causes and consequences of moral failures which, if conducted and received in a spirit of honesty and humility, can only work to benefit and perfect the Church as a temporal social institution charged with a divine mission and responsibility.

But this is only part of the answer. Equally pertinent, though not stressed by Congar, is the *professional* responsibility of the scholar and scientist. Our age seems to have abandoned the true meaning of the word "profession" as a state of life entered upon in a spirit of total commitment to a special set of responsibilities and consecrated to the service of the truth. Except for religion, our professions are no longer marked by a public taking or "profession" of vows; where we do find some remnants of this practice—as in the medical and, to a lesser extent, legal professions—they are generally regarded as little more than ceremonial formalities. Nevertheless, the profession of the scholar must imply a conscious dedication to the service of the truth, the advancement of knowledge, and the correction and, wherever possible, elimination of error. In this light, then, the answer to our question given by the Catholic scholar who would remain true to his professional responsibilities has to be that mistakes and weaknesses—even evils and abuses— must be exposed wherever and whenever they are discovered. And he will expose them in the confident faith that, however much of an embarrassment his revelations might at first present, they will in the long run contribute to the welfare of the Church, which proclaims that Truth is One, and which therefore insists that any apparent divergence between fact and faith must be tested and explored and ultimately reconciled in that unity of truth.

To return to Congar:

The Church considered as a community lives according to laws analogous, *positis ponendis,* to those of any other society. In the disordered conditions and the great tragedies in which a complex and finally collective responsibility must be acknowledged, there are nevertheless some persons responsible in the first degree and others in the second degree. That second-degree responsibility can come from cowardice or connivance. In the Church more than in other societies there is a connection between disordered conditions and great tragedies. One might even say that tragedies are the result of inveterate and accepted shortcomings at the level of everyday practice. Collective responsibility is incurred at the level of pastoral observances, of devotions, by what is preached and by what is *not* preached.[2]

We shall be concerned here with a sociological inquiry which seeks to discover and interpret the operation or the relevance of certain theories as they apply to a particular national segment of the religious community known as the Roman Catholic Church. Our inquiry has to do with behavior relating to the Second World War, certainly one of the greatest tragedies the world has suffered; and it will offer evidence to support the suggestion that this great tragedy was in fact largely the result of inveterate and accepted shortcomings at the level of everyday practice. It will present data showing the extent to which the behavior patterns under study can be traced to pastoral observances and devotions, to what was not preached and, most particularly, to what *was* preached. As a sociological inquiry, however, it will not seek to pass direct or definitive judgment upon the degree of responsibility involved in these actions—though it will certainly hope to open up new lines of inquiry to which the theologian and others who are more properly concerned with questions of moral responsibility might well address themselves.

Other limitations of scope, too, deserve a brief statement here despite the fact that they will be restated in the course of the study itself. First, this is not a historical inquiry. It does not pretend to present a full and complete account of the relationships between the Catholic Church in Germany and the National Socialist regime. Thus, while it will acknowledge and refer to patterns of opposition and resistance evidenced in other areas of civic activity, this study concerns itself primarily with the behavior of German Catholics with respect to participation in the series of conflicts constituting World War II. If, in the process, it should also contribute to a more accurate evaluation of the history of Church-state relations in Nazi Germany (inasmuch as most of the histories published since the collapse of the Third Reich have tended to overlook or ignore the areas of co-operation and compromise on the part of the Church leaders), this would be an incidental contribution and not a primary aim. Similarly, since this is not a historical inquiry, the data and documentation need not be presented in any strict chronological order. The sociological approach stresses themes and consistencies; therefore, the data will be presented as they best reveal such themes and consistencies. There will be instances, of course, where a specific historical event is immediately relevant to a given pattern of behavior; such chronological connections will be noted when they are encountered.

This study cannot offer any basis for a definitive comparison of the behavior of German Catholics with the behavior of other German religious communities, nor, indeed, of the Catholic Church in other countries. However, the writer would offer two assumptions in this connection. First, he assumes that a similar investigation of the behavior of German Protestants, with the minor exceptions of some of the more "radical" Protestant sects, would reveal at least the same degree of support for the Hitler war effort as was manifested by German Catholics. Second, he assumes that the behavior of Catholics of other nations—including his own—would have duplicated the patterns to be described here had they been presented with the same circumstances; and that these patterns could be traced to the same or at least comparable motivations. These are assumptions and nothing more; because of the restricted focus of investigation set for this study, no empirical data were gathered or sought to support or disprove their validity. Again, these assumptions may well serve as hypotheses for future empirical research by others; if so, such research would be welcomed as a much needed expansion of the findings to be presented here.

For many reasons the customary array of individual acknowledgments of those who served as sources for much of the data to be presented or who have offered encouragement and personal confirmation of the interpretations and conclusions based on these data will be omitted. However, even though they cannot be listed by name, the author must express his deep appreciation and sense of indebtedness to the hundred and more individuals who were interviewed or who furnished much valuable supplementary information through correspondence; to the people in libraries and similar agencies who assisted him in obtaining copies of the wartime publications and similar documentation used in the research; and to those friends and colleagues who have given him such open and consistently strong support in the preliminary controversies that have already developed. Much credit and appreciation are due to his publishers and editors who have been so helpful in the preparation of the manuscript for final publication. And most grateful acknowledgment must be made to the administrators of the Fulbright Program for the opportunity offered by the research grant which enabled the author to pursue his study of this topic at the Julius Maximilian Universität in Würzburg and elsewhere throughout Germany during the 1956-57 academic year. It should not be necessary to stress the obvious fact that the sole responsibility for the interpretations and conclusions—as well as the discussion of possible sociotheological implications—of this study rests with the author. Neither the Fulbright Program nor the University with which he is associated has been in any way involved in the organization of the research project or the preparation of the study itself.

During his year of research in Germany, the author lived in a *Gasthaus* operated by a Catholic family, and he breakfasted almost daily under the picture of an only son who had been killed in action shortly before the end of the war. This picture of a proud and dedicated young man in his military uniform reminded the author of another young man, a onetime schoolmate, who had been equally proud and dedicated in his American Air Force uniform—and who had also been killed in action. Both men were Catholics and, therefore, bound by the same theological value system according to which they would be permitted to fight and kill in none but a "just war." Whatever their subjective interpretations may have been— and this is really the crux of the sociotheological problem exposed by this study—one (or both), *objectively* speaking, had to be fighting in an unjust war and, therefore, guilty of a material sin against the Fifth Commandment. In a sense, since both were members of opposing military machines, it can also be said that each played some part in the killing of the other—though, certainly, it would be too much to expect that either was ever aware of the other's existence, whether as a person or as a fellow member of the community Catholics believe to be the Mystical Body of Christ.

A noted German theologian to whom this ever-recurring dilemma was presented dismissed it as "the mystery of the Cross." This somewhat easy view, which seemed to be too simple an answer to a complex problem, did not satisfy the author then, nor does it satisfy him now. The "mystery of the Cross" may indeed explain the dying; for, Catholics believe, it will ever be the lot of the Christian to suffer injustice. But it cannot explain the killing; for, again in the terms of the Catholic value system, it can never be the role of the Christian to perpetrate injustice.

Certainly, this dilemma is not new. It has always been and will continue to be encountered whenever the Christian believer is called to arms in the service of the secular ruler. The greater demands of the modern state and the modern weapons of total destruction have only sharpened and magnified the dilemma to the point that the attempts to rationalize it have become ever more ludicrous and grotesque. It is the author's sincere hope that his effort to throw some light upon the sociological dimensions of a moral *and social* problem which has been treated in the past almost exclusively in terms of its theological dimensions may force a new consideration, however more difficult it may be, of the scandal which finds fellow members of the same Mystical Body periodically engaging in their mutual destruction—in the belief that they are thereby fulfilling a "Christian duty."

*NOTES*

1. *Perspectives,* Vol. 6 (1961), p. 4.
2. *Ibid.*

**Part 2**

Part 2

# CHAPTER 5

# Statement of the Problem

WE BEGIN with a paradox. One of the more colorful traditions observed in Germany, especially in the predominantly Catholic Rhineland, is the annual *Kinderzug* in honor of St. Martin of Tours. In small town and metropolitan center alike, the feast day is celebrated by parades of gaily costumed children led by a man on horseback representing the saint, "the glory of Gaul and a light to the Western Church in the fourth century." The children carry candlelighted lanterns, often the product of their own handiwork; and, once the ceremonial parade is finished, they disperse into small groups and go from house to house, reciting little verses or singing simple songs to test the generosity of the householder in a manner similar to the pattern followed in the "trick or treat" preliminaries to Halloween in the United States.

The passage of the centuries has undoubtedly secularized the form and meaning of the festival, so that it may now be viewed as more a matter of national or regional culture than as a strictly religious observance or tradition. Nevertheless, its essential symbolism still attests to its originally religious nature and to the honor and devotion accorded to a beloved saint. It is obvious, for example, that the "test of generosity" is associated with the acts of charity performed by Martin; similarly, the costuming of rider and entourage, the color of the horse, and other details are intended to serve as direct representations of the man and the legends associated with his life.

But our paradox arises from another aspect of this saint's personal history, an aspect which offers a sharp contrast to the militarism and submissiveness to state authority so frequently attributed to German culture and national character. St. Martin was not noted only for his acts of heroic charity. Of far greater significance, as far as the present study is concerned, is the fact that he was also a "conscientious objector," a man who defied his ruler and refused to perform military duties required of him because he believed such duties incompatible with the teachings of his Christian Faith. A standard reference work includes a biographical sketch in which it is recorded that Martin

has, rather curiously, come to be looked on as a "soldier saint." At the age of fifteen he was, as the son of a veteran, forced into the army against his will and for some years, though not yet formally a Christian, he lived more like a monk than a soldier. It was while stationed at Amiens that is said to have occurred the incident which tradition and image have made famous. One day in a very hard winter, during a severe frost, he met at the gate of the city a poor man, almost naked, trembling and shaking with cold, and begging alms of those that passed by. Martin, seeing those that went before take no notice of this miserable creature, thought he was reserved for himself, but he had nothing with him but his arms and clothes. So, drawing his sword, he cut his cloak into two pieces, gave one to the beggar and wrapped himself in the other half. . . .

This, of course, is the act of charity commemorated in the tradition and image maintained by the parades of German children and the begging for candies and other treats which follows. The narrative continues, however, to relate how some of the bystanders laughed at Martin's generosity while others felt ashamed that they had not done likewise. That very night, he is reported to have had a vision in which Jesus appeared to identify Himself as the poor man he had helped. This experience made such a deep impression on the young man, who was then only a catechumen, that he thereupon "flew to be baptized." His baptism set the stage for the later developments which will interest us here.

Martin did not at once leave the army, and when he was about twenty there was a barbarian invasion of Gaul. With his comrades he appeared before Julian Caesar to receive a war-bounty and Martin refused to accept it. "Hitherto," he said to Julian, "I have served you as a soldier; let me now serve Christ. Give the bounty to these others who are going to fight, but I am a soldier of Christ and it is not lawful for me to fight." Julian stormed and accused Martin of cowardice, who retorted that he was prepared to stand in the battle line unarmed the next day and to advance alone against the enemy in the name of Christ. He was thrust into prison, but the conclusion of an armistice stopped further developments and Martin was soon after discharged. He went to Poitiers, where St. Hilary was bishop, and this doctor of the Church gladly received the young "conscientious objector" among his disciples.[1]

The paradox presented by German Catholic devotion to a conscientious objector saint attains its fullest measure of irony in the context of the greatest tragedy of recent world history.

In 1933 the naming of Adolf Hitler as Chancellor of the Weimar Republic marked the appearance of a new and, as events were to prove, more terrible Caesar on the world scene. In the years to follow this man and his followers would succeed in their efforts to consolidate all civil authority into one mighty totalitarian order and, through a program of systematic repression and outright terror, subjugate or eliminate all who might dare to oppose them or their objectives.

Not the least among the victims of the internal policies and programs initiated by the rulers of the National Socialist Third Reich was the Roman Catholic Church. After a brief honeymoon of comforting assurances designed to forestall religious opposition while the amassing of power proceeded, the new secular authority gradually revealed its essentially anti-religious character in an unfolding pattern of interference, restriction, and repression. Beginning with the fabrication and exploitation of scandals reputedly involving financial or moral irregularities on the part of the clergy and members of religious orders, the assault moved on to formal suppression of Catholic organizations and spiritual activities; interferences with Catholic schools, the Catholic press, even with the performance of ordinary pastoral duties; and, finally, confiscation of Church properties and direct attacks upon the Catholic Faith and the spiritual leaders of the Catholic Church.* Thus, the neopaganism represented by the Nazi Caesar, and its dedicated opposition to Christianity, was if anything more systematic and thoroughgoing than the paganism of Julian's Rome.

* Even today the world is not fully aware of the full extent of the Nazi attack upon the Catholic Church in Germany. Overshadowed by the stark inhumanity of that regime's planned liquidation of European Jewry, the campaign against Catholicism and the other Christian churches tends to be noted only in passing. Two references of particularly great value in correcting this situation are Johannes Maria Lenz, *Christus in Dachau* (Vienna: Buchversand "Libri Catholici," 1957) and Johannes Neuhäusler, *Kreuz und Hakenkreuz* (Munich: Verlag Katholische Kirche Bayerns, 1946). The first book is the history of the experiences undergone by the hundreds of priests sent to a Nazi concentration camp as written by one of those so imprisoned. The second book is a heavily documented account of the step-by-step attack against the Catholic Church, written by a man who held a prominent post in the Munich chancery and is now an auxiliary bishop of that archdiocese. Bishop Neuhäusler, too, experienced extended detention at Dachau.

In this connection, however, it must be noted that Neuhäusler's book has been rather sharply criticized in a recent article which presents evidence that the texts of several documents have been altered by omissions without the customary indication of deletion and, in some instances, by changes in wording. See Hans Müller, "Zur Behandlung des Kirchenkampfes in der Nachkriegsliteratur," *Politische Studien,* Vol. 12 (July 1961), pp. 474-481. However much this somewhat shocking discovery may weaken the over-all reliability of the literature he subjects to careful scholarly review, Müller's findings do not necessarily affect the description of the actions taken against the Church as presented by Neuhäusler and others. These breaches of scholarly integrity seem to be more an attempt to suppress potentially embarrassing instances of compromise or conformity on the part of religious leaders; there is no evidence that the Nazi assaults described in this literature have been fabricated or exaggerated.

In its external affairs the "New Germany" of Adolf Hitler could boast of an impressive series of bloodless victories which incorporated the whole of Austria and Czechoslovakia (first the *Sudetenland* area under terms of the 1938 Munich Agreement and then, barely six months later, the remainder by engineered coup) into the Third Reich, thereby creating the *Grossdeutschland* of his chauvinistic writings and ravings. By 1939 only Danzig and the pre-Versailles German territory of the Polish Corridor remained outside Hitler's contemplated European boundaries; and the provocations and incitements involved in his program to "correct" this situation furnished the spark that set the world aflame in what would ultimately become World War II.

The blitzkrieg victory over Poland brought about the lull of the so-called "phony war" against Poland's British and French allies. This came to an end in May 1940 with the sudden German attack in the West which involved the violation of the neutral territories of Belgium and the Netherlands (Norway and Denmark having already fallen before invading Nazi forces a month earlier). Yugoslavia and Greece were the victims of German assaults in April 1941, and the final major aggression took place in June of that year with the attack upon the Soviet Union, Germany's partner in a 1939 non-aggression pact. The declaration of war against the United States on December 11, 1941, was more of a recognition of a state of involvement in the Japanese attack upon Pearl Harbor and should not be viewed as a direct aggression on the part of Nazi Germany.*

Thus, when in September 1939, the new Caesar called the youth of Germany to battle for the swastika colors of the Third Reich, it was not to repel "a barbarian invasion" but, instead, to overrun

* In the present study the war involvement of Hitler's Third Reich is seen as having three separate and somewhat distinct major phases: the aggression against Poland and the consequent involvement of Poland's treaty allies, Britain and France; the aggressions against the European neutrals in 1940 and 1941; and, finally, the aggression against the Soviet Union. Taken together, all these constitute the total conflict referred to as World War II; but for the purposes of this study, they are viewed as separate wars in a single integrated series.

and conquer the predominantly Catholic nation of Poland* under what might be termed a share-the-victim arrangement with the Soviet Union, the very nation which had previously been described by Nazi spokesmen (with the enthusiastic concurrence of German Catholic leaders) as the archenemy of the German state, Western civilization, and all that was of ultimate human value.

The official publication of the Münster diocese reported that in 1939 the Catholic population of "Greater Germany" numbered 31,943,932 or 40.3 per cent of the total population.[2] Of these, 15.5 million were males, the majority of whom were ultimately subject to the call to serve in the legions of the new Caesar. Unfortunately, it is not possible to furnish accurate statistics as to the number of German Catholic men who actually did bear arms for the Third Reich, but it is clear that most of them who were called to the "defense of *Volk* and *Vaterland*" answered that call.

Despite repeated inquiries among chancery officials and Catholics who had been active in the pre-Hitler peace movement, the writer was able to learn of no more than seven Catholics who openly refused military service. Six of these men were executed for their refusal. The seventh man, charged with a capital offense, was fortunate enough to escape death only by being placed in indefinite custody in what one informant described as a military mental institution, where he remained until the Soviet forces reached Berlin.

---

* It is true, of course, that the Nazis officially claimed that Poland's armed forces were the official aggressors. William L. Shirer in *The Rise and Fall of the Third Reich* (New York: Simon and Schuster, 1959, pp. 518-520), furnishes a detailed report of the faked attack upon the Gleiwitz radio station carried out by SS men wearing Polish uniforms. Several of the present writer's informants referred to this ruse, but, interestingly enough, they tended to differ in their evaluations of its effectiveness. One claimed that publication of "photographic evidence" of the "Polish attack" did dupe German Catholics into believing at first that the war was a just war of defense against unprovoked aggression; other informants insisted that German Catholics were never taken in by the clumsy fabrication. It is obviously impossible to verify the accuracy of either evaluation. Perhaps it is safest to assume that both are partly true, that some Catholics did accept the propaganda story at face value while others rejected it as a trick. None of the informants, however, was of the opinion that even the former were long deluded as to the true nature of Hitler's wars.

It would be extremely unjust, however, to assume that these were the only cases of such refusal; far more likely is the interpretation that others who may have done the same went to their death with no record being made of their heroic sacrifice.* Nevertheless, however great the total number may have been, it would still represent the merest handful when compared with the number of German Catholics who did accept service in the military forces.

The paradox is now complete. Thousands of German Catholics who as young boys had marched in the gay processions honoring the conscientious objector to Julian's war had grown into men who willingly responded to the call to march in Hitler's wars of conquest. In doing so, each of them had sworn "a sacred oath" to

---

* Not all would make such allowances. In the course of an interview with the author, a former general secretary of the *Friedensbund deutscher Katholiken* rather bitterly expressed the pessimistic conviction that the author's research would fail to uncover *a single German* who made such a refusal to serve. In a strict sense, this prediction was almost substantiated by the facts. Of the six executed men who would seem to fit the "conscientious objector" designation, three (a Pallotine priest, Franz Reinisch; the peasant, Franz Jägerstätter; and the Catholic Action leader, Josef Mayr-Nusser) were Austrians. The three who were associated with the religious community *Christkönigsgesellschaft* (Max Josef Metzger, its founder; Brother Maurus; and Brother Michael) were also, for at least a significant part of their adult lives, residents of Austria. Josef Fleischer, the only conscientious objector to escape the executioner, seems to be the only true German of the seven (see below, p. 147 n.).

Information on these men and their wartime stand is rather sparse. The Reinisch and Jägerstätter stories are reported in Kreuzberg, *op. cit.;* Jägerstätter is also mentioned in Jakob Fried's *Nationalsozialismus und katholische Kirche in Oesterreich* (Wien: Wiener Dom Verlag, 1947). The best account of Father Metzger's history is provided in the introductory section to his collected *Gefangenschaftbriefe* (Meitingen: Kyrios Verlag, 1948), and in Lillian Stevenson, compiler and translator, *Max Josef Metzger, Priest and Martyr* (New York: Macmillan, 1952). Information about his two followers and Mayr-Nusser was obtained in the course of interviews with present leaders of the *Christkönigsgesellschaft* and with Bishop Johannes Neuhäusler of Munich. Dr. Fleischer's story was obtained through correspondence and interviews with him and his family, and the perusal of documents and periodical articles made available to the writer.

The present writer has published a summary of the Jägerstätter case, based on the writings cited and supplemented by a visit with the man's widow and pastor, under the title, "He Would Not Serve," in *America,* Vol. 99 (July 5, 1959), pp. 388-390.

render "unconditional obedience" to Adolf Hitler personally*—a striking contrast to St. Martin's rejection of the claims of the Roman emperor. It is the aim of this study** to seek some understanding of how and why such a situation could come to pass, and the conclusion to which I have come is simply this: The German Catholic supported Hitler's wars not only because such support was required by the Nazi rulers but also because his religious leaders formally called upon him to do so; not only because the actions and opinions of his fellow citizens made him feel obligated to share the nation's burdens and sorrows but also because, by example and open encouragement, the Catholic press and Catholic organizations gave their total commitment to the nation's cause; not only because of deep-felt fears of the terrible price nonconformity would bring or the warm surge of satisfaction accompanying nationalistic or patriotic identification with the war effort, but also because his most cherished religious values had been called into play to encourage him to take his post "on the field of honor" in the "defense of *Volk* and *Vaterland*."

A German Catholic who was troubled by doubts about the war's justice would find those doubts considerably eased by reading the strongly patriotic contents of his *Kirchenzeitung* (assuming the Nazis still permitted its publication), or by giving his careful attention to the *Hirtenbriefe* or other episcopal pronouncements that might be read to him from the pulpit. And as he left the church, he might also pick up such doubt-quieting material as the pamphlet (written by a prominent theologian and bearing the imprint of a familiar Catholic publisher) in which the answer to the challenging title *What Is To Be Done?* reads in part:

* The text of this military oath, as included in the *Katholisches Gesang-buch,* edited by Chaplain Felix Gross for distribution to Catholic servicemen under the auspices of the Military Bishop, reads: "I swear before God this sacred oath that I will render unconditional obedience to the *Führer* of the German nation and *Volk,* Adolf Hitler, the Supreme Commander of the armed forces, and that, as a brave soldier, I will be ready at all times to stake my life in fulfillment of this oath."

** The research upon which this study has been based was made possible by a senior research grant under the Fulbright Program.

Now there is no point in raising the question of the just war and introducing all sorts of "ifs," "ands," or "buts." A scientific judgment concerning the causes and origins of the war is absolutely impossible today because the prerequisites for such a judgment are not available to us. This must wait until a later time when the documents of both sides are available. Now the individual has but one course open to him: to do his best with faith in the cause of his *Volk*. For this, one cannot demand mathematical proof. This would no longer be faith but, instead, a reckoning; and service to the *Volk* is based on faith and trust, not on calculation. Today that is self-evident to all patriots.[3]

Such advice would have been a source of great comfort to the man troubled by doubts. To any German Catholic who was already *convinced* in conscience that the war was unjust and that he was obliged to refuse to take part in it, such advice and the reasoning behind it would have constituted a distinct hardship. Such a man would have found himself facing the dire consequences of his decision with the knowledge that he could count on no clear expression of unequivocal support from any recognized leader of his Church. Indeed, as has already been noted,[4] he might even have found himself being denied the sacraments as a penalty for refusing to perform his "Christian duty."

Once again a note of balance must be introduced. Except for the position taken by some minor Protestant groups—the Jehovah's Witnesses and the traditional "peace churches," for instance—there is reason to believe that German Protestantism matched the Catholic record of support for the Nazi war effort. If anything, there were indications that the Protestant commitment was even more thorough and enthusiastic. This was especially true of the Müller wing of the dominant Evangelical (Lutheran) Church; but even the dissident *Bekenntniskirche* (Confessional) segment of Lutheran Protestantism was loyal to the nation's cause despite its record of heroic opposition to the Hitler regime. There is, for example, the familiar story of the efforts of its leader, Martin Niemöller, to resume voluntarily his World War I submarine duties as soon as the new war began (despite the fact that Niemöller was in one of

Hitler's concentration camps at the time).* None of the German bishops appears to have matched this dramatic show of nationalistic identification with the Hitler war effort.

Nevertheless, members of the Catholic hierarchy did assume a significant role in marshaling the support of the Catholic population and bolstering the war morale of the Catholics in active service and on the home front. In the more impassioned words of E. I. Watkin, the charge can be made that "the German bishops tarnished the luster of their noble resistance to Hitler's tyranny at home by giving their flocks to understand that it was their Christian duty to fight for the triumph of the Nazi antichrist, the inhuman fiend who tortured and murdered millions of men, women and children."[5]

This support can and should be thoroughly documented in the more detached tone proper to the sociological approach by specific reference to episcopal statements and actions. In presenting this documentation, the material will be organized to reveal, first, the support given the war effort by the bishops in general; second, the support given the war effort by those bishops who are generally accorded the reputation of having been the most outspoken representatives of German Catholic resistance to Hitler and his policies; and, finally, the support given the war by the Catholic Military

---

* The research upon which this study is based was limited to the behavior of German Catholics with respect to Hitler's wars. It is the writer's hope that the results of his investigations may inspire other scholars to undertake a parallel study of the behavior of German Protestants with respect to those wars.

As far as the Niemöller incident is concerned, one of his biographers suggests that the pastor's request in 1941 to be recalled for submarine service might have resulted from one of the "moments of despair" all prisoners experience. The incident, complete to Field Marshal Keitel's rejection of the request as well as some of the other interpretations that have been offered to explain Niemöller's action, is discussed in Dietmar Schmidt, *Pastor Niemöller*, trans. by Lawrence Smith (New York: Doubleday & Co., 1959), pp. 120-121. Of some special interest in the present context is the reported comment of a friend of Niemöller's, Ludwig Bartning, who claimed that he and other friends had prevailed upon the Confessional leader to make the offer. Bartning is quoted as saying in retrospect, "He was not allowed to bear arms in an unjust war under the most unjust of 'Leaders.' We ought to have realized that, instead of trying to gain petty advantages for him. . . ."

Bishop, the religious leader holding immediate spiritual authority over and responsibility for the Catholic men in Germany's armed forces.

## NOTES

1. Butler's *Lives of the Saints,* edited, revised, and supplemented by Herbert Thurston, S.J., and Donald Attwater (New York: P. J. Kenedy & Sons, 1956), Vol. 4, p. 310.

2. *Kirchliches Amtsblatt für die Diözese Münster,* Vol. LXXV (December 12, 1941), p. 113. This statement by the episcopal ordinariate cites as its source the May 17, 1939, census as reported in a special supplement, *Wirtschaft und Statistik,* issued by the government statistical office in 1941. The population totals were for "the present German area, excluding Memel, Danzig, and the region of Eupen, Malmedy and Moresnet."

3. M. Laros, *Was Ist Zu Tun?* (Dülmen: Verlag Laumann, 1940), pp. 3-6. "Es hat jetzt keinen Sinn, den Fragen des gerechten Krieges nachzusinnen und überall ein Wenn und Aber anzubringen Ein wissenschaftliches Urteil über Ursachen und Veranlassung des Krieges ist heute noch gar nicht möglich, weil uns die Voraussetzungen dafür noch nicht gegeben sind. Das kann erst in späterer Zeit geschehen, wenn die beiderseitigen Dokumente zugänglich sind. Jetzt heisst es für den einzelnen handeln, sein Bestes tun im Glauben an die Sache seines Volkes. Dafür kann man keine mathematischen Beweise verlangen. Dann wäre es kein Glaube mehr, sondern eine Berechnung, und der Dienst am Volke ist auf Glaube und Vertrauen, nicht auf Berechnung gestellt. Das ist heute bei allen Patrioten selbstverständlich."

4. See above, p. 17 n.

5. E. I. Watkin, "Unjustifiable War," in Charles S. Thompson, ed., *Morals and Missiles* (London: James Clarke & Co., Ltd., 1959), p. 58.

# CHAPTER 6

# The Bishops

*"Our heart belongs to our Volk."*\*

UNDOUBTEDLY one of the most important documents bearing upon the question whether the official leadership of the Catholic Church in Germany operated as an agency of social control inspiring and strengthening Catholic support for the Nazi war effort is the 1941 pastoral letter issued by the eight Bavarian bishops. Accompanying instructions directed that it be read from the pulpit on the First Sunday in Lent. The date is important. Appearing as it did *after* the victories over Poland, France, and the neutral Low Countries (the latter campaign having been the subject of indirect Vatican criticism\*\*), and *before* the Nazi attack upon the Soviet Union

---

\* *Unser Herz gehört unserem Volke.* As we have seen,[1] the word *Volk* is not adequately translated into English by "people," nor can *Vaterland* be translated as "Fatherland" nor *Heimat* as "homeland." Hence, I have retained these and other terms in my translations of the German texts. Similarly, the word *Führer* will be used in the German, since it was invested with a distinctive mystique and involved both the concept of leader and the person of Adolf Hitler.

\*\* In his messages *Au moment* to the King of the Belgians and *Apprenant* to the Queen of the Netherlands, both issued on May 10, 1940, Pius XII referred to their nations as having been involved in the broadening conflict "against their will and their rights." Several German informants mentioned these papal letters as evidence that German Catholics, certainly their episcopal leaders at the very least, could have been aware of the injustice of this phase of Hitler's wars.

reintroduced the "crusade against Bolshevism" aspect of the National Socialist program, this episcopal message and its appeal for unity and unstinting support of the war offer incontrovertible evidence that Bavarian Catholics would have received little encouragement from their bishops had they even considered refusing to take part in the Hitler war effort. The letter reads in part:

Beloved: the time in which we live is one full of decision for many years to come, full of decision for our national, economic, spiritual, and religious life. We have already lived through a similar time in the First World War and, therefore, we know from hard and bitter experience how vitally important it is in such a situation for everyone to fulfill his duty fully and willingly and loyally, to maintain a calm presence of mind and a firm trust in God, not to begin to waver or to complain. For this reason, beloved flock, we are today directing a word of exhortation to you in our fatherly love and concern, that it may inspire you to devote your full efforts to the service of the *Vaterland* and the precious *Heimat* in conscientious fulfillment of duty and serious awareness of your mission. We Germans constitute one great community of life and destiny; we Christians constitute a community of belief in Christ and the love of Christ. And if the commandment to love is always the greatest commandment of all, this is especially true in times of danger and need. . . .

In the first years of the World War we saw with joy and pride the greatness that unity brings; but at the end of that war we had to learn how disunity can destroy all that greatness again. To be united is, therefore, the great commandment of this serious hour. To be united in the love and in the service of the *Vaterland* is our wish, so that we may form one single community of sacrifice and effort for the protection of the *Heimat*. We wish to be united, too, in an elevated and devout interpretation of life. Though, unfortunately, we are not united in the same Faith, it is nevertheless a self-evident duty—even more so in wartime than in days of peace—that we respect every honorable religious conviction. We trust, however, that we, too, will be left free to acknowledge and practice our Faith, that we will not suffer injury to our most sacred sentiments and rights. To the free recognition of our religion guaranteed us in the Concordat belongs the freedom to remain loyal to the Faith and to defend it in every situation and circumstance, to attend Mass, to receive the sacraments, to edu-

cate and instruct our children and young people in the Catholic Faith
as is required of parents and clergy as a matter of duty and conscience.
The freer and happier men are in the fulfilling of their duty to God,
the more sacred to them will be the duties to the *Vaterland*. . . .[2]

It will be noted, of course, that the bishops are taking the occasion offered by this morale-strengthening appeal to register at the
same time their public protest against the anti-Catholic policies and
programs of the Nazi regime. Coupling the two served the purpose
of reminding the Nazi rulers that religious toleration would work
to their benefit in the long run. In this sense, then, the pastoral
can be viewed as a "resistance" document in that it clearly suggests
to the faithful that all may not be well in the area of Church-state
relationships as far as the enumerated rights are concerned. But this
very protest feature actually adds emphasis to the patriotic morale
content; for the Catholic who heard this call to duty could easily
(and correctly) conclude that, despite the antireligious aspects and
policies of the Nazi government, of which he might have become
aware, the official leaders of his Church continued to stand united
behind the national war effort.

This patriotism-combined-with-protest theme is also to be found
in the pastoral issued by the combined German Catholic hierarchy
at its annual Fulda conference in 1942. The message itself em-
bodied a declaration that Catholics must remain true to the Church
and the Ten Commandments. However, the morale theme was
given a prominent place in the opening paragraphs:

You know that we bishops are remembering [in the religious services
at Fulda] . . . the German soldiers who with so much heroism and
patience have taken upon themselves the burden of extraordinary
dangers and deprivations. Filled with gratitude, we stand in spirit with
those whose bravery and loyalty bear the seal of serious wounds. Out
of the depths of our hearts we pray for the many who have sacrificed
their lives for *Volk* and *Vaterland,* and for the missing and captured
as well. . . .

The message went on to make specific mention of the priests and religious who had offered much both at the front and at home in their service to the sick and wounded, and it also commiserated those who "under the terrifying air assaults have experienced and continue to experience the severest sufferings."

We sorrow, too, with the wives and mothers, with the brothers and sisters, who have lost their husband, their son, their father, their brother. We remember, too, the millions working on the home front who often drive themselves to the very limits of physical endurance. We lift our hands in prayer to the Almighty and All-Worthy God that He may grant the war dead the favor of eternal peace in Heaven and send us all on earth a peace full of blessings for *Volk* and *Vaterland*.[3]

Even in what must be regarded as the most courageous and outspoken of all the Fulda statements, the 1943 pastoral, the pattern holds true. The letter, taking as its subject the Ten Commandments as the "law of life for all peoples," included some astonishingly direct applications to the situation prevailing in Nazi Germany. At the outset, in a discussion of the First Commandment, the message stressed the limits of secular authority and the necessary dependence of that authority upon its divine source, God's grace. An *Obrigkeit* which depended entirely upon its own might and failed to recognize God as its source and justification ceased to be an "authority" in the sense of possessing a legitimate power to issue commands binding not only the bodies of its subjects but also their consciences. The Sixth and Ninth Commandments were developed into a strong defense of the Catholic family ideal; the fact that this ideal was under strong attack was quite clearly indicated, and a particularly direct application defended "the so-called racially mixed marriage," declaring that such a marriage concluded in the sight of God could not be broken by any law of man. The discussion of the Fifth Commandment stressed the rights of the innocent to life. While the statement did point out that the state as the "servant of God" may take to the sword to punish criminals and to set up armed defense against "unjust attacks upon the *Vaterland*," it included among those innocents specifically protected by the Commandment "innocent hostages, disarmed prisoners of war and other prisoners, people of foreign races or origin." The same solicitude for the innocents was repeated toward the end of the statement when the bishops turned to a consideration of the general commandment to love God and neighbor: "Inspired by this love, we speak, too, in behalf of those who are least able to help themselves —for the innocent people who are not of our *Volk* and blood, for the displaced persons, for the imprisoned or foreign (conscript) laborer and for their right to treatment befitting their human dignity. . . ."

But even this message struck the already familiar keynote in its opening paragraph:

> We memorialize here the brave soldiers on all fronts and in the field hospitals, and thank them in the name of the entire *Volk* for the high courage and never-failing strength which they bring to the task of surrounding us with a strong wall against the enemy. We remember in prayers full of thanksgiving the dead heroes *"who gave their lives for their brethren"* and thereby demonstrated that they had the greatest love in their hearts: "Germany must live, even if we have to die" (italics in original).[4]

There is no need to pursue this theme through all the wartime Fulda pastorals.\* The course was already set in the bishops' pronouncement of September 1939 specifically devoted to the outbreak of war. At that time they stated their intention "to encourage and exhort our Catholic soldiers to do their duty in obedience to the *Führer,* ready for sacrifice and with the commitment of the whole being."[5] Indeed, Strobel, in introducing the war years section of his documentation of episcopal resistance to Nazism, makes the point for us:

\* The selection of episcopal quotations presented in this chapter is based upon *Hirtenbriefe* and other statements reported or reproduced in the German Catholic press. In this, no claim is made for the more thorough coverage of the type that did obtain for succeeding sections which deal with individual members of the hierarchy. One assumes, however, that a complete review of all wartime statements issued at these Fulda meetings would have produced still other examples of the support, indirect and direct, indicated by the quotations presented here.

With respect to the pastorals issued during the war years, the following should be made clear in advance: it goes without saying that they contained no attempt to call for resistance to military service and so forth. The bishops were much more likely to preach to the Catholics in favor of the fulfillment of their patriotic duties, although reference was made at least once to "the war which has been forced upon us" (Gröber's Lenten Pastoral, 1940) in which the Catholics must loyally fulfill their soldierly duties.[6]

Strobel's explanation that the Catholic Church must always and in all places take such a position is more pertinent to a later discussion. Here it is enough to note that his findings confirm those of the present study—both in the direct statement quoted here and, perhaps more significantly, in his obvious inability to find even a single episcopal statement departing from the general pattern of support for Hitler's wars.

The objection might be advanced that these expressions of support of the Catholic fighting men who were "defending the *Heimat* in heroic battle and protecting her from incalculable ills" were merely a matter of form and were not intended to rally German Catholic support for the war. But such statements, made in the most authoritative fashion by the combined spiritual leadership of the Church, cannot be so lightly dismissed—especially when, as in the case of the declaration of the Bavarian hierarchy, direct emphasis is placed on the moral dimensions of support for the nation's military cause. This, coupled with the Fulda praise for the men actually involved in the military operations, could only have meant that such participation was, to say the very least, *permissible* or, to be more accurate, actually *recommended* and even *obligatory*.

These general statements have been introduced first, since they clearly represent the official and most carefully deliberated judgment of the combined hierarchy. From the very beginning of the new world conflict, however, the Catholic press reported many other individual episcopal statements—some of them considerably less circumspect in tone—dealing with the war and the obligations of the Catholic faithful. In introducing brief extracts from one such statement, issued by Cardinal Bertram, the then ranking member of the German hierarchy, in which he told of lessons to be drawn from a reading of letters written by soldiers during World War I, one editor noted that

In recent weeks the German bishops have again lifted their voices in words of guidance and comfort for the faithful in the *Heimat* and at the front concerning the tasks and the sacrifices the present demands of us. One common theme runs through these pastoral writings: in times that demand of men the fullest dedication and ultimate surrender of self, the Catholic turns to the sources of spiritual strength and grace which surmount mere natural powers and perfect the heroism of fighting men.[7]

Cardinal Bertram's message itself stressed spiritual considerations: the power his correspondent-soldiers had found in the Faith, in the practice of prayer, and in the frequent reception of the sacraments. These lessons, taken by themselves, would make for the general edification of the reader; but in the context of the existing military situation (and especially in the context of the glowing editorial introduction), they constituted an obvious and direct contribution to wartime morale.

Other items reported in the Catholic press made even more explicit "morale appeals" in their stress upon the obligations of Catholics, priests as well as laymen, concerning the war. Bishop Rackl of Eichstätt addressed himself to his clergy, declaring that "we priests" would share the burdens of the time of emergency in full and conscientious performance of "our patriotic duty."[8] The same Catholic periodical published another boxed item, reporting a 1940 message addressed by Rackl to his entire diocese stressing (1) the debt of gratitude owed to the German army and "its awe-inspiring leadership and, above all, its fallen heroes," and (2) the obligation to support the annual *Winterhilfswerk* collections.[9] The reference to the army and its leadership was apparently prompted by the successful conclusion of the Polish campaign. As for the

national charity collection, it should be noted that Archbishop
Gröber of Freiburg referred to these collections in the course of a
postwar survey of the evils of the Nazi regime as collections which
were scarcely ever used for the alleviation of suffering but, instead,
were almost entirely devoted to the production of war matériel.[10]
It is unlikely that the Bishop of Eichstätt would have been any less
aware of this fact than was his Freiburg colleague.

Bishop Kumpfmüller of Augsburg directed a message to the men
serving at the front in which he stressed the particular dedication
of the Christian soldier. Since he derives special strength from his
Faith, "the Christian is always the best comrade; the Christian
remains loyal to the flag to which he has sworn allegiance, come
what may."[11] The same theme is given further elaboration by
Bishop Bornewasser of Trier. His message called for a clear recognition that the readiness to bear what must be borne in days of trial
"is, for the Christian, not only a patriotic but also a religious
obligation." Admitting that devotion and loyalty to *Volk* and
*Vaterland* are not the monopoly of the Christian, he added, nevertheless, that making these qualities a religious concern roots them
more firmly in the conscience. Quoting St. Thomas Aquinas and
Pope Leo XIII as teaching "He sins who fails to do his part for the
*Volk* and its problems," he applied this principle to the existing
situation:

But when could the cares of a *Volk* be more trying and the need for
each one to do his part more pressing than in times of war? Therefore,
we must now put all of our inner and external powers at the service of
the *Volk,* not only as Germans but also as Christians following the
principles of our Faith; we must make every sacrifice that the situation
demands of us; we must patiently bear every cross that is placed upon
us. . . .[12]

The Bishop of Würzburg, Matthias Ehrenfried, felt similarly
obliged to issue a call to his flock "for trust in God and self-
sacrificing loyalty to the *Vaterland.*" The soldiers, he declared,
"fulfill their duty to *Führer* and *Vaterland*" by "pledging their whole

personality according to the teachings of Holy Scripture"; and those who stay behind at home are obliged to "stand together in love and unity, in calm and trust, a source of strength and a comfort to the fighting men at the front."[13]

Nowhere in these episcopal statements does one encounter the question, or even a hint of any question, of whether or not the Hitler war effort met the conditions set for a "just war." This silence on what one might expect to be a bishop's first and most troubling concern is crucial to our analysis. The German Catholic who listened to or read these messages could only conclude that either the war was "just" or, if not, that the "just war" question held little or no immediate behavioral relevance for him; that the mere fact that the war was in progress obligated him *as a Christian* to give it his fullest support, even to the point of offering up the ultimate sacrifice of his own life. Unquestioning service to *Volk* and *Vaterland* and the protection of the *Heimat* emerge as virtually the only two standards for determining the individual Catholic's obligations with regard to the war.

But there were some specific issues that did receive attention in episcopal messages, and many of these tended to reinforce the impression that German Catholics had actually been called to service in a just war. Among the principal objectives set in the National Socialist program from the earliest days of the movement's existence were the undoing of the harsh provisions of the Versailles Treaty and the restoration of *Grossdeutschland*. It follows that, whenever these themes are encountered in pastoral letters and episcopal sermons, something of an aura of legitimacy to Hitler's foreign policy of aggrandizement and aggression was provided. And these themes did appear in such episcopal messages, both before and during World War II.

The results of the Saar plebiscite of 1935 which returned that territory to full German administration were greeted with pride and enthusiasm by Bishop Sebastian of Speyer as enduring proof that "he who remains loyal to God will never fail in his loyalty to his country."[14] From time to time other statements would call attention to the fact that the efforts of Catholics, and in particular members of the Catholic clergy, constituted one of the strongest forces for preserving the ties of allegiance to German *Volk* and *Vaterland* on the part of the "separated" populations of territories surrendered by Germany under the terms of the Versailles Treaty. The point most relevant here is not the legitimacy (or lack of it) of these German territorial aspirations; for, certainly, the treaty did contain territorial adjustments of at least questionable justice. What is extremely relevant, though, is the fact that, in discussing these events, the bishops placed their principal emphasis upon the evidence they offered of the ardent patriotism of German Catholics and not on the rectification of injustice the territorial changes of the years just before World War II presumably represented.

The 1938 settlement of the *Sudetenland* dispute was greeted by another burst of episcopal enthusiasm. One can, of course, credit the congratulatory telegram sent to Hitler by the three German Cardinals as having been motivated in great part by the sincere joy they felt over the narrow averting of a threatened armed conflict.[15] But a distinctly nationalistic tone takes precedence in Cardinal Bertram's greeting to the 30,000 Sudeten Germans who had formerly been part of his Breslau diocese and in his frank avowal of unqualified submission to secular authority as a civil and moral duty of the citizen:

How could the Catholic Church, which is a *Volk* church in the most exalted sense, silently ignore a development so rich in meaning for all in the bosom of the *Volk*? . . . Gratitude to God for the preservation of international peace is joined in your community with the second blessed sensation of joy that you are once again united with the rest of Germany. All of us share your joy in the depths of our heart and pray to God that the new arrangement will bear richest blessings for the spiritual and temporal welfare of all communities. . . . There is no need to urge you to give respect and obedience to the new authorities of the German state. You all know the words of the apostle: let every man be subject to the powers placed over him.[16]

The same issue of this periodical reported that Bishop Anton Weber of Leitmeritz (the only formerly Czechoslovakian diocese with a German bishop) was one of the honored guests attending a military parade held in Leitmeritz by order of General von Brauchitsch to mark the return of the *Sudetenland* region to *Grossdeutschland*.[17]

Both the Saar and Sudentenland "home-comings" were bloodless and accomplished through peaceful means and diplomacy—reinforced though they were by massive military threats. The 1938 *Anschluss* with Austria and the military occupation of the Memel region of Lithuania (March 23, 1939), following shortly upon the entry of German troops into the remainder of Czechoslovakia (March 15, 1939), were also peaceful in that they were accomplished so suddenly and so completely that any real threat of active resistance was completely forestalled.

The "restoration" of Danzig and the Polish Corridor to the Greater Reich was quite another matter, coming as one of the first fruits of Nazi Germany's early military success in World War II. A boxed item in a Catholic periodical offers the following description of this turn of events by Bishop Splett of Danzig. Under the heading "Of the Christian Contribution to Germany's Greatness," the item reads:

We are today experiencing how our *Volk* is once again trying to find its way back to all the values that once permitted it to become so great and powerful that as the Holy [Roman] Empire it offered protection and order, not only for Germans but for the whole of Western civilization. That such a turning back and the reinvigoration of the old values that rests upon it cannot be accomplished without disturbances, struggles, and sorrows is, of course, clear enough to us; but over all these there stands nevertheless the happy faith and certain hope that our *Volk* will be granted a time of new greatness and bloom. . . .

In this context the Bishop went on to stress the special responsibility of Catholics to preserve and extend their heritage of the Faith, which had contributed so much to past German greatness.[18]

Perhaps the major contribution made by the German hierarchy toward assuring Catholic conformity to the demands of Hitler's war effort is one that can be traced back to the earliest days of the Third Reich. For by its original act of recognizing and supporting the new Nazi regime as the repository of legitimate authority, the hierarchy bound the individual German Catholic to a moral obligation to obey that authority or, at the very least, to give it the benefit of every reasonable doubt in any apparent conflict of values.

The tendency to explain the episcopal approval extended to the Hitler regime in terms of a presumed helplessness in the face of some horrible reprisal potential, or in terms of a need to follow the pattern set by the Holy See in concluding its Concordat with the new government, is not entirely convincing in either respect. It took a considerable period of time and the most intricate manipulation of events before Hitler was able sufficiently to consolidate his power in order to dare to mount any kind of serious threat to the Catholic Church in Germany. Yet the statements referred to here were issued almost immediately, the first statement of this kind issued by the combined hierarchy appearing on March 28, 1933, just five days after full dictatorial powers were granted to Hitler. It would be every bit as legitimate, perhaps more so, to hold that the Concordat was more the consequence of the enthusiastic welcome given the new regime by the Catholic hierarchy than to regard it as the source of the support furnished that regime by the bishops of Germany.

There might be little doubt that what can now be viewed as an unseemly haste in extending its legitimation to so consciously revolutionary and authoritarian a regime—coupled with what one theologian-informant described to this writer as an addiction to a blind obedience to the secular power in German Catholic moral teaching —did serve, as later history would prove, to assure all-out support for the German cause in World War II long before the grim parade of actual Nazi aggressions began.

This should not obscure the fact that the Catholic Church in Germany did show a strong and often effective resistance to certain Nazi policies and programs:[19] one need only mention Cardinal Faulhaber's rigorous defense of the Old Testament in the face of early Nazi efforts to "de-Judaize" the Christian religion,[20] or Bishop von Galen's heroically direct denunciations of the euthanasia program and Nazi interferences with Church properties.[21] Other occasions of open protest and refusal to co-operate arose from the enforced secularization of schools and the attempt to establish a Nazi monopoly over youth groups and their activities. The attack upon the basic tenets of the Christian Faith posed by Alfred Rosenberg's *Mythus des 20. Jahrhunderts* and the related efforts to promote a neopagan state religion were accepted as a direct challenge and energetically opposed by the Catholic bishops, individually and collectively. Many an issue of the Catholic periodicals was officially confiscated because its contents were offensive to the regime; many such periodicals found their publication rights suspended or withdrawn altogether for daring to report and justify the Church's counterattack in those areas of opposition. And many a Catholic priest found his way into a Nazi concentration camp under charges of "misuse of the pulpit" because he dared to reply to these challenges or protest the assaults upon the Church.

In short, we must recognize that the position taken by the Catholic Church on the Nazi Third Reich was one of mixed support and opposition. While due honor is to be given great Churchmen like Galen and Faulhaber (and even *their* positions, as we shall see, reflected the same mixture of support and opposition), any true assessment of the history of the Church under Nazism must also include the contribution of enthusiasts like Osnabrück's Bishop Berning, who reportedly continued to take pride in his official rank as Prussian *Staatsrat* and Senator of the German *Akademie*.

Such a historical balance might well reveal that the support actually outweighed (in a purely quantitative sense, of course) the opposition represented by the famous leaders of the German Catholic resistance and the hundreds of priests and laymen who suffered and died in Dachau and other concentration camps.* Certainly it

---

* A very useful survey of the experiences of Roman Catholic priests and laymen in concentration camps is to be found in Johannes Maria Lenz's *Christus in Dachau,* cited above on p. 52 n.

is an indisputable historical fact that *at no time was the German Catholic population released from its moral obligation to obey the legitimate authority of the National Socialist rulers under which those Catholics were placed by the 1933 directives of their spiritual leaders; at no time was the individual German Catholic led to believe that the regime was an evil unworthy of his support.* Long after the hollow hypocrisy of the words had become brutally evident, the official spokesmen of the Church continued to quote Hitler's early assurances of support for the Christian Faith in their formal and public appeals against oppressive Nazi actions—thereby helping to perpetuate, unintentionally we may assume, the impression that Hitler somehow stood apart from the evil acts of his associates and underlings. To this extent every such protest contained the risk of actually serving to strengthen the dictator's personal hold over his Catholic subjects.

In 1933, of course, there may have been some excuse for taking these assurances at their face value. We can understand the position taken by Cologne's Cardinal Schulte when, after reminding his flock of the frankly condemnatory tone taken at past Fulda conferences toward the Nazi movement and Catholic participation in it, he described the shift in attitude as follows:

It is now, however, to be acknowledged that public and formal declarations have been made by the foremost representative of the national regime, who is also the authoritarian leader of that movement, that the regime guarantees to respect the integrity of Catholic teachings and the unchangeable mission and rights of the Church, as well as all provisions of the formal agreements concluded between the Church and the various states of Germany [e.g., Bavaria, Baden, and other *Länder* of the German federation]. Therefore, without lifting the judgments concerning specific religious and moral errors on which these former measures [anti-Nazi edicts] were based, the hierarchy now feels it can act in the confidence that it is no longer necessary for these previously designated general proscriptions and warnings to be observed.

There is no need at this time to issue any special call to Catholic Christians, to whom the voice of their Church is holy, to be loyal to the legitimate authority and conscientiously fulfill their civil duties, rejecting on principle all illegal or revolutionary nonco-operation.[22]

The 1933 Fulda pastoral was also devoted to a discussion of the events of "this serious hour of ferment and upheaval." It declared that there was  no need to proclaim a new relationship between Catholics and their *Volk* and *Vaterland;* Catholics had always been obliged to recognize and meet their civil responsibilities. Nor was the strong emphasis upon authoritarianism in the new order viewed as much of a problem: "Only if the individual sees himself as a part of an organism and places the common good ahead of individual good, will his life once again be marked by the humble obedience and joyous service that Christian Faith demands. . . ."

The Church's authoritarian structure is advanced as a model to support this argument; but, lest the authoritarian principle be carried too far, the defense of secular authoritarianism was tempered somewhat by the limiting principle that "human freedom be no more restricted than the common good demands." The new regime's dedication to the aim of regaining Germany's freedom and her proper place in the sun was also welcomed: "We deplore the fact that the victor nations in their blind selfishness shoved justice aside and, by placing a frightful burden on German shoulders, increased the manifold sufferings which, since the end of the war, we have borne to the limit of all endurance. . . ."

But, again, there is no call for a politics of revenge or a new war to rectify these injustices; instead, the bishops limited themselves to an appeal for the peaceful correction of existing inequities. Later issues were anticipated in this message by its explicit warning against an overemphasis on the unity of blood and race "which leads to injustice," even as assurances were offered the new rulers that Catholics would be understanding and self-sacrificing coworkers in the attempt to end the divisions and dissensions within the German *Volk*. After making the point that the well-being of the *Volk* is necessarily founded upon religion, the letter continued: "To our great joy, the leaders of the new state have specifically declared that they place themselves and their work on the foundation of Christianity. This is a public and formal avowal that deserves the heartfelt gratitude of all Catholics. . . ."

The message then specified some of the expectations held by the Church, including recognition of its essential freedom of worship and belief; its right to maintain its own school system; its right to organize religious associations of individuals in the various professions and states of life; its right to be unhindered in its organized works of charity; its right to sponsor and support a Catholic press. But the message hastened to add:

If we German bishops present these enumerated claims, they do not, of course, imply any hidden reservations with regard to the new state. Under no circumstances would we seek to deprive the state of the virtues of the Church, and we may not do so; for only the power of the *Volk* combined with the power of God inexhaustibly streaming forth from the spiritual life can rescue and restore us.[23]

Thus the pattern was set of giving recognition to Hitler and his National Socialist regime as the legitimate secular authority possessing full claim upon the loyalty and obedience of the individual German Catholic, not only as a civil duty but specifically as a *moral* obligation.* This pattern was fixed ever more firmly under the terms of the Concordat concluded in July 1933 and ratified that September, barely eight months after Hitler's accession to power.

* Since this was written a trenchant analysis of the issue has been published in Germany: Ernst-Wolfgang Böckenförde, "Der deutsche Katholizismus im Jahre 1933," *Hochland,* Vol. 53, No. 3 (February 1961), pp. 215-239. An English translation of this article has been published in *Cross Currents,* Vol. 11, No. 3 (Summer 1961), pp. 283-304. The author offers a much more systematic summary of the position taken by the German bishops and other Catholic leaders and reaches the conclusion that it would have been best for German Catholics not to have followed the official advice and directives concerning their political responsibilities offered them by their bishops. The article provides a wealth of revealing quotations—some of them echoing the Nazi ideological concept of the *Volk* state—and proceeds to relate these to traditional "theological-political" teachings which, Böckenförde suggests, require serious re-examination in the light of later history. A rejoinder to Böckenförde's article was published in *Hochland,* Vol. 53, No. 6 (August 1961), pp. 497-515.

And the pattern was maintained, despite the continued unfolding of the antireligious and peace-endangering nature of National Socialism and its objectives; indeed, as noted above, the pattern was specifically extended to the Catholics of other populations drawn into the orbit of Nazi rule.

At no time was there any serious possibility that the German Catholic hierarchy would openly denounce the Nazi regime in such a manner as to imply that it was no longer to be considered legitimate authority—although these eminent Churchmen were not deluded for long as to the essentially unchristian and even anti-Christian quality of that regime, its *Weltanschauung,* and its programs, judged by the moral standards these Churchmen were to uphold and protect. Nor did the Vatican ever take any formal action which would have withdrawn its recognition of the legitimacy of the Hitler regime, although his famous 1937 encyclical, *Mit brennender Sorge,* furnishes ample evidence that Pius XI was well aware of the course of developments in Germany.* Considerations of prudence and a

---

* Bishop Neuhäusler, the eminent author of *Kreuz und Hakenkreuz,* told the writer about some of the efforts made by the Nazis to block the circulation of this document among Germany's Catholics, and of the severe punishments meted out to publishers who had anything to do with printing it. He also described the often fantastic stratagems employed by the German hierarchy to circumvent the attempts of the Nazis to suppress the encyclical. Copies were delivered by secret courier to priests for public reading; sometimes they were not delivered until the moment before the priest was ready to ascend the pulpit. The length of the document presented a special problem because this was also the time of the lengthy Easter season observances; this led some priests to read the opening paragraphs and then announce that the remainder of the encyclical would be read at the evening service, thereby forcing the authorities to choose between permitting the completion of the reading and making their suppression of the document a matter of public record.

The encyclical itself was a stirring protest against the Third Reich's violation of the Concordat and, in particular, its assaults against Christian teachings. In censuring Nazi attacks on Christianity, Pius condemned Rosenberg's direct attempt to introduce a new religion of heathenism, and the more subtle efforts to "purify" Christianity by removing its Jewish components and the "weakness and humility" image, which was regarded as unsuited to the "heroic" image deemed more proper to the *Herrenvolk* ideology. Other aspects of the Nazi government program condemned by the Pope were the Nazi efforts to win children away from the Church by secularizing the schools and absorbing all youth activities under the Hitler Jugend move-

regard for the benefits to be gained through continued diplomatic contact argued against punitive action on the part of the Holy See; yet, in effect, as long as papal recognition continued, the German Catholic was in the difficult position of being morally obliged to render obedience to a presumably legitimate authority dedicated to the destruction of the moral values represented by his Church. And when war finally came, this difficult position became one of impossible confusion in which the confusion would be compounded by the guidance offered by the spiritual leaders of German Catholicism.

Resistance on the part of the Catholic Church in Nazi Germany there was, and it was a truly heroic resistance. But the scope of resistance was most generally limited to those issues involving direct

---

ments; and the elevation of racist and national values to absolute priority. It would, of course, be an exaggeration to regard *Mit brennender Sorge* as a formal condemnation of the Nazi regime by which German Catholics were released from their obligations of obedience to it as "legitimate authority." Indeed, the encyclical did not even go so far as terminating Vatican-Reich diplomatic relations. However, it did include some strong instructions that might be applied to the present study. In his exhortation to the clergy, Pius XI called for a "comprehending and merciful charity towards the erring, and even towards the contemptuous," but cautioned that this "does not mean and cannot mean that you renounce in any way the proclaiming of, the insisting on, and the courageous defense of the truth and its free and unhindered application to the realities about you. The first and obvious duty the priest owes to the world about him is service to the truth, the whole truth, the unmasking and refutation of error in whatever form or disguise it conceals itself. To fail in this would be not only treason against God and your vocation, but a crime against the true welfare of your people and of your fatherland." He went on to express his concern and gratitude for the sacrifices being made by priests who were already in prisons and concentration camps. See text in Terence P. McLaughlin, C.S.B., ed., *The Church and the Reconstruction of the Modern World* (New York: Doubleday, 1957), p. 356.

The Nazi reaction could be interpreted as evidence of an awareness of a serious potential threat to their security through the possibility that German Catholic opinion might be mobilized against them. This raises the intriguing conjecture that German Catholics and their bishops were not really as powerless as they thought themselves to be. While such a hypothetical question can never be answered, there is, of course, no question but that a more concerted opposition on the part of German Catholics would have provoked drastic reprisals by the Nazis. Nevertheless, there is some reason to question how effective these reprisals would have been had the bishops chosen to rally the Catholic faithful to a more thoroughgoing opposition—and had they been successful in the effort.

assaults upon Church rights and property or those government programs which in the eyes of the Catholic hierarchy clearly contradicted Catholic moral principles. Active participation in or other
forms of support for Hitler's wars of aggression were apparently
not recognized as such a contradiction of principle—indeed, quite
a contrary view is indicated by the tenor of their wartime directives.*

On the basis of this brief survey of the positions taken publicly
by the general Catholic hierarchy—at least as those positions were
reported in the Catholic religious periodicals of the time—one must
conclude that two of the important social controls inducing Catholic
conformity to the demands of the Hitler war effort were to be found
in the external pressures exerted by leading Church officials and
the internal conviction of moral responsibility that the words and
examples of these leaders would be expected to instill in the hearts
and consciences of individual German Catholics.

*NOTES*

1. See above, pp. 21 ff.

2. *Amtsblatt für die Erzdiözese München und Freising* (February 25,
1941), pp. 29-30.

"Liebe Diözesanen! Die Zeit, in der wir leben ist entscheidungsvoll für
eine lange Zukunft, entscheidungsvoll für unser vaterländisches, wirtschaft-
liches, geistiges und religiöses Leben. Wir haben eine ähnliche Zeit schon
durchlebt in Weltkrieg und wissen daher aus einer harten und bitteren
Erfahrung, wie notwendig und wichtig es ist, dass in solcher Lage jeder-

---

* Actions, too, may be cited in this connection. Brief biographical
sketches of Franz Jägerstätter, the Austrian Catholic peasant who was beheaded for refusing to serve in what he believed to be an unjust war, tell
of the direct instructions he received from his bishop to the effect that he
had no right to reach such a judgment nor to take such a stand. Only when
Jägerstätter persisted in his refusal did the bishop relent to the point of
saying that he would be morally permitted to accept such martyrdom only
if he were absolutely certain that his decision was the result of a personal
revelation and not motivated by selfish or personal considerations. These
brief accounts may be found in Kreuzberg, *op. cit.*, pp. 184-187, and Fried,
*op. cit.*, pp. 82-83.

mann ganz und gern und treu seine Pflicht erfüllt, ruhige Besonnenheit und festes Gottvertrauen bewahrt und nicht anfängt zu zagen und zu klagen. Darum richten wir heute an euch, liebe Diözesanen, in väterlicher Liebe und Sorge ein Wort der Ermahnung, das euch ermuntern möchte, in gewissenhafter Pflichterfüllung und ernster Berufsauffassung die ganze Kraft einzusetzen im Dienste des Vaterlandes und der teuren Heimat. Wir Deutsche bilden eine grosse Lebens- und Schicksalsgemeinschaft, wir Christen bilden auch eine Gemeinschaft im Glauben an Christus und in der Liebe Christi. Und wenn das Gebot der Liebe immer das grösste Gebot von allen ist, dann ganz besonders in Zeiten der Gefahr und der Not. . . .

"Wir haben in den ersten Jahren des Weltkrieges mit Freude und Stolz gesehen, was die Einigkeit Grosses vollbringt, wir haben am Ende des Weltkrieges aber auch erfahren müssen, wie die Uneinigkeit alles Grosse wieder zerstört. Einig zu sein, ist daher jetzt das grosse Gebot der ernsten Stunde. Einig wollen wir sein in der Liebe und im Dienste des Vaterlandes —, wollen zum Schutze der Heimat eine einzige Opfer- und Arbeitsgemeinschaft bilden. Einig wollen wir sein auch in gläubiger und hoher Lebensauffassung. Sind wir leider nicht einig im gleichen Glauben, so ist es doch im Kriege noch mehr als im Frieden eine selbstverständliche Pflicht, dass wir jede ehrliche Glaubensüberzeugung achten. Wir vertrauen aber auch, dass wir selbst unseren Glauben frei bekennen und betätigen können und dass wir in unseren heiligsten Gefühlen und Rechten nicht verletzt werden. Zum freien Bekenntnis unserer Religion, das uns im Reichskonkordat zugesichert ist, gehört die Freiheit, den Glauben in jeder Lage und Stellung treu zu bewahren, den Gottesdienst zu besuchen, die heiligen Sakramente zu empfangen, die Kinder und die Jugend im katholischen Glauben zu erziehen und zu unterrichten, wie es Pflicht und Gewissen von katholischen Eltern und von den Seelsorgern verlangen. Je freier und freudiger die Menschen ihre Pflichten gegen Gott erfüllen, um so heiliger sind ihnen auch die Pflichten gegen das Vaterland. . . ."

3. *Kirchlicher Anzeiger für die Erzdiözese Köln* (1942 volume, exact date not noted), p. 141.

"Ihr Diözesanen wisst, dass wir Bischöfe in diesen Tagen an den Altären des Domes . . . der deutschen Soldaten gedenken, die mit soviel Heldenmut und Ausdauer Not und Gefahren sondergleichen auf sich nehmen. Voll dankbarer Ergriffenheit stehen wir im Geiste bei denen, die mit schweren Wunden ihre Tapferkeit und Treue besiegelt haben. Wir beten aus Herzensgrund für die vielen, die ihr Leben für Volk und Vaterland zum Opfer brachten, nicht weniger für die Vermissten und Gefangenen. . . .

"Wir trauern mit den Frauen und Müttern, mit den Brüdern und Schwestern, die ihren Mann, ihren Sohn, ihren Vater, ihren Bruder verloren haben. Wir gedenken auch der Millionen, die ihre Kräfte in der Heimatarbeit oft bis zu den Grenzen ihrer Kraft zum Einsatz bringen. Betend erheben wir unsere Hände zum allmächtigen und allgütigen Gott mit der Bitte, Er möge den Gefallenen den ewigen Frieden im Himmel und bald einen für Volk und Vaterland segensreichen Frieden uns allen auf Erden schenken. . . ."

4. The text of the 1943 pastoral is found in Fried, *op. cit.,* pp. 213-220. "Wir gedenken der tapferen Soldaten auf allen Fronten und in den Lazaretten und danken ihnen im Namen des ganzen Volkes für den hohen Mut und die immer gleiche Kraft, die sie alle aufbringen, um uns mit einem starken Wall gegen die Feinde zu umgeben. Wir gedenken im Gebet voll Dankbarkeit der toten Helden, die *"ihr Leben hingaben für die Brüder",* und damit zeigten, dass sie in ihrem Herzen die grösste Liebe hatten: "Deutschland muss leben, auch wenn wir sterben müssen."

5. "Erklärung der deutschen Bischöfe zum Kriegsausbruch, September 1939," cited in Ferdinand Strobel, *Christliche Bewahrung* (Olten Switzerland : Verlag Otto Walter AG, 1946), p. 116.

6. *Ibid.,* pp. 59-60. "Zu den *Hirtenbriefen* während der Kriegsjahre ist folgende Vorbemerkung am Platz: Es ist selbstverständlich verfehlt, in ihnen Aufforderungen zum Widerstand gegen den Kriegsdienst usw. suchen zu wollen. Die Bischöfe predigen vielmehr den Katholiken immer wieder Erfüllung der vaterländischen Pflichten, reden wohl auch einmal von einem "uns aufgezwungenen Krieg" *(Fastenbrief Gröbers,* 1940), in welchem der Katholik seine soldatischen Pflichten treu erfüllen müsse."

7. *Münchener Katholische Kirchenzeitung,* Vol. 32, No. 41 (October 8, 1939), p. 545. "In den letzten Wochen haben die Deutschen Bischöfe wieder ihre Stimme erhoben, um den Gläubigen in der Heimat und an der Front Worte der Wegweisung und des Trostes zu geben für die Aufgaben und Opfer, die die Gegenwart von uns verlangt. Durch diese Hirtenschreiben zieht sich das eine Gemeinsame: In Stunden, die vom Menschen vollen Einsatz und letzte Hingabe verlangen, geht der Katholik zu den Quellen der Gnadenkräfte, die unsere natürlichen Kräfte überhöhen und das Heldentum der Kämpfenden vollenden."

8. *Klerusblatt* (Organ der Diozesan-Priestervereine Bayerns und ihres Wirtschaftlichen Verbandes), Vol. 20 (September 27, 1940), p. 511.

9. *Ibid.,* Vol. 21 (November 20, 1939), p. 58.

10. *Amtsblatt für die Erzdiözese Freiburg.* No. 4 (May 12, 1945), p. 15. "Darum auch die geheime und öffentliche Kriegsrüstung und die Sammlung zum Winterhilfswerk, die kaum je zur Linderung der Armut, sondern fast ausschliesslich zur Beschaffung von Kriegsmaterial verwendet wurde."

11. *Münchener Katholische Kirchenzeitung,* Vol. 33, No. 1 (January 7, 1940), p. 3.

12. *Ibid.,* Vol. 33, No. 8 (February 25, 1940), p. 45. "Wann aber wären die Sorgen eines Volkes schwerer und der Einsatz eines jeden notwendiger als in Kriegszeiten? Daher müssen wir nicht nur als

Deutsche, sondern auch als Christen aus unserem Glauben heraus jetzt alle unsere äusseren und inneren Kräfte freimachen zum Dienste am Volke, müssen jedes Opfer bringen, das die Zeitlage von uns verlangt, müssen geduldig jedes Kreuz tragen, das uns auferlegt wird. Wir müssen das tun, indem wir das ewig vorbildliche Gebet des Erlösers wiederholen: 'Vater, nicht mein, sondern dein Wille geschehe.' "

13. *Würzburger Diözeseanblatt,* Vol. 85 (September 4, 1939), page not noted.

14. *Bayrische Katholische Kirchenzeitung,* Vol. 11 (February 4, 1935), p. 31.

15. *Ibid.,* Vol. 14 (October 9, 1938), p. 288.

16. *Ibid.,* Vol. 14 (November 6, 1938), p. 316.

"Wie könnte die katholische Kirche, die eine Volkskirche im edelsten Sinne ist, an solchen für alle Volkskreise hochbedeutsamen Wendungen schweigend vorübergehen? . . . Mit dem Dank an Gott für die Sicherung des Völkerfriedens verbindet sich in euren Gemeinden als zweites beglückendes Empfinden die Freude darüber, dass ihr wieder mit dem übrigen Deutschland vereinigt seid! An dieser eurer Freude nehmen wir alle herzinnigen Anteil und beten zu Gott, dass die Neugestaltung von reichstem Segen für das geistliche und weltliche Heil in allen Gemeinden werden möge. . . . Es bedarf nicht der Mahnung, der neuen Obrigkeit im deutschen Staat Ehrerbietung und Gehorsam zu erweisen. Ihr alle kennt die Worte des Apostels: Jedermann sei untertan den obrigkeitlichen Gewalten."

17. *Ibid.*

18. *Klerusblatt,* Vol. 22, No. 8 (February 19, 1941), p. 59.

"Wir erleben heute, wie unser Volk wieder zu all den Werten zurückzufinden sucht, die es einmal so gross und mächtig werden liessen, dass es als Heiliges Reich nicht nur den Deutschen, sondern dem ganzen Abendland Schutz und Ordnung bot. Das eine solche Rückbesinnung und die darauf beruhende Verlebendigung alter Werte nicht ohne Erschütterungen, Kämpfe und Sorgen vor sich geht, spüren wir zwar deutlich genug, aber über all diesem stehen doch froher Glaube und sichere Hoffnung, dass unserem Volk eine Zeit neuer Grösse und Blüte geschenkt werden möge. . . ."

19. For a fully documented review of this Catholic resistance, see Neuhäusler, *op. cit.*

20. See below, p 108.

21. See below, pp. 85-87.

22. *Kirchlicher Anzeiger für die Erzdiözese Köln* (April 1, 1933), p. 53. "Es ist nunmehr anzuerkennen, dass von dem höchsten Vertreter der Reichsregierung, der zugleich autoritär Führer jener Bewegung ist, öffentlich und feierlich Erklärungen gegeben sind, durch die der Unverletzlichkeit der katholischen Glaubenslehre und den unveränderlichen Aufgaben und Rechten der Kirche Rechnung getragen sowie die vollinhaltliche Geltung der

von den einzelnen deutschen Ländern mit der Kirche abgeschlossenen Staatsverträge durch die Reichsregierung ausdrücklich zugesichert wird. Ohne die in seinen früheren Massnahmen liegende Verurteilung bestimmter religiössittlicher Irrtümer aufzuheben, glaubt daher der Episcopat das Vertrauen hegen zu können, dass die vorbezeichneten allgemeinen Verbote und Warnungen nicht mehr als notwendig betrachtet zu werden brauchen.

"Für die katholischen Christen, denen die Stimme ihrer Kirche heilig ist, bedarf es auch im gegenwärtigen Zeitpunkte keiner besonderen Mahnung zur Treue gegenüber der rechtmässigen Obrigkeit und zur gewissenhaften Erfüllung der staatsbürgerlichen Pflichten unter grundsätzlicher Ablehnung alles rechtswidrigen oder umstürzlerischen Verhaltens."

23. *Ibid.* (Special number), No. 15 (June 9, 1933), pp. 92, 93, 94, 96. "Nur wenn der Einzelne sich als ein Glied eines Organismus betrachtet und das Allgemeinwohl über das Einzelwohl stellt, wird sein Leben wieder ein demütiges Gehorchen und freudiges Dienen, wie es der christliche Glaube verlangt. . . . Wir bedauern es, dass die Siegernationen in verblendeter Selbstsucht die Gerechtigkeit hintansetzen und durch eine ungeheure Belastung der deutschen Schultern das mannigfache Elend vermehren, unter dem wir seit dem Kriegsende bis  zur Unerträglichkeit leiden. . . . Zu unserer grossen Freude haben die führenden Männer des neuen Staates ausdrücklich erklärt, dass sie sich selbst und ihr Werk auf den Boden des Christentums stellen. Es ist das ein öffentliches, feierliches Bekenntnis, das den herzlichen Dank aller Katholiken verdient. . . .

"Geliebten Diözesanen! Wenn wir deutschen Bischöfe die aufgezählten Forderungen erheben, so liegt darin nicht etwa ein versteckter Vorbehalt dem neuen Staat gegenüber. Wir wollen dem Staat um keinen Preis die Kräfte der Kirche entziehen, und wir dürfen es nicht, weil nur die Volkskraft und die Gotteskraft, die aus dem kirchlichen Leben unversiegbar strömt, uns erretten und erheben kann. . . ."

# CHAPTER 7

# Clement August von Galen

*"It is better to die than to sin."*\*

FEW NAMES will outrank that of Clement August von Galen, the Bishop of Münster, in any roll of honor registering the names of opponents of Hitler and his National Socialist regime. The postwar elevation to the dignity of the Cardinalate of the "Lion of Münster" (together with Bishop von Preysing of Berlin) is rightly regarded as a mark of papal recognition for his heroic stand in the face of the totalitarian demands of the Third Reich. In fact, many of his devoted wartime flock and other ardent admirers have already instituted preliminary efforts to promote the cause of his canonization.

These honors and this devotion, let it be said at once, are fully deserved. If the Old Testament narrative of Abraham's pleas that Sodom be spared were applied to the course of these events so that the presence of even ten just and good men might have saved Germany and its Catholic community, a strong argument can be made for including this man in even so small a number. In July and August 1941, Galen mounted the pulpit and thundered a series of open and direct challenges to the Nazi terror-state in terms that still stir

\* *Lieber sterben als sündigen.*

a note of wonder and admiration. The first of these, delivered July 13, listed specific acts taken by the government against convents and religious orders, and expressed his public and official protest against these assaults. The protest rested upon the principle that "Justice is the foundation of the State," and its concluding section amounted to a spiritual call to arms in defense of that principle:

And, therefore, in the name of the righteous German *Volk,* in the name of the majesty of justice, in the interests of peace and the solidarity of the inner front, I raise my voice; as a German, as an honorable citizen, as a representative of the Christian religion, as a Catholic bishop, I publicly declare: We demand justice! If this call remains unheard, if the rule of Justice, the Queen, is not restored, then our German *Volk* and *Vaterland* will perish of inner decay and rottenness despite the heroism of our soldiers and their glorious victories.[1]

The following week the Bishop faced the congregation of Münster's *Liebfrauenkirche* (Überwasser) and delivered what is properly regarded as the single most stirring statement of episcopal opposition to the Nazi rule. Enumerating the additional assaults suffered by his diocese at the hands of government officials since the previous Sunday's sermon, he called for patient endurance on the part of his spiritual flock. To make his point with greatest effect, he set his appeal in terms of a highly dramatic figure of speech:

Be strong! Stand firm! Right now we are not the hammer, but rather the anvil. Others, for the most part enemies and apostates, beat upon us seeking to bend us by force from our true relation to God and to impose a new form upon our *Volk,* ourselves, and our children. But take a lesson from the forge! Ask the smithy and learn from him this truth: that which is hammered out on the anvil takes its form not only from the hammer but also from the anvil. The anvil cannot and need not strike back; it need only stand firm and strong. If it is tough enough and firm enough, the anvil usually outlives the hammer. And no matter how forcefully the hammer may strike, the anvil stands there in quiet firmness and will long continue to shape that which is being forged anew. . . .

The hammer-anvil metaphor was not, of course, original with the Bishop.* The sermon proceeded to outline and describe some of the things "that are being beaten into form today" by the Nazi hammer and called upon Münster's Catholics to bear the hardships of the day in the calm confidence that theirs would be a certain and eternal reward, even though "it may be that obedience to God will cost you or me our life, freedom, or *Heimat*. But it is better to die than to sin!"[2]

The third in this series of sermons, delivered again in St. Lambert's Church, the scene of the first, was primarily concerned with a public denunciation of the Nazi *Sterbehilfe* (euthanasia) program as an open violation of the Fifth Commandment. This special focus did not, however, keep him from attacking other government-encouraged or sponsored activities which violated other commandments as well. Building upon the Gospel lesson of the day, the incident of Jesus weeping over the prophetic vision of the destruction of Jerusalem, the Bishop warned:

My Christians! I hope there is still time, but time is running out. Let us recognize right now, this very day, what makes for our peace! What alone can save us, can spare us from the divine wrath:

That we completely and without reservation accept God's revealed truth and acknowledge it in our lives;

That we must take the divine commandments as the guidelines of our lives and earnestly live according to the word: It is better to die than to sin!

That through prayer and sincere penance we call forth God's forgiveness and mercy upon us, our city, our country, and our whole beloved German *Volk*.[3]

It is not difficult to understand why these sermons furnished a

* The writer's colleague, Dr. Edward Gargan, has pointed out that the same metaphor was used in an almost parallel context by Voltaire in his article on "Tyranny" in the *Philosophical Dictionary*. In translation the passage reads, in part, "I fear that in this world one must be either hammer or anvil; for it is indeed a lucky man who escapes these alternatives" (Ben Ray Redman, ed., *The Portable Voltaire* [New York: Viking, 1949], p. 218).

source of new inspiration to those Germans who, singly or as members of groups, were active in the underground resistance to Hitler. Informants described how copies were duplicated throughout Germany by every available means and furtively passed from hand to hand, always at the certain risk of the loss of freedom and possibly life for both the distributor and the reader. As for the Bishop himself, stories abound of the threats of, and actual preparations for, arrests that never took place. Legends still circulate telling of Galen's bold declarations to the threat-bearing Gestapo that he would willingly submit to arrest—in the full regalia of his episcopal office! Legend or not, it is clear that the Bishop held so firm a place in the hearts of his people that the better part of prudence did indeed impose forbearance, however frustrating it might have been, upon those who felt the biting lash of his now famous sermons.

But however joyously these sermons were welcomed by the men and women of the German resistance, no evidence was encountered to suggest that Galen ever gave any public or official support to the movement. The extent of his contributions to any such resistance seems to have been limited to protesting specific Nazi aggressions against the Catholic Church and its teachings. Beyond this he did not go. Indeed, the same "hammer-anvil" sermon that ended on a note certain to quicken the enthusiasm of the men in the resistance forces included a paragraph that would constitute a serious obstacle to any effort to win Catholic support for a program of direct action against the Nazi rulers:

Of course, we Christians make no revolution! We will continue to do our duty in obedience to God, out of love for our German *Volk* and *Vaterland*. Our soldiers will fight and die for Germany, but not for those men who wound our hearts and bring shame upon the German name before God and before man by their cruel acts against their brothers and sisters of the religious orders. Bravely we continue the fight against the foreign foe; against the enemy in our midst who tortures and strikes us, we cannot fight with weapons. There is but one means available to us in this struggle: strong, obstinate, enduring perseverance.[4] *

The quotation already cited from the July 13 sermon included specific mention of the "glorious victories" won by the German soldiers. A similar note is struck in his protest against the eviction of religious orders from their convent properties. Stressing the patriotism displayed by members of the orders, he cited the fact that 161 religious were actually serving "as German soldiers in the field, some of them in the front lines," and he went on to complain that

While these German men fight for the *Heimat* in true comradeship with their other German brothers, at the risk of their lives and obedient to their duty, their *Heimat* is being taken away from them, the convent that is their family home is destroyed—ruthlessly and without any justification.[5]

Thus, even these most forceful expressions of opposition to Hitler and his regime were at one and the same time clear indications to the Bishop's hearers that it was a duty—indeed an honored duty —to fight in the wars undertaken by that regime. It is true that the

* Here we have a striking example of the kind of text alteration in Neuhäusler's *Kreuz und Hakenkreuz* discussed by Müller (see note on p. 52 n. above). Neuhäusler, too, furnishes the text of this sermon by Galen. But as he has it (Vol. II, p. 262), this quoted portion reads: "Of course we Christians make no revolution! We will continue to do our duty in obedience to God, out of love for our German *Volk* and *Vaterland*: 'Against the enemy in our midst who tortures and strikes us, we cannot fight with weapons. There is but one means available to us in this struggle: strong, obstinate, enduring perseverance!'"
It is quite significant to the thesis being presented here that Galen's stirring appeal for continuation of "the fight against the foreign foe" was apparently viewed by Neuhäusler as a potential source of embarrassment.
But Bierbaum, from whose biography of the Bishop we have quoted in this chapter, is also guilty of some omissions. In his appendix giving the supposedly complete texts of Galen's sermons of July 13 and July 20, he omits the closing prayers, in the first instance for "our German *Volk* and *Vaterland* and its *Führer*," and in the second for "our *Volk* and *Vaterland* and its *Führer*." These prayers are given in Heinrich Portmann, *Bischof von Galen Spricht*, included in the series *Das christliche Deutschland, Katholische Reihe*, No. 3 (Freiburg: Herder, 1946), pp. 52, 61. Portmann also (p. 112) includes a letter from Galen to Göring in which the Bishop closes "mit deutschem Gruss," the term referring to the "Heil, Hitler!" salute.

statement of support does make an explicit distinction between the Nazi cause at home and the German cause on the war front; but the validity of this distinction and its implications present another analytical problem which will be discussed more fully in connection with the general analysis and conclusions to be presented later.[6] At this point, however, it is proper to note that these messages of Galen's—including the distinction—would certainly have served to induce continued conformity to the demands associated with the war even as they established his claim to honor and recognition as an outspoken opponent of National Socialism.

The sources of this apparent paradox can be traced to his life history. Born in 1878 a member of the German nobility (as the eldest son he inherited the title of Count upon the death of his father in 1906), he never really abandoned the aristocratic system of values, with its particular affinity to the hyperpatriotic and militaristic trappings of the old order. Galen's personal reactions to the outbreak of World War I were already a foreshadowing of the support he would later give as a Bishop to World War II. In his eyes, that earlier war was a "struggle for our existence," and he wrote his beloved younger brother of the joy and pride he took in the latter's military career.[7] His biographer tells of the certainty then prevailing in Germany of the nation's just cause and of the unity of will marshaled behind the defense of the *Vaterland*. The day following the outbreak of hostilities in 1914 found Galen, then chaplain of a young men's society in Berlin, volunteering his services to the Military Bishop because, as he put it, "I believe that every one who is able must now put himself in the service of the *Vaterland*."[8] A week later, he wrote another letter to his brother saying, "Each of us at his proper place in devotion to duty and readiness to sacrifice will want to implore God's mercy upon our *Vaterland* and God's protection for our soldiers."[9] His application for duty as a military chaplain denied, he found solace in the thought that even in Berlin there would be war work he could do.[10]

As the First World War progressed, American demands upon Germany were greeted with the opinion, "I cannot feel that we should give in to America. Of what help to us is a sham neutrality that in reality supports our enemies and strikes the last weapons from our hands?"[11] Even the August 1917 peace appeal issued by Benedict XV received somewhat critical comment; the young Galen conceded that the Pope was trying to help Germany but noted that there was an implication that Germany should admit defeat—a dismal thought, since "I dare not share the Holy Father's hope that from now on Right, rather than Might, will reign." Nevertheless, "we must place all our trust in God and prepare ourselves to accept whatever He sends with humility."[12]

Bitter sarcasm marks the letter of October 7, 1918, in which he told his brother, "We are now going to be governed 'democratically' and in a 'parliamentary' fashion. The enemies who did not succeed in defeating us militarily have known how to wear away our unity on the home front with phrases and slogans." Scornfully, he ticked off the elements of "the new line": antimilitarism, self-determination of peoples, creation of a League of Nations—"all attractive ideas which one could easily support with enthusiasm but which are suspect from the start because they are promulgated by the Freemason Wilson and bound up with the notorious thirst for vengeance, the greed, and the hunger for power that paved the way for war in the first place." This letter proceeded to describe the forces contributing to the downfall of the imperial regime and dismissed as "unfortunate" the *Reichstag* session at which the appeal for peace on the basis of the Wilson proposals was approved.[13] The fact that this same stab-in-the-back theory was exploited by Hitler in *Mein Kampf* and elsewhere (the latter was even more displeased with the "November criminals" who finally signed the agreements ending World War I) is not without significance for an understanding of Galen's position when this war would "break out anew" in 1939.

For the present, however, these statements provide sufficient basis for understanding that Galen was not overmuch disturbed by the ultimate collapse of the Weimar Republic—though it is also uncontested that he did give it his support as the embodiment of legitimate authority. Again, as a member of the nobility who was dedicated to its aristocratic value system, he probably found the rabble-rousing associated with the Nazi movement and the support it drew from the *Lumpenproletariat* extremely distasteful. It is clear, however, that once Hitler came to power, the mantle of legitimate authority would descend upon his regime in Galen's eyes. It was a nice irony of fate, therefore, that the newly named Bishop of Münster—the man who was later to become a center of opposition to certain aspects of the Hitler regime—was the first German bishop to be sworn to the oath of allegiance prescribed under the terms of the Concordat. Named bishop on September 5, 1933, Galen was consecrated on October 28. Five days earlier he had taken the civil oath before Göring in Berlin.

Widely circulated and officially inspired charges impugning the loyalty of Germany's Catholics played a major part in the Nazi campaigns to discredit and undermine the position of the Church. In 1935 Galen issued a statement repudiating these charges:

We are good Germans and we are at the same time good Catholics. This involves no contradiction, no inconsistency within ourselves or in our intentions. And this is why we protest when people attack the belief in a personal and supernatural God as un-German. . . . It is truly not only a religious but also a national duty for us continually to protest such action, continually to lift our voice in warning against the propaganda of an ostensibly "German-minded" heathenism.[14]

Later in that same year, the Bishop returned to this theme, spelling out the relationship between German Catholics and the Nazi state in the course of an address delivered to a conference of his deans. After describing some of the difficult circumstances in which the Church in Germany found itself, he declared that it was not his place "to pass judgment upon the political organization and form of government of the German *Volk* or upon official government measures and proceedings, to yearn for previous forms of government, or to criticize contemporary politics." To add further weight to this position, he specifically cited the fact that a Concordat had been concluded with "the present authoritarian state" as evidence that the Holy See recognized it as the legitimate authority for Germany.[15]

In the light of the foregoing, then, it is not at all surprising that this most outspoken of all the opponents of Hitler consistently restricted his protests to official actions which directly violated the rights and teachings of the Catholic Church—and that these protests were coupled with the restraining caution that "we Christians make no revolutions."

Still another factor of singular importance in explaining this pattern of outspoken protest in the context of loyal support may be found in the fact that the Catholic Church and National Socialism found a common ground in their antagonism toward Bolshevist Communism. In 1939 Galen issued an exultant pastoral greeting the end of the Spanish Civil War. He found an immediate cause for joy in the mere fact that the bloody conflict was over, a conflict that had divided a people to whom Germans owed a particular debt of gratitude for its refusal—despite all the propaganda efforts of Germany's enemies in World War I—"to take part in that war of annihilation waged against our *Volk* and *Vaterland*." But a further cause for rejoicing lay in the fact that the Communist forces had been vanquished. Recalling past evidences of the Catholic Church's unwavering opposition to Communism, he described the offenses attributed to the defeated Spanish government and continued:

Thus did godless Communism and Bolshevism rage in Spain for more than three years! That was the enemy who now, with God's help, has been thoroughly defeated and stripped of all his power. What dangers would have faced the Christian West, our *Volk*, too—indeed, the whole world—had Moscow emerged victorious and succeeded in erecting and establishing a new center of militant atheism and disruptive agitation affecting Christian states on both sides of the Mediterranean!

That is why we join with the heroic and liberated Spanish people in their jubilation and gratitude toward God Who gave the victory to the brave warriors against the legions of the antichrist. . . .[16]

The Franco rebellion may indeed have been accomplished "with God's help," but the German Catholic would not have been unimpressed by the fact that considerable "help" was given by the Nazi forces dispatched by Hitler to become part of "the brave warriors against the legions of the antichrist." If God and Hitler were on the same side in this struggle, might it not be easy to assume that their alliance continued into World War II?

One might well think so when one turns to Galen's message of September 1944, in which he dedicated the annual "Prayer-and-Penance" holiday to *Volk* and *Vaterland*. Lacking are the joyous overtones of victory, but the sentiments are the same:

In this hour I must direct a word of greeting and acknowledgment to our soldiers. I wish to express our gratitude to them for the loyal protection they have furnished the *Vaterland* and its borders at the price of unspeakable strains and sheer superhuman effort. In particular for the defense against the assaults of godless Bolshevism! And a word of deep-felt remembrance for those who, in the performance of their duty, have offered their lives and the last drop of blood for their brothers. May these all-sacrificing efforts succeed in winning for us an honorable and victorious peace![17]

His biographer, Bierbaum, speaks of the special problems presented by the outbreak of World War II, one of them being the fact that the efforts of the Catholic peace movement in Germany had raised many strong doubts as to the legitimacy of war. These doubts had been reinforced by the deliberations of a 1932 Freiburg (Switzerland) conclave of Catholic theologians and their formal statement that modern war had ceased to be an instrument proportional to the ends of achieving order and peace, that the moral permissibility of even defensive war had been reduced to stringently narrow limits. Another of these "special problems" centered upon the moral doubts associated with this war and the opportunity it afforded the Nazis to further hinder the work of the Church by disguising restrictive and punitive actions as "emergency war measures" and labeling any attempt to resist them as acts of treason.[18] These problems may have been in the mind of the Bishop, but there was no hint of them in his first wartime message to his clergy, a message which often reads like a résumé of his World War I correspondence with his officer brother. Indeed, the outbreak of hostilities was not viewed as the opening of a new conflict:

War, that outwardly was ended by an imposed peace in 1919, has now broken out anew and has drawn our *Volk* and *Vaterland* into its clutches. Once again a large part of our men and youth has been called to arms, and they are engaged in bloody conflict or stand guard on the borders in firm determination to shield the *Vaterland* and to risk their lives to win for our *Volk* a peace of freedom and justice. And those who remain behind have been called and are ready, each at his proper place, to join in, selflessly giving of his person, his strength, and all other means of assistance so that our *Volk* will meet the test and may soon enjoy the fruits of peace once more.[19]

Neither Bierbaum nor Galen makes the slightest mention of what must have been a very special problem connected with the war, namely, the newly found friendship between the Nazi state and the representatives of "godless Communism and Bolshevism." This message was issued before Soviet forces moved in to claim their share of Polish territory, but there is no record of public protest on Galen's part when the Nazi-Soviet friendship did become an open and active partnership.

It must be acknowledged that the Münster diocesan journal apparently did not publish all of the Bishop's statements; indeed, it seems that relatively few of them appeared in its pages. Even the 1941 sermons cited earlier were not encountered in its issues for that period. This may be due to the sharp surveillance of the Nazi censors, or it may reflect the Bishop's own decision not to jeopardize the continued publication of the journal.* Nevertheless, the few

* There is some indirect evidence that such was the case. A file of wartime issues of the Münster *Amtsblatt* was obtained from a Franciscan convent in that city on an interlibrary loan arrangement with the library of the Julius Maximilian Universität at Würzburg. Several 1941 issues were missing, and these might have included references to or texts of the sermons. Also, the first 1943 issue carried the Bishop's acknowledgment of the many congratulatory messages he had received concerning his pastoral letter of the previous December 13; however, no text of any such letter is found in the 1942 volume of the *Amtsblatt* (which, incidentally, did appear to be complete). The secrecy with which the 1941 sermons were duplicated and circulated by interested parties similarly supports the conclusion that, while the Bishop undoubtedly did continue to deliver sermons and issue pastoral directives throughout the war years, prudence dictated that they not always be published in the pages of his *Amtsblatt*.

Galen statements that are published there always manage to introduce a note of support or admiration for those engaged in the actual war effort. A 1940 message, for example, sadly announced that two traditional religious processions had been canceled by Nazi officials, ostensibly because of the possibility of enemy air attacks and the pressure of war needs; but part of his sadness was explained by the fact that the cancellation came just at the time when "we all feel impelled to join in communal songs of thanksgiving to offer our public adoration to the Lord God, Who has given our soldiers the strength and the bravery needed to win those glorious victories that have led to the armistice in France and to a rebirth of hope for an early peace. . . ."[20]

In another published message, the 1944 Lenten pastoral, Galen elaborated upon the Ash Wednesday theme, "Remember, O man, that thou are dust and unto dust shalt thou return." The overwhelming tragedies of the day are interpreted, not as a sign that God has forsaken man, but as the bitter fruit of placing too much faith in earthly riches and human powers. All these things have now turned to dust as was foretold, to the dust of bombed cities fallen victim to a war whose destructiveness had long since extended far beyond the actual war fronts. "No city, no house, no man can be certain that on the morrow this will not have become literally true for him —'unto dust shalt thou return.' " But it was not true, as the non-believer contended, that such death was the final end, that there was no afterlife. In his most masterful style, Galen rejected that thesis as unthinkable, and, in rejecting it, he struck all the emotional chords associated with the familiar "fallen heroes" theme. Once again we find an unquestioning acceptance of the soldier as model German and model Christian, as "our wonderful, idealistic young men who, dying in loyal performance of duty, have offered for us all their worldly goods, all their loved ones in the *Heimat,* all their hopes and prospects for the future." The reward was set forth with a reference to the writings of St. Thomas Aquinas where "one learns that the death in battle of a believing Christian ranks in merit and honor alongside that of the martyr for the Faith and immediately opens the way into the everlasting blessedness for the witness for Christ."[21] Even as late as 1944, this comforting assurance would help to resolve whatever moral doubts his hearers may have had as to the justice of the war.

This review of Bishop von Galen's references to World War II would not be complete without giving some attention to two truly extraordinary statements. The first, the 1944 New Year's message, was devoted to the theme of charity and love for one's neighbor. This virtue was proclaimed as a Christian obligation, and the point was specifically made that it ought to be observed *even with respect to the enemy,* difficult as that may seem. The Lord's Prayer was offered as evidence of this because it sets as the measure of forgiveness one may seek from God the same measure of forgiveness he is willing to extend toward others. Therefore, "let us never go to sleep at night without first banishing from our hearts all antipathy, all resentment, all hatred, and all thirst for vengeance and in their place sending a prayer to heaven for our opponents."[22] In much the same vein, a promise made the previous summer by Goebbels to the effect that the destruction of German cities would be matched by reprisal assaults upon enemy centers of population had drawn the following comment from the Bishop in a sermon delivered at Tegel:

Is it really a comfort for a mother whose child has been killed in an air raid if someone guarantees that soon we will also kill the child of an English mother? No, such a proclamation of vengeance and reprisal offers no comfort. . . . To desire to destroy nonmilitary objectives and noncombatants just to take vengeance or to practice reprisal would be a denial of decent thinking, soldierly chivalry, yea, the honorable manliness which prides itself on not giving way to primitive and unworthy impulses but rather on standing in manly self-mastery and doing battle only against real enemies who are capable of defending themselves.[23]

These are both truly Christian statements. But even as they testify to the heroic proportions of Galen's Christianity, they testify to something else: his tragic failure to come to terms with the real nature of the war itself. World War II was certainly no *ritterlich* engagement between armed warriors fighting under the rules of a bygone chivalry; and to treat it as such, even in the realm of theological abstraction, meant that Bishop von Galen was ill prepared to give German Catholics the guidance they should have had and may have sought from him. For the "glorious victories" for the German *Volk* and *Vaterland* to which he so often referred with pride were actually an extension of Hitler's power and Nazi programs and policies to new lands and new victims. It is quite clear that Galen never came to terms with this fact; the entry of advancing Allied troops into his cathedral city was to prove a "shattering experience" for him that would "always remain a sad memory."[24]

Seen in this light, then, the wartime writings of this most revered opponent of National Socialism clearly contributed to the social controls inducing German Catholic conformity to the German military cause. The German Catholic who thrilled to the thundering challenge, "It is better to die than to sin!" in the context of sermons that praised the devotion to duty exhibited by the soldiers who were "defending *Volk* and *Vaterland*" against the evils of "godless Bolshevism" would obviously be led to conclude that the war was a just war and that he had a moral obligation to give it his every support.

*NOTES*

1. Max Bierbaum, *Nicht Lob Nicht Furcht, Das Leben des Kardinals von Galen* (Münster: Verlag Regensberg, 1957), pp. 317-324. The Appendix contains the complete texts of von Galen's three famous 1941 sermons. "Und darum erhebe ich im Namen des rechtschaffenden deutschen Volkes, im Namen der Majestät der Gerechtigkeit, im Interesse des Friedens und der Geschlossenheit der inneren Front meine Stimme, darum rufe ich laut als deutscher Mann, als ehrenhafter Staatsbürger, als Vertreter der christlichen Religion, als katholischer Bischof: Wir fordern Gerechtigkeit! Bleibt dieser Ruf ungehört, wird die Herrschaft der Königin Gerechtigkeit

nicht wiederhergestellt, so wird unser deutsches Volk und Vaterland trotz des Heldenmutes unserer Soldaten und ihrer ruhmreichen Siege an innerer Fäulnis und Verrottung zu Grunde gehen!"

2. *Ibid.*, pp. 325-335.

"Hart werden! Fest bleiben! Wir sind in diesem Augenblick nicht Hammer, sondern Amboss. Andere, meist Fremde und Abtrünnige, hämmern auf uns, wollen mit Gewaltanwendung unser Volk, uns selbst, unsere Jugend, neu formen, aus der geraden Haltung zu Gott verbiegen. Seht einmal zu in der Schmiede! Fragt den Schmiedemeister und lasst es euch von ihm sagen: Was auf dem Amboss geschmiedet wird, erhält seine Form nicht nur vom Hammer, sondern auch vom Amboss. Der Amboss kann nicht und braucht auch nicht zurückzuschlagen, er muss nur fest, nur hart sein! Wenn er hinreichend zäh, fest, hart ist, dann hält meistens der Amboss länger als der Hammer. Wie heftig der Hammer auch zuschlägt, der Amboss steht in ruhiger Festigkeit da und wird noch recht lange dazu dienen, das zu formen, was neu geschmiedet wird."

3. *Ibid.*, pp. 337-347.

"Meine Christen! Ich hoffe, es ist noch Zeit, aber es ist die höchste Zeit! Dass wir es erkennen, noch heute, an diesem Tage, was uns zum Frieden dient! Was allein uns retten, vor dem göttlichen Strafgericht bewahren kann:

"Dass wir rückhaltlos und ohne Abstrich, die von Gott geoffenbarte Wahrheit annehmen und durch unser Leben bekennen.

"Dass wir die göttlichen Gebote zur Richtschnur unseres Lebens nehmen und Ernst machen mit dem Wort: Lieber sterben als sündigen!

"Dass wir in Gebet und aufrichtiger Busse Gottes Verzeihung und Erbarmen herabflehen auf uns, auf unsere Stadt, auf unser Land, auf unser ganzes, liebes deutsches Volk."

4. *Ibid.*, p. 330.

"Gewiss, wir Christen machen keine Revolution! Wir werden weiter treu unsere Pflicht tun im Gehorsam gegen Gott, aus Liebe zu unserem deutschen Volk und Vaterland. Unsere Soldaten werden kämpfen und sterben für Deutschland, aber nicht für jene Menschen, die durch ihr grausames Vorgehen gegen unsere Ordensleute, gegen ihre Brüder und Schwestern, unsere Herzen verwunden und dem deutschen Namen vor Gott und den Menschen Schmach antun. Wir kämpfen tapfer weiter gegen den äusseren Feind; gegen den Feind im Innern, der uns peinigt und schlägt, können wir nicht mit Waffen kämpfen. Da bleibt uns nur ein Kampfmittel: starkes, zähes, hartes Durchhalten!"

5. *Ibid.*, p. 326-327.

"Während diese deutschen Männer, in treuer Kameradschaft mit den anderen deutschen Brüdern, unter Einsatz ihres Lebens, gehorsam ihrer Pflicht, für die Heimat kämpfen, wird ihnen im Vaterland rücksichtslos und ohne jeden Rechtsgrund die Heimat genommen, das klösterliche Elternhaus zerstört. Wenn sie, wie wir hoffen, siegreich wiederkommen, finden sie ihre Klosterfamilie von Haus und Hof vertrieben, ihre Heimat von Fremden, von Feinden besetzt!"

6. See below, pp. 175 ff.

7. *Ibid.,* p. 138.

8. *Ibid.,* p. 136.

9. *Ibid.,* p. 137.

10. *Ibid.,* p. 138.

11. *Ibid.,* p. 146.

12. *Ibid.,* p. 152

13. *Ibid.,* pp. 162-163.

14. *Bayrische Katholische Kirchenzeitung,* Vol. 11 (1935), p. 199.

"Treudeutsch sind wir, wir sind auch treukatholisch, das ist kein Gegensatz, dast ist kein Zwiespalt in unserem Wesen und Wollen! Und darum protestieren wir, wenn man den Glauben an den einen persönlichen, überweltlichen Gott als undeutsch bekämpft, und mit der Autorität jede Autorität, auch die staatliche Autorität untergräbt. Es ist wahrhaftig nicht nur religiöse, es ist auch nationale Pflicht, wenn wir immer wieder gegen solches Tun protestieren, wenn wir gegen die Propaganda eines angeblichen "deutschgläubigen" Heidentums immer wieder warnend unsere Stimme erheben."

15. Bierbaum, *op. cit.,* p. 216-217.

16. *Kirchliches Amtsblatt für die Diözese Münster,* Vol. LXXIII (April 3, 1939), pp. 36-37.

"So hat der gottlose Kommunismus und Bolschewismus durch mehr als drei Jahre in Spanien gewütet! Das war der Feind, der mit Gottes Hilfe jetzt gänzlich besiegt und seiner Macht beraubt ist. Welche Gefahren wären dem christlichen Abendland, auch unserem Volke, ja der ganzen Welt erwachsen, wenn Moskau gesiegt und ein neues Zentrum der kämpfenden Gottlosigkeit und der zersetzenden Wühlarbeit in allen christlichen Staaten diesseits und jenseits der Meere im Südwesten Europas errichtet und ausgebaut hätte!

"Darum stimmen wir mit dem heldenhaften und befreiten spanischen Volk in den Jubel ein und in den Dank gegen Gott, der den tapferen Kämpfern gegen die Scharen des Antichrists den Sieg geschenkt hat. . . ."

17. *Ibid.,* Vol. LXXVIII, No. 21 (September 1, 1944), p. 111.

"In dieser Stunde drängt es mich, ein Wort des Grusses und der Anerkennung an unsere Soldaten zu richten. Ich möchte ihnen unser aller Dank aussprechen für den wirksamen Schutz, den sie unter unsäglichen Anstrengungen und in schier übermenschlichen Leistungen dem Vaterland und seinen Grenzen schenkten. Besonders für den Schutz vor dem Anstürmen des gottlosen Bolschewismus! Und ein Wort ganz innigen Gedenkens für jene, die in Pflichterfüllung bis zum letzten ihr Blut und Leben opferten für die Brüder! Möge es diesen hingebenden Anstrengungen gelingen, einen ehren- und segensvollen Frieden für uns alle zu erkämpfen!"

18. Bierbaum, *op. cit.,* pp. 228-229.

19. *Kirchliches Amtsblatt für die Diözese Münster,* Vol. LXXIII, No. 23 (September 19, 1939), pp. 99-100.

"Der Krieg, der 1919 durch einen erzwungenen Gewaltfrieden äusserlich beendet wurde, ist aufs Neue ausgebrochen und hat unser Volk und Vaterland in seinen Bann gezogen. Wiederum sind unsere Männer und Jungmänner zum grossen Teil zu den Waffen gerufen und stehen im blutigen Kampf oder in ernster Entschlossenheit an den Grenzen auf der Wacht, um das Vaterland zu schirmen und unter Einsatz des Lebens einen Frieden der Freiheit und Gerechtigkeit für unser Volk zu erkämpfen. Und die Zurückgebliebenen sind aufgerufen und gewillt, ein jeder an seinem Platz, in selbstlosem Einsatz seiner Person, seiner Kraft und aller Hilfsmittel mitzuwirken, dass unser Volk die Prüfung bestehe und bald die Früchte des Friedens wieder geniessen möge."

20. *Ibid.,* Vol. LXXIV, No. 17 (July 4, 1940), p. 91.

"Wir alle fühlen gerade jetzt uns angetrieben, in gemeinsamen Dankesliedern öffentlich Gott dem Herrn unsere Huldigung darzubringen, der unseren Soldaten die Kraft und den Mut gegeben hat, jene glorreichen Siege zu erringen, die zum Waffenstillstand in Frankreich und damit zu einer Belebung der Hoffnung auf baldigen Frieden geführt haben. . . ."

21. *Ibid.,* Vol. LXXVIII, No. 6 (February 15, 1944), p. 35.

"Es steht ja nach der wohlbegründeten Lehre des hl. Kirchenlehrers Thomas von Aquin der Soldatentod des gläubigen Christen in Wert und Würde ganz nahe dem Martertod um des Glaubens willen, der dem Blutzeugen Christi sogleich den Eintritt in die ewige Seligkeit öffnet."

22. *Ibid.,* (January 12, 1944), pp. 10-11.

"So lasst uns denn Ernst machen auch mit diesem schwersten Teil des Gebotes der Nächstenliebe. Lasst uns, eingedenk unserer eigenen Armseligkeit vor Gott, immer bereit sein, Kränkungen unserer Mitmenschen geduldig zu ertragen und ihnen aufrichtig die Hand zur Versöhnung zu reichen. Lasst uns, nach der Mahnung des Apostels: "Die Sonne soll nicht untergehen über eurem Zorn.", keinen Abend zur Ruhe gehen, ohne dass wir zuvor alle Abneigung, allen Groll, allen Hass und alle Rachsucht aus unseren Herzen verbannt und statt dessen ein Gebet für unsere Gegner zum Himmel gesandt haben."

23. Bierbaum, *op. cit.,* pp. 234-235.

"Ist das wirklich ein Trost für eine Mutter, deren Kind einem Bombenangriff zum Opfer fiel, wenn man ihr versichert: Demnächst werden wir auch einer englischen Mutter ihr Kind töten? Nein, solche Ankündigung von Rache und Vergeltung ist wahrlich kein Trost! Sie ist unchristlich, undeutsch . . . Nur um Rache zu nehmen, nur um Vergeltung zu üben, nichtmilitärische Ziele, nichtkämpfende Menschen schädigen wollen, das verleugnet auch anständiges Denken, ritterliches Soldatentum, ja edles Mannestum, dessen Stolz es ist, nicht primitiven und niedrigen Rachegefühlen zu unterliegen, sondern in mannhafter Selbstbeherrschung nur den wahrhaften und sich wehrenden Feind zu bekämpfen!"

24. See below, p. 193.

# CHAPTER 8

# Michael Cardinal Faulhaber

*"If you want peace, prepare for peace!"** 

LIKE BISHOP VON GALEN, Michael Cardinal Faulhaber, the titular leader of the Bavarian hierarchy, has earned the world's sincere respect for the integrity and bravery he displayed in opposing Hitler and his policies, in particular, those relating to the secularization of Catholic schools and youth movements; the confiscation of religious property and the scandalous exploitation of currency manipulation and moral turpitude libels to discredit religion; and the Nazi efforts to promote the "new paganism" associated with Alfred Rosenberg's anti-Christian attacks.

He is best remembered, perhaps, for the famous series of sermons during Advent 1933 in which he pointedly reaffirmed the worth and validity of the Old Testament and stressed its essential links to the Christian dispensation. In the context of an already mounting and obviously official anti-Semitism, which was to culminate in the total horror of the *Führer*'s "final solution" through the deliberate and carefully organized liquidation of Europe's Jewry, these sermons were widely interpreted as a public rebuke of a crucial segment of Adolf Hitler's program. Such a rebuke was a

* *Wenn du Frieden willst, rüste den Frieden!*

telling blow in two respects: first, as the leading Catholic spokesman in Bavaria, the most heavily Catholic state of Germany, the Cardinal's opposition could have proved fatally decisive; second, to have such opposition voiced in the very city where the successful Nazi movement had had its birth was certain to be a source of personal embarrassment to Hitler. It was to be expected, then, that Munich's Cardinal became one of the first targets of vilification and even violence organized and carried out under Nazi auspices.

With respect to Catholic support for Hitler's wars, however, Faulhaber's record reveals the same pattern already observed for the German hierarchy in general and for Bishop von Galen in particular. That this was a source of grave disillusionment and disappointment to Catholics who had looked to him for antiwar leadership was made clear to this writer in the course of several of his interviews. One such informant, a free-lance journalist, rather bitterly recalled that Faulhaber had at one time accepted the honor of being designated the official protector of the *Friedensbund deutscher Katholiken;* yet, when the Nazis turned upon this Catholic peace movement in 1933, its protector made not the slightest move to come to its defense.

Nor was his acceptance of that honorary title the only basis for expectations that the Cardinal Archbishop of Munich would take a positive stand against Hitler's program of rearmament and preparation for war, and even lead the opposition to any war that might ultimately develop out of that program. In February 1932 Faulhaber had greeted the opening of the Geneva Disarmament Conference with a powerful sermon calling for "a new ethic of war and preparation for peace." This remarkable document assumed a distinctly pacifist tone and stressed the urgent need for disarmament coupled with prayers and active work for peace. At one point in this sermon, he went so far as to invite all "apostles and front-line soldiers for peace" to enroll themselves in the ranks of the *Friedensbund.* Among the essential changes he publicly recommended were the following:

Moral disarmament must precede the military disarmament. The nimbus surrounding the uniform and the military parade has faded. The old songs of war can now be quietly laid to rest in the war museums. The heroism of the sword is not the only form of the heroic life. Even moral theology will speak a new language. It will remain true to the old principles, but in the question of the permissibility of war new facts will be taken into account. . . .

The "new facts" identified by the Cardinal were three: (1) the great advances in communications technology which made it easier for potential combatants to reach amicable settlement of threatening conflicts before these could develop beyond a point at which war was unavoidable; (2) the technology of war itself which had reached such levels of destructive potential that it was "no longer human, not to mention Christian," and thus guaranteed that any war once begun would soon perish of its own excesses; and, finally, (3) the awareness that the aftermath of such a war would find the victor as much the loser as the vanquished, thus destroying all possibility of achieving the proportionality between objectives and their price required under the traditional Catholic morality of war. In this vein, the Cardinal repudiated the old adage, "If you want peace, prepare for war," and demanded that it be replaced by a new principle: If you want peace, prepare for peace![1]

Bishop Neuhäusler, at the time a member of Faulhaber's chancery staff, reports the adverse reaction on the part of the Nazis to a sermon preached by the Cardinal at Munich's Basilica of St. Boniface, again in behalf of the *Friedensbund* and its activities. Whether this was the sermon discussed above or (as is more likely) still another evidence of support for the Catholic peace movement is not clear. Neuhäusler merely indicates that it was delivered before Hitler became Chancellor and that it was greeted by a Party newspaper with the threatening comment, "Once we come to power, the *Herr Kardinal* will no longer be able to deliver such sermons." The prediction proved a sound one. It is noteworthy, too, that Neuhäusler adds a footnote to that threat: "Actually, this particular Catholic peace movement was liquidated at the beginning of the Nazi rule and its leader, the Dominican Father Stratmann, sent to a concentration camp. . . ."[2] One may assume from this that the *Friedensbund's* protector was not unaware of the drastic steps taken against his ward.

When the war began in 1939, the new language promised by the Cardinal in 1932 was not heard. Instead, the only language spoken in official Catholic circles was composed of the old familiar words *"christliche Pflicht"* (Christian duty), *"Heldentum"* (heroism), *"Ehrentod"* (death with honor), and so on. And the voice of Munich's Cardinal spoke them too. As one of Germany's three Cardinals, he led the list of episcopal signatories to the annual Fulda messages which, as we have already seen, contained significant contributions to Catholic war morale. Similarly, his position as its leader must be noted in connection with the official call to arms issued by the combined Bavarian hierarchy quoted earlier in Chapter 6.[3]

It is true that only a few evidences of personal messages issued by the Cardinal during the war in his own name were encountered in the course of this research. This is explained in part by the fact that he was in ill health at the outbreak of the war and for much of the time thereafter; but perhaps he maintained a prudent silence or, at least, withheld his statements from publication in anticipation of possible Nazi reprisal against his diocesan paper. In any event, it would be rash to interpret this scarcity of published material as evidence that the Cardinal opposed the war more than his fellow bishops. Neuhäusler's extensively documented review of Faulhaber's official resistance to Hitler and the Nazi regime offers negative evidence of this, since it makes no mention of any opposition to the war or to the support given it by Bavarian Catholics. Indeed, it is highly significant that the index to the two volumes of this admirable study does not contain a single reference to the morality of war in general or of Hitler's wars in particular. The closest any indexed item comes to this critical subject is to report a Faulhaber statement (issued before Hitler came to power) calling upon secular rulers to use every means to prevent a new world war.

One final bit of interpretative evidence to support the conclusion that the Cardinal joined his fellow bishops in their support for the German war effort may be gleaned from the fact that three Catholic publications associated with the area under his influence (i.e., the *Münchener Katholische Kirchenzeitung*, the *Bayrische Katholische Kirchenzeitung*, and the *Klerusblatt*) were nothing less than strident in their all-out support for the war. We may grant that such a tone was almost a necessary concession to assure continued publication; but this does not mean that it could not, at the same time, reflect the actual commitment of the editors and the writers of the articles responsible for that tone. And it is certain that, had the Cardinal interpreted such a necessary concession as one likely to mislead the Catholic reader into sinful participation in an unjust war, he would have refused to comply on the grounds that such a price was too high to pay for the privilege of continued publication. We can infer this from a somewhat parallel situation, his refusal "on grounds of conscience" to approve the appointment of a Nazi Party member to a chair in Church Law at the University of Munich. This refusal resulted in the shutting down of the University's School of Theology, but Faulhaber remained firm in his position.[4] It is permissible to conclude, then, that the continued publication of these periodicals as ostensibly official or, at least, approved Catholic periodicals may be taken as evidence that Faulhaber was not particularly disturbed by or opposed to the extremes of nationalism often manifested in their tone and contents.

To turn now to what may be taken as more direct evidence of the Cardinal's position, the beginning of Hitler's wars with the aggression against Poland was noted in an official chancery directive issued in the name of the vicar-general of the archdiocese, the Cardinal being ill at the time. There is no basis whatsoever to suspect that this strong appeal for full support of the war was in any way out of keeping with Faulhaber's personal feelings and intentions. Certainly there was never the slightest effort to repudiate or modify the instructions contained in this message; and its author continued to hold his post of responsibility at as late a date as 1949. Vicar-General Buchweiser's *Oberhirtlicher Aufruf* declared:

The *Vaterland* has entered upon a fateful hour of decision. Responding to the seriousness of the hour, the faithful are being summoned to lift their hands trustingly to God, the Ruler of all history, that He may protect *Volk* and *Vaterland* in their present emergency and danger; that He may stand by their responsible leaders in the hour of life-and-death decision; that He may strengthen our soldiers and accompany them along the difficult paths of war; that He may comfort the families who are sorely anxious over members and providers; that He may lend His strength and help to all those who will be hit the hardest by the trials of war.

In such difficult times, when everything is at stake, *it is absolutely imperative that everyone faithfully discharge his religious, patriotic, and civic duties at whatever post he is assigned;* and that one and all stand side by side in the spirit of true Christian charity and consciousness of community [italics added]. . . .[5]

A month later, another statement, this time issued in the Cardinal's name, called upon Catholics to support the national *Winterhilfswerk* collections. The customary appeals in terms of the virtue of charity were given a new dimension in the argument that

We owe it to the relatives of those who stand at the battle front and risk their lives for the *Vaterland* that they be protected against need, hunger, and cold. It will be a truly special comfort to the fighting men in the field to know that their loved ones at home are spared from worry and care through the active assistance provided by the *Winterhilfswerk* whenever needed. Therefore, the voice of the Church is joined with the government's appeal in pursuance of the direct commission she has received from her Lord and Master to regard every man in need as a brother and to feed, clothe, and shelter him. . . .[6]

On other occasions, too, similar appeals of a patriotic or even nationalistic tone were introduced to strengthen or supplement some other principal theme. Sometimes, as above, it was a call to charity; more often, it was a protest against some action taken by the Nazis which was deemed detrimental to the Church or its teachings. The Cardinal's 1941 New Year's Eve sermon noted, for example, that

Between religious confessions there is peace. But in other respects, the wildest dissension rages in the *Heimat* in the form of that most tragic and most unnecessary of all struggles—the *Kulturkampf* against the Church. While Catholic soldiers serve at the front standing shoulder to shoulder with other German men, bearing the same burdens and trials, and bringing the same heroic sacrifice of blood; while the Catholics at home make the same sacrifices, contribute to the same collections whether required or voluntary (in this particular instance, the current collection of warm winter garments for our soldiers in the field)—the Church is being treated with constant suspicion, spied upon and subjected to special regulations; Church and parochial facilities are commandeered as if they were nothing more than private residences. . . .[7]

This, again, is the familiar patriotism-and-protest combination. But we approach an area of more direct relevance to the present analysis when we turn to the Cardinal's official opposition to the Nazi euthanasia program in that, as might be expected, his opposition is stated in terms of the Fifth Commandment. In a direct appeal to Reichsminister Gürtner, in 1940, Faulhaber accords to the state the right to take the life of a criminal in punishment for his crime and also "to call upon the men capable of bearing arms to come to the defense of the *Vaterland,* even to the point of sacrificing their lives." But he goes no further than this; there is no mention at all of such a right being limited to service in a war which can meet the theological requirements of the just war. Of course, any detailed excursion into the morality of war would have been out of place in so specific a protest. Nevertheless, there is some added significance for us in the reference he does make to the war which had then been in progress for more than a year.

We understand when extraordinary measures are taken in wartime to assure the security of the nation and sustain the *Volk.* And we instruct the *Volk* that it must be prepared to assume the burden of wartime sacrifices, even that of blood, in the Christian spirit of sacrifice and to honor the women they encounter on the streets of the city who wear the veil of sorrow signifying that they have offered the sacrifice of a precious life for the *Vaterland.*[8]

Since this was a formal letter personally addressed to a Nazi official, the ordinary German Catholic would never have been aware of its contents; therefore, as a direct control upon his behavior relative to the war it would hold no significance for the present study. But since it does contain a direct statement on the part of the Cardinal to the effect that he considered it one of the functions of his spiritual leadership to "instruct the *Volk* that it must be prepared to assume the burden of wartime sacrifices, even that of blood," this letter assumes an extremely critical significance for us.

The private appeal became a matter of public protest in the 1942 Passion Sunday sermon, in which the euthanasia program was openly branded as a violation of the Fifth Commandment. The sermon touched upon other Nazi policies as well and included a highly emotional defense of the individual's "right to the protection of his honor against lies and slander." Faulhaber was referring most immediately to the problem faced by members of the religious orders who had in the past suffered from all sorts of vicious lies and slanders and were now, in many instances, being evicted from their convents. For greater effect, the Cardinal set this protest in terms of the contributions being made by men of these orders:

In war, too, on the battlefield and in the *Heimat,* the members of Catholic religious orders have done their duty, as is shown by the frequent awarding to them of military citations and honors. Despite this, many of them find their convent home taken from them. We Catholics demand effective protection for the honor of every countryman, including the faithful Catholic and the member of the Catholic religious order.[9]

Consider this combination. The Catholic who heard this sermon in which (a) violations of the Fifth Commandment were officially identified and condemned and (b) support of Hitler's wars was identified and praised would take renewed confidence in the assumption that taking part in these wars did not constitute service in an unjust war which would also be a violation of the Fifth Commandment—if, indeed, he gave the matter any thought at all.

Two published summaries of Faulhaber's life history afford some insights into his position on the war.[10] For one thing, we may assume that his World War I appointment to the post of Chaplain General of the armies of the Kingdom of Bavaria had a lingering influence upon his point of view concerning that war and its outcome. The *Kirchenzeitung's* biographical sketch declared that "In the World War, the Bishop, who was completely convinced of the justice of our cause, had to provide an answer to the questions posed by the bleeding *Volk* as to how war can be reconciled with the Gospel teachings. . . ." The answer he gave them at that time affirmed his belief in world peace, but also allowed for the fact that legitimate national needs often could not be met without resorting to violence and war. To him, obviously, World War I was such a situation. The same article noted that Faulhaber's war service—in providing his troops with "spiritual ammunition," as the article put it—earned for him the honor of being the first Catholic bishop ever to receive the highly prized Iron Cross decoration.

The years of hardship following World War I found Faulhaber devoting his full energies to efforts to meet the critical needs of the suffering German population. At one point he traveled to the United States and toured the country begging for financial assistance for German children. Thoughout these same years, Bavaria, now a part of the Weimar Republic, was a focal point of Communist agitation; indeed, immediately following the war there had been a short-lived Communist seizure of power. Needless to say, the Archbishop of Munich (elevated to the rank of Cardinal in 1921) threw himself into a dedicated effort to combat that social and political movement which, in his eyes, would lead to the destruction of family and *Volk*.

Both his personal experiences with the military order and his attachment to its ideals and values, as well as his total rejection of Communism, undoubtedly contributed to the support he was later to give the Nazi war effort.

To the extent that Faulhaber was "completely convinced of the justice" of Germany's cause in World War I, the harshness of the settlement arising from her defeat in that conflict would have to be regarded as a further violation of justice. Thus, to the extent that success in World War II promised to undo these injustices, it is permissible to assume that the Cardinal would have been personally disposed toward supporting that war as actively as his position would permit. The content of the 1939 statement of the Bavarian hierarchy certainly supports the validity of this interpretation.

Another factor which would have inclined him in this direction is his personal attitude toward the military life and its traditions. This attitude is quite clearly revealed in an interesting little article he contributed in 1930 to *Der 9-er*, the regimental newspaper published for veterans of the "Wrede" Ninth Infantry of the former Bavarian Royal Army. Recalling his own service with that regiment while stationed at Würzburg in 1888-89 and his later encounters with some of its men during World War I, Faulhaber paid particular honor to this famous military unit and proceeded to explain his current interest in the *Friedensbund* and its activities:

I work for peace today because I am convinced that it is no longer human to wage war with clouds of gas that smother all personal bravery, with airborne poison bombs which destroy all life, from nursing infant to aged invalid, in a few brief hours. But I still recall with wonderment that devotion to duty and self-sacrifice I witnessed [in 1915] and, even today, I am moved to the depths of my soul when I think back on those encounters with regimental comrades in the trenches or in the field hospitals.[11]

But, compelling as the fruits of such personal associations may have been, an even more important clue to Faulhaber's wartime position is provided by his personal commitment to the principle of unquestioning obedience to legitimate authority as a moral obligation of the Christian citizen. This has obvious relevance to his favorable attitude toward the military life and its traditions; however, its effect went beyond this to color his thinking in other areas as well. Certainly, the continued recognition by the Cardinal (as well as by his fellow bishops and the Holy See) of the legitimacy of the Hitler regime, could leave little room for Catholic opposition to the war. The extent to which this commitment to obedience to

the secular authority could lead can be illustrated by two com-
memorations deserving of some special note.

In the first, the Bavarian Catholic papers, following the pattern
set for the secular press, devoted extensive and prominent coverage
to Hitler's fiftieth birthday in April 1939. Of course, such coverage
was required of them in the sense that any paper which failed to do
justice to this important event could expect its future publication
rights to be limited or suspended. However, it is doubtful that this
fact alone accounts for the warm enthusiasm displayed by the
*Kirchenzeitung* in its full-page spread adorned with a photograph
of the *Führer* in uniform. The text of the article provided a brief
review of the severe trials suffered by Germany in the postwar years
and noted the particular threat of Bolshevism that had arisen. That
these troubles had now been overcome was due to the man being
honored.

> Thus we have truly sufficient cause to thank Divine Providence that,
> after the bloody international strife of the World War and the subse-
> quent years of defeat, the German *Volk* was again favored and the
> nation's leadership entrusted to a statesman who understood how to
> unite a power without historical parallel in his hands. Only thus was
> it possible to rise up against Bolshevism in the decisive hour and to
> bring our full strength to the fray. . . . Divine Providence spared us
> the terrible fate that was visited upon the Spanish people two-and-a-
> half years ago.[12]

Again, the article itself is not directly attributable to the Cardinal
personally. Nevertheless, its publication in a paper under his jurisdiction must be taken as indirect evidence that he was not ill disposed to its contents and emphasis.

It is useful to attempt a logical reconstruction of the situation,
to make an effort to see this article through the eyes of the ordinary
Catholic reader of 1939. Even if he were aware of the public denunciations directed against the Cardinal by leading Nazi spokesmen; even if he knew of the threats, indignities and physical assaults that had been made upon the person of the Cardinal, his en-

tourage, and his episcopal palace; even if he gave careful attention to the Cardinal's public protests against certain specific aspects of the Nazi program—despite all these incidents, such an article in his diocesan paper attributing the advent of Hitler to no less a source than Divine Providence would have gone far to quiet any misgivings he may have developed about the *Führer*. Reading this, and knowing that it could not have appeared without at least the tacit approval of the Cardinal, such a Catholic would most likely have been led to conclude that all of these things, unpleasant and unfortunate though they were, were a sacrifice that had to be made to assure the greater good of the elimination of the Bolshevist threat. He would have been inclined, too, to take refuge in the comforting assumption that these hardships and trials visited upon the Church were really the handiwork of lesser officials; for, certainly (or so it would seem to him), such enthusiastic praise would not be showered upon the *Führer* if he were personally responsible for these offenses. One thing is certain: Faulhaber did enjoy great popularity among the Catholics of the Munich archdiocese. In 1936, at the height of the demonstrations against him, the Cardinal had been obliged to make a *third* public appeal to Catholic youth groups that they not engage in public demonstrations when he appeared, or even greet him with cheers and shouts of praise, lest these be used by "others" as a pretext for organizing counter-demonstrations.[13] This devotion to a revered spiritual leader, coupled with his clearly evidenced acceptance of the Hitler regime as legitimate authority, guaranteed the loyalty of Bavaria's Catholics to that regime. And when, in less than six short months after the appearance of this highly laudatory article, war became a reality, this loyalty would be manifested in the wholehearted support of the war on the part of Faulhaber's devoted followers.

An even more dramatic occasion for the display of this acceptance of Hitler and his regime arose shortly after the war broke out. Munich's *Bürgerbräukeller* became the scene of an unsuccessful—and, there is some reason to believe, staged—attempt to assassinate the *Führer*. The official Catholic reaction was noted in a news report published in boldface type:

On November 12, in conjunction with Solemn High Mass in the Cathedral, a *Te Deum* was held in order to thank Divine Providence in the name of the archdiocese for the *Führer's* fortunate escape in connection with the criminal attempt made upon his life. With grateful hearts, the assembled congregation joined in the hymn of thanksgiving and jubilation. We Catholic Christians are united with the entire German *Volk* in the burning wish that God may protect our *Führer* and *Volk*.[14]

In an interview with the writer, Bishop Neuhäusler explained that the real purpose of the *Te Deum* was to offer public thanks to God that the people had been spared the blood bath that would almost certainly have followed upon a successful assassination. Without questioning in the least the sincerity or the validity of this explanation, one might still question whether this somewhat cryptic intention could have been at all obvious to the ordinary Catholic who joined in the song of thanksgiving and jubilation that November morning. It is also proper to note in this connection that Neuhäusler himself fails to mention this event and its explanation in his well-documented history of the struggle between the followers of the Cross and the followers of the Swastika in the Munich archdiocese.

If Cardinal Faulhaber's high regard for the military calling (reinforced by his own military background and associations) plus his firm commitment to the legitimate authority represented by the Hitler regime exerted a powerful influence upon him and his wartime position, the Nazi opposition to Communism must also be considered as still another major influence. Many of his personal statements—and a continuing flood of articles appearing in the Bavarian Catholic press—play upon the "Crusade against Bolshevism" theme which is often mistakenly advanced as the total explanation of the support given Hitler and his wars by German Catholics and, in particular, by the hierarchy. One of the most explicit references to this theme in a wartime pronouncement is found in Faulhaber's 1941 message concerning the confiscation of church bells for use as scrap in the production of war matériel. In his eyes the taking of the bells represented another major sacrifice demanded of the German Catholic community, but

> This sacrifice, too, we are willing to make for the precious *Vaterland* if it is now needed to assure a happy conclusion to the war and the defeat of Bolshevism. Horrifying is the picture of Bolshevism as our soldiers are learning to know it. Frightful and intense is the struggle against this world enemy, and we owe the deepest gratitude to our death-defying soldiers for all the great and difficult things they have accomplished and endured in this conflict. . . .

Departing from this theme, he referred to the troubling fact that assaults against the Christian Faith were still continuing at home and warned that there is danger in all forms of godlessness and infidelity. The message ended:

> May the final ringing of our departing bells sound a clear and serious admonition: "Watch and pray!" Remain ever loyal to your Almighty God, your Savior, and your Church! May God protect our precious *Heimat,* our holy Church, our brave soldiers, our beloved children on the battlefield. This is the heartfelt Christmas wish and the fervent Christmas prayer of your Archbishop.[15]

In the final analysis, however, anti-Communism must be regarded as only a part of the explanation of Faulhaber's support of the war. This is true because inferences drawn from articles published in April 1939 or episcopal messages issued in December 1941 omit a very significant segment of world history. As has already been noted, from August 1939 to June 1941 the Third Reich and the Bolshevist "world enemy" were treaty partners and had actually joined in the dismemberment of Poland and other territorial adjustments in Eastern Europe. Throughout these intervening years, Catholic leaders—and this includes the onetime protector of the Catholic peace movement—supported the war and called upon their followers to perform whatever duties were demanded of them. And when the Nazi *Führer* did decide to resume his anti-Communist "crusade" in 1941, this decision, too, took the form of a surprise aggression in violation of solemn treaty responsibilities. Thus, the issue was not really "solved" by this action; for Hitler's war against the Soviet Union, like his earlier aggressions against Poland and her allies and against the European neutral nations whose misfortune it was to lie in the conqueror's path, would be of highly questionable justice when measured according to the conditions of the just war set forth in traditional Catholic moral teachings.

## NOTES

1. *Friedenskämpfer,* Vol. 8, No. 3 (March 1932), pp. 41-46.
"Wir leben in einer Zeitenwende, und wie in anderen Fragen wird sich auch in der Frage, Krieg oder Frieden, eine Wandlung der Geister vollziehen. Die öffentliche Meinung muss umlernen, wenn es auch nicht ohne Gegenstösse abgehen wird. Der militärischen Abrüstung muss die moralische Abrüstung vorausgehen. Der Nimbus der Uniform und Militärparade is verblasst. Die alten Kriegslieder können ruhig zum alten Eisen im Kriegsmuseum gelegt werden. Das Heldentum der Waffen ist nicht die einzige Form heldischen Daseins. Sogar die theologische Sittenlehre über den Krieg wird eine neue Sprache sprechen. Sie wird ihren alten Grundsätzen treu bleiben, in der Frage nach der Erlaubtheit des Krieges aber den neuen Tatsachen Rechnung tragen. . . .
"Das alte Sprichwort: "Wenn du den Frieden willst, rüste den Krieg" muss wie ein altes Kriegsboot abgetakelt werden. Die endlosen Rüstungen während des Friedens sind kein Schutz vor dem Krieg, keine Sicherung des Friedens. Das Rüsten um die Wette gibt die ständige Bereitschaft zum Kriege, und von der Bereitschaft ist der Weg nicht weit zum wirklichen Losschlagen. Was man heute Bereitschaft zum Kriege nennt, ist selber schon ein stiller Krieg und eine Finanzlast wie früher ein Krieg. Statt 'Rüste den Krieg' sagen wir heute: Wenn du den Frieden willst, rüste den Frieden!"
2. Neuhäusler, *op. cit.,* Vol. I, p. 44.
3. See above, pp. 60-61.
4. Neuhäusler, *op. cit.,* Vol. I, p. 105.
5. *Münchener Katholische Kirchenzeitung,* Vol. 32, No. 38 (September 17, 1939), p. 531.
"Das Vaterland ist in entscheidende Schicksalsstunden eingetreten. Dem Ernst der Zeit entsprechend werden die Gläubigen aufgerufen, ihre Hände vertrauensvoll zu Gott, dem Lenker aller Geschichte, emporzuheben, auf

dass er Volk und Vaterland schütze in Not und Gefahr, auf dass er seinen verantwortlichen Leitern beistehe in Stunden lebenswichtiger Entscheidungen, auf dass er unsere Soldaten stärke und geleite auf ihren schweren Kampfeswegen, auf dass er die Familien aufrichte, die in banger Sorge sind um ihre Angehörigen und Ernährer, auf dass er allen jenen seine Kraft und Hilfe verleihe, die von den harten Folgen des Krieges am schmerzlichsten betroffen werden.

"In solch schweren Zeiten, wo es um alles geht, ist es unabweislich notwendig, dass jeder an dem Platze, wo er hingestellt ist, seine religiösen, vaterländischen und staatsbürgerlichen Pflichten vollauf erfülle und dass einer dem anderen im Geiste echt christlicher Nächstenliebe und wahren Gemeinschaftsbewusstseins zur Seite stehe. . . ."

6. *Ibid.*, No. 44 (October 29, 1939), p. 568.

"Gilt es doch die Angehörigen derjenigen, die im Felde stehen und fürs Vaterland ihr Leben einsetzen, vor Not, Hunger und Kälte zu bewahren. Es wird den Kämpfern im Felde ein ganz besonderer Trost sein zu wissen, dass von ihren Lieben zu Hause, soweit notwendig, die Sorge auch durch die tatkräftige Mitwirkung des Winterhilfswerk gebannt ist. Darum vereinigt sich mit dem Aufruf der Reichsregierung auch die Stimme der Kirche, die von ihrem Herrn und Meister den Auftrag erhalten hat in jedem Notleidenden den Bruder zu sehen und ihn zu speisen, zu bekleiden und zu beherbergen. . . ."

7. Neuhäusler, *op. cit.*, Vol. II, p. 143-144.

"Zwischen Bekenntnis und Bekenntnis ist Friede. Sonst aber herrscht in der Heimat der wildeste Unfriede, der unnötigste und traurigste aller Kriege, der Kulturkampf gegen die Kirche. Während die katholischen Soldaten an der Front Schulter an Schulter mit den anderen deutschen Männern stehen, mit gleichen Lasten und gleichen Leistungen, mit heldenmütigen Blutopfern, während die Katholiken in der Heimat die gleichen Opfer bringen, an den gleichen Sammlungen sich beteiligen, an den pflichtmässigen wie an den freiwilligen, besonders in diesen Tagen an der Sammlung von warmen Wintersachen für unsere Soldaten im Felde, wird die Kirche in der Heimat mit ständigem Misstrauen behandelt, von Spionen umlauert, mit Ausnahmebestimmungen bedrückt, werden kirchliche und klösterliche Räume ungleich mehr als Privatwohnungen beschlagnahmt. . . ."

8. *Ibid.*, pp. 361, 363.

"Wir verstehen, wenn in Kriegszeiten ausserordentliche Massnahmen getroffen werden, um die Sicherheit des Landes und die Ernährung des Volkes sicherzustellen. Wir sagen dem Volk, dass es bereit sein muss, in Kriegszeiten auch grosse Opfer, auch Blutopfer, in christlichem Opfergeist auf sich zu nehmen, und begegnen mit Ehrfurcht im Strassenbild der Stadt den Trägerinnen des schwarzen Schleiers, die für das Vaterland das Opfer eines teueren Lebens gebracht haben."

9. *Ibid.*, p. 149.

"Die katholischen Ordensleute haben in Feld und Heimat, auch im Kriege heldenmütig ihre Pflicht getan, wie vielfach durch die Verleihung von Kriegsauszeichnungen anerkannt ist. Dennoch hat man vielen von ihnen die klösterliche Heimat genommen. Wir Katholiken fordern wirksamen Ehrenschutz für jeden Volksgenossen, auch für die glaubenstreuen Katholiken und katholischen Ordensleute."

10. "Und was halten wir vom Kardinal?" *Bayrische Katholische Kirchenzeitung,* Vol. 12, No. 7 (February 16, 1936), pp. 54-55, is an article summarizing the Cardinal's life experiences and issued in commemoration of his 25th anniversary as bishop. The other source is a biographical pamphlet issued on the occasion of his 80th birthday: Joseph Weissthanner, *Michael Kardinal Faulhaber, 80 Jahre* (Munich: Verlag Katholische Kirche Bayerns, 1949).

11. Weissthaner, *op. cit.,* pp. 14-15.

"Ich trete heute für den Frieden ein, weil es nach meiner Überzeugung nicht mehr menschlich ist, in dieser Art Krieg zu führen, mit Gaswolken, die alle persönliche Tapferkeit ersticken, mit Fliegergiftbomben, die in ein paar Stunden alles Leben vom Säugling bis zum Greis vernichten. Aber ich erinnere mich heute noch mit Bewunderung dessen, was ich an Pflichttreue und Ergebung damals gesehen habe, und heute noch ergreift es mich in tiefster Seele, wenn ich an jene Begegnungen mit Regimentskameraden in den Schützengräben oder in den Lazaretten zurückdenke."

12. *Bayrische Katholische Kirchenzeitung,* Vol. 15 (April 16, 1939), p. 113.

"So haben wir wahrlich Grund genug, Gottes Vorsehung zu danken, dass sie nach dem blutigen Völkerringen des Weltkrieges und der darauffolgenden Zeit des Niederganges dem Volk der Deutschen wieder gnädig war, und die Führung des Reiches einem Staatsmanne anvertraute, der es verstand, eine in der Geschichte beispiellose Machtfülle in seiner Hand zu vereinigen. Nur dadurch war es möglich in entscheidungsvoller Stunde das Haupt gegen den Bolschewismus zu erheben und alle Kräfte auf den Plan zu rufen. Gerade das Beispiel Spaniens aus der jüngsten Weltgeschichte ist uns ein deutlicher Beweis dafür, wie sehr der richtige Augenblick von entscheidender Bedeutung ist. Die göttliche Vorsehung hat uns vor dem furchtbaren Schicksal bewahrt, das uns 2½ Jahre für das spanische Volk bangen liess."

13. *Ibid.,* Vol. 12, No. 46 (November 15, 1936), p. 363.

14. *Münchener Katholische Kirchenzeitung,* Vol. 32, No. 47 (November 19, 1939), p. 588.

"Im Anschluss an den feierlichen Gottesdienst im Dom an 12. November wurde ein Te Deum gehalten, um im Namen der Erzdiözese der göttlichen Vorsehung zu danken, dass der Führer dem verbrecherischen Anschlage, der auf sein Leben gemacht wurde, glücklich entronnen ist. Dankerfüllten Herzens stimmte die versammelte Gemeinde in das Dank- und Jubellied ein. Wir katholischen Christen sind mit dem ganzen deutschen Volk in dem heissen Wunsche einig, dass Gott Führer und Volk schützen möge."

15. *Amtsblatt für die Erzdiözese München und Freising,* (December 23, 1941), pp. 162-163.

"Für das teuere Vaterland aber wollen wir auch dieses Opfer bringen, wenn es nun notwendig geworden ist zu einem glücklichen Ausgang des Krieges und zur Ueberwindung des Bolschewismus. Schrecklich ist das Bild des Bolschewismus, wie es unsere Soldaten kennenlernen. Gewaltig und furchtbar ist das Ringen gegen diesen Weltfeind und tiefsten Dank sollen wir unseren todesmutigen Soldaten für alles, was sie in diesem Kampf Grosses leisten und Schweres dulden. . . . Daher möge das letzte Geläute unserer scheidenden Glocken die laute und ernste Mahnung sein: "Wachet und betet!" Bleibt treu euerem Herrgott, euerem Heiland und euerer Kirche! Gott schütze unsere teuere Heimat, unsere heilige Kirche, unsere tapferen Soldaten, unser lieben Angehörigen im Feld! Dies ist der herzliche Weihnachtswunsch und das heisse Weihnachtsgebet eures Erzbischofs."

# CHAPTER 9

# Conrad Gröber

*The "brown" bishop*[*]

THE LAST OF THE resistance figures of the German Catholic hierarchy to be discussed here is Archbishop Conrad Gröber of Freiburg (Breisgau).[**] In many respects, his official acts offer the

[*] *Der "braune" Bischof.*

[**] A brief note is in order to explain the omission of another German bishop noted for his outspoken opposition to certain aspects of the Nazi regime, Bishop (later Cardinal) von Preysing of Berlin. Although attempts were made to locate copies of the official diocesan journal covering the war years, these attempts did not meet with success. The only materials upon which an evaluation of Preysing's attitude toward World War II could be based were (a) limited personal interviews with Berlin informants who had some firsthand recollections of the war period, and (b) a published collection, apparently highly selective, of some of Preysing's official statements (*Dokumente aus dem Kampf der katholischen Kirche im Bistum Berlin* [Berlin: Morus Verlag, 1946] ).

The *Dokumente* publication, prepared and distributed under chancery auspices, contains only four wartime documents: a sermon attacking the euthanasia program, with emphasis on a defense of the sanctity of human life, and three pastoral letters—the first (June 17, 1941) protesting the confiscation of certain diocesan properties; the second (September 8, 1941) protesting the enforced closing of Berlin monasteries and convents and the removal of religious symbols from school classrooms; and the third (December 13, 1942) constituting a more general repudiation of the basic principles behind the Nazi *Weltanschauung*. None of these documents reveals any significant support for (nor of course any opposition to) the war. The sermon

greatest challenge to accurate evaluation and explanation. It appears, for example, that he did not take at all unkindly to the National Socialist surge to power. Indeed, his attachment to the movement was apparently so close that anti-Nazi Germans reportedly referred to him sarcastically as "the brown [-shirt] bishop." One informant described him in a published article as a promotional or sponsoring member (*förderndes Mitglied*) of the hated SS. Another informant, a well-known journalist of the pre-Hitler period,

---

(November 2, 1941) included two references to the legitimacy of taking life in war. The first (p. 108) stated the three circumstances in which the killing of a human person is permitted and includes as one of them: "The soldier may employ weapons in a just war to protect the *Vaterland.*" The second reference (p. 109) discussed the prohibition of suicide (including under this term the appeal for a "mercy death") and declared: "A man may have the right and the duty to offer his life in witness to his Faith, in the defense of the *Vaterland;* he may not take his own life." It is obvious that these few documents—which, in addition to their scarcity, may have undergone some diminution of scholarly value in the course of editing for postwar publication—are not a sufficient basis for any conclusions as to Preysing's personal or official position regarding participation in Hitler's wars. To the extent that they may be at all suggestive of his general attitude, it must be granted that they display an unusual degree of episcopal restraint—if only in that they do not even include the customary prayers for the well-being and safety of the heroes on the battlefield. However, this, too, might be more a matter of editorial omission.

The impressions obtained in the course of interviews are similarly inconclusive. One informant, for instance, reported that the Bishop had issued some letters calling for an end to the "senseless" war, and she referred the researcher to the *Dokumente* publication as a source where these letters might be found. Not only were they not there, but the prelate responsible for the preparation of that volume denied that any such statements had ever been made by Preysing. He then went on to describe the difficult situation in which the bishops were placed by the war. Elements of this situation included: the awareness that opposition to the war would certainly provoke a wave of extreme anti-Catholic persecution; recognition of the fact that even an evil government incorporates areas of legitimate and binding authority; a fear that successful opposition to Hitler might result in opening vast areas of Europe to Communist domination; and, finally, the fact that, as men, bishops were subject to human weakness and could not be expected to display a degree of omniscience not demanded of other men. This analysis has value in its own right and will be referred to again. In the present context, however, it may be taken as evidence that Preysing shared in the general episcopal support for the war effort. This informant had been one of the Bishop's close associates; the fact that he did not specifically exclude Preysing from the general tenor of his analysis holds obvious meaning and significance to the present analysis.

volunteered the same information, explaining the SS membership in terms of the then current power struggle between Himmler's SS and the even less palatable SA; his interpretation was that Gröber wished to influence the outcome in favor of the lesser of these two particular evils. While they made no reference to any such formal ties to the Nazi movement, two other informants furnished evaluations that would tend to support the Bishop's reported attraction to the promised new order. The first, himself a bishop, described Gröber as originally a believer in the possibility of working with the new regime and quite willing to accept the legitimacy of its ends. The other, a prominent Jesuit interviewed in Rome, interpreted Gröber's early support of the Nazi cause as the product of nationalistic sentiments which made certain of the goals set for the movement attractive to him, so attractive in fact that he deluded himself into believing that the passage of time would bring the less desirable aspects of Nazism under control.

But the clearest evidence of an over-eager acceptance of Hitler and his program is found in Gröber's own words, written in 1945 following Nazi Germany's total defeat. Looking back upon the trials and upheavals of the Weimar period, he recalled that

In spite of this, none of us could escape the fear that the hardest times were yet to come for our young people as well as for the whole *Volk* unless the extremely insecure internal political situation, then bordering upon revolution, was brought under control by some strong hand.

And then, at the beginning of 1933, it seemed, in the eyes of many, as if the longed-for pacification and ordering of the divided and discontented German community had arrived. . . .

According to Gröber's summary, the "good example" found in the reports emanating from Mussolini's Italy (especially those telling of official promotion of the religious formation of Italian youth by means of regular group attendance at church and monthly reception of the sacraments by the *giovanezza*) and the public assurances made by Hitler that he, too, would protect religion and help to re-

Christianize German youth won him the support of many sincere Catholics. But, he admitted, not all were fooled right away:

Despite this, powerful voices were raised warning that the new state, with all of its many and vocal promises—and precisely because of these—should be watched with gravest mistrust. But then we were taken by surprise at Eastertide by the first report that Herr von Papen, the Vice-Chancellor of the young Third Reich, was in the Eternal City to negotiate a concordat with the Holy See. And in the course of that summer, this treaty actually came into being without encountering any exceptional obstacles from the German regime. . . .[1]

We have here a remarkably frank and honest admission of a mistake, one deserving of the fullest respect. Many others outside of Germany were similarly deceived by Hitler's glowing promises, even though they were not in Gröber's position of being open to the lure of nationalistic sentiments and haunted by the overriding fears of an apparently imminent social upheaval. One point, however, does not quite ring true. It is difficult to believe that any German bishop who had evidenced even the suggestion of a friendly attitude toward National Socialism—and certainly not one as closely identified with the movement as Gröber allegedly was—would have been kept uninformed about the impending concordat negotiations. In a 1942 pastoral, Gröber had reviewed his personal experiences and had noted, "In 1932 I was in Rome for the conclusion of the Baden Concordat, and in 1933 I took part in the deliberations over the German Concordat."[2] How extensive a part he played in these deliberations is not indicated, but apparently the Archbishop of Freiburg was not one of those to whom Papen's mission came as a complete surprise.

If we are to accept the considered opinion of the editor of a Freiburg diocesan paper, Gröber learned his lesson relatively early and thereafter was one of the more active opponents of the Hitler regime. This informant advanced an interesting comparison between Gröber and Faulhaber, one favorable to the former in that he felt that Faulhaber was strongly anti-Nazi at the beginning and then tended to quiet down, whereas Gröber's opposition came later, at a time when the risk was greater. There is evidence of Gröber's recorded opposition on a wide range of issues. Neuhäusler recalled incidents in which advance copies of secret Nazi orders inimical to the Church found their way into the hands of Catholic leaders. In such instances, the hierarchy turned to Gröber, who then bombarded the responsible officials with telegrams threatening full publicity before the orders went into effect—with the result that they were remanded. Perhaps one might infer from this that Gröber continued to maintain some connections even after his enthusiasm for the regime had waned; or, failing this, that the Nazi officialdom preferred to avoid too open a break with so prominent an erstwhile supporter.

It is not clear exactly when the disillusionment set in, but as early as 1934, the Archbishop felt obliged to take public issue with the so-called "new heathenism" sponsored by the Nazi leaders:

As bishop, I say to you: the German *Volk* will not attain its future greatness by forgetting its Christian past but, instead, only by continuing to build upon the foundations of Christianity. I call upon you, therefore, to be and to remain loyal Catholic men and women, come what may.

But in what must be viewed as either a refusal to face facts or an overoptimistic appraisal, he added

The great *Führer* of our *Volk* wants no *Kulturkampf*, and I think he will do all he can to avoid a *Kulturkampf*. But to those others who do toy with the idea of a *Kulturkampf*, we want to make it clear on the basis of our Christian conviction that they will find us ready should they dare to try to tear the Cross from our Church and our souls, or the Faith from our hearts.[3]

Three years later, in the preface to his *Handbook for the Religious Questions of the Day,* the Archbishop exhibited the same strain between support for the legitimate authority, as represented by the Nazi regime, and firm opposition to the Nazi assaults against the Catholic Church:

The Church shares the responsibility for truth and right, for order and peace. In our nation's present fateful hour, the leaders of the Church take their place in explicit loyalty at the side of the men of the state, dedicated to their own defense against the common enemy. Since they fight for Christianity and the true faith in God on the part of the German *Volk,* they are, in their way, giving surest support for the ramparts the *Führer* has erected against Bolshevism in our *Vaterland.*

Recalling the obstacles earlier religious divisions had presented to "our national development," he denounced the new form of threatening religious strife then current and declared that: "only through honorable discussion, carried on in love for the common *Vaterland* and respect for the truth and rights of conscience, can we hope to overcome the present religious emergency."[4]

Like Cardinal Faulhaber, Gröber had been associated with the *Friedensbund deutscher Katholiken.* In November 1931 he had addressed the national conclave of that peace movement. Gröber's message—he was Bishop of Meissen at the time—was even stronger evidence of support than was Faulhaber's 1932 sermon calling for a "new ethic of war."

True international peace is not founded on the old saying, if you want peace, prepare for war; but, rather, on the universal and open intention to block a new murderous war *at any price.* Military preparedness is a form of dynamite that needs but a single spark to unleash its fearful devastation. Therefore, there is *no justification before man or God* for devoting billions to armaments while millions of people in virtually every country on earth suffer from unemployment and physical as well as spiritual hunger. But I do not overlook the fact that the whole idea of disarmament will become unworkable if even one of the major powers circumvents it, whether openly or in secret. For this reason an irresistible world conviction must be created that would view war as a scandal to all culture and civilization, as mass fratricide and a source of unspeakable sufferings, and would block any such attempts to undermine general disarmament [italics added].

Expressing his warm greetings and heartfelt wishes for the "far-reaching and practical success" of the *Friedensbund* meeting, he complimented it as "an outstanding work of Catholic love and action in the sense of the motto of our Holy Father Pius XI: the Peace of Christ in the Reign of Christ."[5]

A distinctly pacifist statement. However, the complexity of the "Gröber problem" finds further illustration four years later in his published reaffirmation of the traditional teachings on the just war —a reaffirmation which included an explicit rejection of pacifism and a willingness to surrender the final determination of a war's justice or injustice to the secular ruler.

In her almost two thousand years of existence, the Church has never yet absolved her members from military duty, as have several sects— for instance, the Manichaeans and the followers of Wycliffe. She has, on the contrary, rejected the extreme and helpless pacifism which sees war as something forbidden and unchristian and thereby surrenders power to the unjust. . . . Catholic theologians have always distinguished between the just and unjust war and have never left it to the judgment of the individual, with all of his shortsightedness and emotionalism, to decide the justice of any given war. Instead, the final decision has been left to the legitimate authority.[6]

It may be of some passing interest to note that the book from which this quotation was taken was ultimately placed on the Nazi list of forbidden books, as was another Gröber book, *You Have But One Teacher, Christ,* which contained criticism of extreme racist ideologies.

In 1934 the same rejection of pacifism had been sounded in an address given to a group of priests attending a university class. "The Church," he said, "wants no 'Hurrah patriotism,' but neither does she want an unlimited and enfeebling pacifism." The Catholic, according to Gröber, is loyal to his *Vaterland* precisely because he is a Catholic.[7]

It should come as no surprise, then, to find the Archbishop (by now a Nazi opponent) registering his full support of the German cause in World War II and proclaiming at its start that: "With God's strength and Christ's solace, we will bear the burdens of war and fulfill our duty with honor, dedication, and loyalty whether we serve on the battlefield or remain in the *Heimat*." Religious freedom, he took the occasion to declare, was now more important than ever to enable the blessings of the Almighty to descend upon "the just cause of our *Volk*."[8]

A 1939 letter to the men called into service charged each of them to "work as a good soldier of Christ" and reached peaks of nationalistic fervor matched only by the messages of the Catholic Military Bishop which are to be discussed in the next section of this analysis:

You belong to the German *Volk* as its guardian and protector. Blood, language, culture, natural love and other ties of the most intimate kind bind you to it.

Thus, you live in the *Volk*.

By the same token, the *Volk* lives in you. For you are the firm wall of defense that protects our *Volk* and *Vaterland* in its most serious trials. All other barriers are down. Only through you can they live and fight, thunder and blaze forth in the battle.

In your soldierly mission, you offer the *Volk* all that you prize most highly: time, sweat, strength of will, obedience, love, spirit—and, should fate so decree, your health, your blood, and your life.

It is scarcely possible to give more than this to *Volk* and *Vaterland*. And you assume this all-encompassing service as a duty sworn under oath in God's sight! A duty, however, that is not assumed as an unwanted burden but rather, in keeping with the soldierly character, with a deliberate and manly "I will!"

Should one or another of you lose his life, it becomes far more than the ordinary tribute demanded by Death the Conqueror in repayment of man's mortal guilt. It is the ultimate offering to *Vaterland* and *Volk*. A soldier's death is, therefore, a sacrificial death. A sacrificial death is a hero's death. The hero's death is death with honor, a wreath of glory to adorn the grave of the Unknown Soldier as a mark of a comrade's gratitude.

In this way you redeem your debt to the German *Volk* in full. It gave you the heritage of its glorious blood, and you offer it your own precious life's blood in return. You live through the *Volk;* the *Volk* lives on through you. And you, in turn, live on in it.[9]

Here is what has been termed the "myth" or "mystique" of the *Volk* in its most complete expression

From message to message, the theme of personal identification with the heroic sacrifice of the soldier at the front is given renewed emphasis—even while the constant complaint is voiced that religion is being attacked and that the *Volk* itself is being weakened to the degree that these attacks are successful. But in none of these messages do we find this eminent author of a moral guidance handbook making any attempt to apply the traditional "conditions for the just war" to the Nazi wars.

The victory over France was celebrated by a ringing of the church bells, an action that is at least partly explained as compliance with official government demands and expectations. But along with the ringing of the bells came a special Gröber greeting to his returning parishioners who had been evacuated from this border area for military reasons: "With my whole heart, I thank those who led the German Army to so swift a victory and thereby preserved our German *Heimat* from the destruction of war and freed her from war's dangers. . . ."[10]

January 1940 brought a message to the wives and mothers of men in service assuring them of the Archbishop's unwavering trust "in the tested heroic might of our army" and in God.[11] In May of that year, a message to an assembly of Catholic boys bemoaned the fact that the old war song, "Prayer Before the Battle: Father, I Call to Thee," was no longer sung (an obvious criticism on his part of the de-Christianizing efforts of the Nazi regime); however, the Archbishop voiced his personal confidence that this pious sentiment still mounted heavenward in the form of a silent prayer in the hearts of the German soldiers.[12]

In February 1941, after explicitly disavowing any intention to weaken the war effort, Gröber returned to a discussion of the religious threat of the times and, in the process, cast a glance toward the hoped-for future:

Anyone at all who thinks or feels as a German man will long for an honorable world peace, a peace that will bring stability to our *Volk* and land for a long time to come and will guarantee it undiminished freedom in the *Heimat* as well as the living space it needs and the influence it deserves in the world at large. . . .[13]

It should not be necessary to point out that the term for "living space" (*Lebensraum*) was a favorite rallying cry for the Nazi movement. Whether it was the Archbishop's intent or not, his use of this term in such a context would almost necessarily carry over-tones of acceptance of the Third Reich's war aims to the ordinary Catholic listener.

But the religious problem at home continued to mount. In June 1941, as part of the Nazi-incited program of harassment and general anti-Catholic rowdyism, a cannon cracker was exploded in the Freiburg cathedral in the course of a Sunday night service being held for a Catholic youth group. When order was finally restored, the Archbishop personally took to the pulpit to deliver a scathing commentary.

I can only refer to the so-called "Germans" who are responsible for this impious act as criminals, cowards, and traitors. It is not enough that French and English bombs create panic in our German cities. No! Our magnificent cathedral must also be desecrated by a "cannon cracker" and, in the midst of our prayers for our brave soldiers, our people sent into a panic that could easily have brought tragic consequences.[14]

The Archbishop's indignation notwithstanding, his words illustrate once more the fact that there was scarcely any issue which could not serve as the vehicle for an episcopal lesson in wartime morale or as the occasion to point with pride to the wholehearted commitment of the German Catholic population to the prosecution of the war.

The confiscation of the church bells inspired Gröber, like Faulhaber, to deliver a moving sermon in the course of which he reminded the faithful of the many familiar services the bells had performed: ringing out messages of joy over victories, sorrowfully tolling the news of death, awakening the populace with emergency warnings of impending dangers, and so on. Now these old friends were to become *Wanderglocken,* never to return to the *Heimat.* Not even his beloved bells could find an abiding home on earth. But this leave-taking becomes still another call to arms in a very literal sense:

Fare thee well! We sorrow after you and quiet the pain of loss only through the reassuring thought that you will continue to serve Christ the King in another form since your sacrifice will contribute to the conquest of godless and anti-Christian Bolshevism. . . .

The "other form," of course, was that of munitions destined for direct engagement in the military struggle. To make his point doubly clear, he drew a parallel between the sorrow of parting and loss he felt with those suffered by war-bereaved widows and mothers.[15]

In 1942 Gröber issued a lengthy birthday message in which he summarized the experiences of a long life. Little mention is made of contemporary events; indeed, after telling of the part he played in bringing about the 1933 Concordat he makes what might be a highly significant statement: "What has transpired since 1934 is indelibly recorded in our memory and needs no specific mention here. . . ." Today this suggests an avoidance of unpleasant and possibly dangerous expressions of disappointment and disillusionment; to his hearers at the time, however, it could have just as easily implied the contrary. But there is no question as to the Archbishop's continued commitment to the principle that the Christian is obliged to render obedience to the secular authority. There are, of course, rather clear indications of indirect criticism of the Nazi regime in his recollections of the tragic oppression suffered by Catholics during Bismarck's *Kulturkampf,* as well as in his rejection of total and absolute power in the state, but these points are neutralized by being placed in the context of traditional teachings about *Gehorsam*:

We were no more enemies of the state [in the time of Bismarck] than were Peter and Paul and the early Christians of Rome. Of course, we recognized *and recognize* no total and absolute power in the state, but rather an instrument of the Eternal Ruler Who set Himself as the final and highest end for man, as for all creation. Love of the *Vaterland* was *and is* for us . . . an unalterable obligation under Natural Law and a Christian commandment binding in conscience [italics added]. . . .[16]

That same year's Christmas message to the faithful found Gröber making a specific reference to the scriptural warning that he who takes to the sword will perish by the sword. He hastened to add, however,

This is not, of course, to be taken literally, but only in the sense that almost every armed action can produce an often dangerous and even deadly counteraction, which is also demonstrated by the irresponsibly declared and unjust wars through which entire races and nations of men have already vanished from the face of the earth.

Is this to be read as a dire warning that Hitler's wars were such "irresponsibly declared and unjust wars," and that Germany could be destined to find herself numbered among the races and nations vanishing from the face of the earth? One might be tempted to think so—until one reaches the closing prayer including "the devout wish that burns in all German hearts" that this Christmas "may at last prove to be the very last Christmas not crowned by the just and final victory."[17] In this connection, the term used by Gröber (*Endsieg*) had special overtones for the German Catholic, who would associate that term with the all-out victory of the Nazi New Order it had come to mean in Hitler's Germany.

One other pastoral letter issued during the war must be mentioned, the Archbishop's 1942 commemoration of *Heldengedenktag,* Germany's Memorial Day. It is an extremely touching portrayal of the losses sustained in the war. The tragic fact that many family strains were dying out completely with the death in battle of their last male members caused him to reject indignantly the blithe official assurances that the increased birth rate had already replaced the losses sustained in the war. Such a statistical computation, he charged, ignores the very nature of the great sacrifices being made; for each human life must be seen as a value in itself and can never be viewed as expendable or replaceable. The letter continued at great length to describe the spiritual rewards and blessings earned by the soldier dead—pointing out, of course, that many priests, seminarians, and members of religious orders were included in their number. It would be impossible to exaggerate the potential impact on morale of the entire document. Only two brief citations are necessary here. The first is the explanation of why Germans should find solace in honoring their fallen warriors on this day: "They died for our German *Vaterland*, that is, for something truly wonderful and great, albeit not the very highest and absolutely ultimate good in the scale of values held by the man who believes in God." But not only did they die as patriots: "Yea, God be praised! Our dead heroes died as victors. Seldom in the entire history of the world have armies been so accustomed to victory and so crowned with glory as those in whose ranks these men fought and died." Rejoicing in the fact that these warriors had earned an eternal reward, the Archbishop drew the inevitable lessons for those who remained behind, one of which was that "we, too, fulfill our patriotic duty with Christian fervor."[18] It is important to note that the morale-building effect of this document was not limited to the Catholics of the Freiburg diocese to whom it was directed; instead, it was deemed so effective and significant that it was reprinted in its entirety in the Münster *Amtsblatt*.

The Archbishop's 1942 Christmas pastoral was the last recorded wartime message contained in the issues of the Freiburg *Amtsblatt* placed at the researcher's disposal. It is unlikely that this means that Gröber withdrew in silence rather than continue voicing his support for the war. It is more properly explained as an end to publication of whatever sermons and statements he may have continued to present orally and privately. No evidence was encountered by this writer which would support Mother Gallin's statement, based on OSS documents, that "in February 1943 there was a report that Archbishop Gröber had denounced Hitler's wars as unjust."[19] The Metzger case, to be discussed shortly, would seem to refute any such report; otherwise, we would be forced to conclude that the Archbishop continued to evidence support for a war he actually regarded as unjust.

Even in his postwar messages, filled though they were with detailed admissions of the evil excesses of the Nazi period and his attempts to explain how they could have taken place, Gröber made no open declaration that Hitler's wars had been unjust and should not have been supported by German Catholics. Instead, one finds renewed statements of the moral obligation of Germans to honor their war dead, although the usual references to *Heldentod, Ehrentod,* and so on, are not present. The new and more restrained appeals argued that "in God's eyes the death for the *Vaterland,* which is often a most painful death, atones for much and, in the eyes of the All-knowing and All-just, erases whatever remains of sin and guilt on the soul." The hope (in sharp contrast to earlier statements of absolute certainty) was also expressed that these fallen soldiers had found a merciful judgment at the hands of "the Lord of battles." Calling for prayers for the fallen soldiers, Gröber declared,

I hold that such prayer is actually obligatory upon us all. This does not depend upon the success of arms. Even though these warriors were not permitted to mark the victory upon their banners, they nevertheless gave the *Vaterland* all that they possessed and could give. And they gave it for us—as fathers, sons, or relatives. I do not know if we will ever be permitted to erect war memorials in our communities to honor them, but one thing we know: Stone is stone and remains stone; it is cold and wears and crumbles away. The heart, on the other hand, is life and its prayer is a greeting to the dead, carrying the power through love to win eternal blessedness for them if they do not already possess that blessedness or have not lost it forever through their own fault. . . .[20]

Bearing even more specifically upon this point is the October 1945 letter which was devoted to answering some of the charges that the Allied victors had directed against German Catholics and their spiritual leaders. One of these was the challenging question, Why did not the Christian soldiers of Germany mutiny and thereby quickly end the war, thus saving their own lives and the lives of countless others? The Archbishop's reply stresses two points of considerable importance to the present analysis: (1) the binding quality of the military oath sworn to Hitler and the recognition of the regime as legitimate authority; and (2) the absence of sufficient opportunity to reach a soundly reasoned judgment concerning the war and its justice.* The first point is of most immediate relevance here.

In answering this charge, it is permitted to raise the question as to whether mutiny could be reconciled with the sworn oath of allegiance and the other oaths with which the German *Volk*—even school children—were burdened in order that they might be bound in deepest conscience to the Third Reich. Furthermore, one should not forget the horrible fate of all, including the highest ranking generals, who dared to speak of peace and an end to the war or who tried to eliminate the driving force behind the war by means of assassination. In this connection, we German Catholics know the judgment of our Church regarding tyrannicide, which she forbids just as she forbids murder in general. . . .[21]

The clear implication of an adverse moral judgment upon those officers and others who participated in the July 20, 1944 assassination attempt requires no elaboration. But that such a judgment was publicly stated *after the war was over,* at a time when these men were being honored as martyred heroes of the true German spirit, offers unmistakable evidence that Gröber held fast to his earlier

* The Archbishop made no mention of the obvious fact that one of the major obstacles to reaching such a judgment—at least as far as the Catholic layman would be concerned—was his own and other bishops' continued support of the war, to say nothing of his earlier denial that any such "judgment concerning the war and its justice" *could* fall within the range of individual competence.

definitions of the limited competence of the individual in exercising personal moral responsibility with regard to issues involving demands made upon him by legitimate authority.

A more dramatic illustration of this position may be found in the Archbishop's approach to the charges brought against Father Max Joseph Metzger, a priest of his diocese, in 1943. Founder of *Una Sancta,* a Church reunion movement, and of the *Christkönigsgesellschaft,* a religious community in which he took the name of Brother Paulus, and also cofounder of the *Friedensbund deutscher Katholiken,* Father Metzger was one of the few Catholics openly to register his opposition to Hitler's wars. According to information furnished by the writer's informants, the priest once wrote a letter to Hitler himself demanding an end to his unjust war before more lives were lost; however, efforts to discover a copy of this letter have thus far not been successful. In 1943 Metzger fell into a Gestapo trap and was condemned to death by the Nazi *Volksgericht.* Archbishop Gröber took a personal interest in the case to the extent of sending his own representative to the sessions of the trial and, in addition, writing a personal letter to the court's prosecutor appealing for mercy toward his accused priest.

Several of Metzger's closest associates still recall the joy and comfort they and the condemned man took from the fact that the Archbishop had interceded in his behalf. They also reported other evidences of episcopal interest in the affair. One was the report reaching a superior of Metzger's religious community that, as soon as official word was received that the execution had taken place, Gröber celebrated a private Requiem Mass, at the conclusion of which he added the ejaculation, "Brother Paulus, pray for us." This same informant told the writer that the Archbishop soon became fearful that his actions in Metzger's behalf would be resented by the Nazis or misinterpreted by others of his priests as evidence of personal support for Metzger's stand. This fear led him to issue a private circular letter clearly dissociating himself from Metzger's antiwar sentiments and activities. Neither the incident of the Mass nor the issuance of the letter could be verified in the course of interviews with present chancery officials. Since some of these in-

formants had held chancery posts under Gröber during the war—
one of them was the cleric chosen to be the Archbishop's representative at the trial—it is difficult to determine how much confidence can be placed in these reports.

That Gröber did make an appeal for mercy is, however, a matter
of record; and a copy of this letter is in the Freiburg chancery files.
Its text affords some quite significant clues to the Archbishop's
position. For one thing, the letter does not contain even the slightest
hint of support for Metzger's activities; instead, the document's
prevailing tone is one of prudent disapproval of the "idealism" that
had led Metzger to place his life in jeopardy, and one finds a note
of condescension such as one might associate with an embarrassed
parent's apology for damage done by a child. The letter leaves the
reader with the impression that, if this show of interest was enough
to bring joy and comfort to Metzger and his associates, they must
indeed have held rather pessimistic expectations of the position
Gröber would take. The significant portions of the letter read as
follows:

Metzger is a man of many great talents, an idealist who has grown
ever more estranged from reality. Parochial work in the diocese was
not enough for him; instead, he preferred social and charitable work
and founded a project in Graz with aims and procedures such as only
an idealist who was a stranger to the world could pursue. . . . Metzger
is an idealist who wanted to help his *Volk* and *Vaterland* but who
proceeded from the wrong premises. Unfortunately, I had no opportunity to speak with him in recent months. The last time he was with
me, I limited myself to denying him permission to give lectures in my
diocese advocating the union of the two confessions—a decision he
resented. . . . I beseech you . . . to do everything you can for him. If
you save him, you will not be sparing a criminal from his deserved
punishment, but rather an idealist and super-philanthropist from a
fate that he ought to be spared out of consideration for the reputation
he has both in foreign countries and among broad segments of the
population. . . .[22]

A mild appeal indeed, one marked by episcopal restraint and a
distinct note of practical expediency in its suggestion that the Nazis

might be the gainers if mercy were shown this man. Whether its mildness and restraint reflect a prudent evaluation of the type of appeal that would carry the greatest hope of success, or whether they reflect a personal disavowal of Metzger's principles and position, no one can say.* But one thing can be and must be said: mild, restrained, even disapproving as it was, this letter represents the strongest and perhaps the *only* episcopal support given any German Catholic objector to Hitler's wars.

With the three sections just concluded, attention has been focused upon the support given the Hitler military undertakings by three of the most reknowned and respected opponents of Nazism: Cardinal Faulhaber of Munich-Freising; Archbishop Gröber of Freiburg im Breisgau; and Bishop (later Cardinal) von Galen of Münster. Although, in view of his early support for the Nazi movement, some might take exception to including Gröber in this context, no one could question the right of the other two to the designation as opponents of the Hitler regime. Ardent admirers of Galen's heroic stand have already taken the first steps in the series of actions which, if they are successful, will lead to his ultimate canonization.

This section of the analysis represents a more systematic inquiry into the actual record of wartime acts and statements attributable to these men than the earlier chapter dealing with the hierarchy in general. Instead of relying upon references found in the ordinary Catholic press, all available issues of the official *Amtsblätter* of the

---

* That the latter is more than likely true may be inferred from the interviews conducted with three officials of the Freiburg chancery. All of them had been acquainted with Metzger and indicated a high personal regard and friendship for him; yet all of them spoke of him as an "idealist" who was too far removed from the world of practical reality for his own good. Even today, there is no special official diocesan commemoration of Metzger's sacrifice—an indication, perhaps, that it is still dismissed as an act of excessive idealism. We might note in passing that the Archbishop's use of the term "idealism" did lead to a significant bit of self-judgment on the part of a Nazi spokesman. The notorious judge, Roland Freisler, handled the case and, in the account of the trial given in the volume of Metzger's *Gefangenschaftbriefe,* he is quoted as screaming, "his Archbishop has called him an idealist. But that is an altogether different world, a world we do not understand. . . ."

three dioceses were reviewed, and these were supplemented by the authorized biographical sketches of the lives of Faulhaber and Galen. It is, therefore, of highest significance to note that here, too, the pattern developed for the hierarchy in general holds true. No overt evidence of opposition to the Hitler war effort was encountered; even Galen's dissents concerning the methods being employed were, as has been noted, limited and presented in a context of general support for the national cause. Wherever and whenever references were made to the war or to service in the war, the emphasis was clearly placed upon the moral obligation of the individual Christian to "do his duty" and upon the undying honor and gratitude owed to the men who were engaged in actual battle.

If these men, the most heroic, bitter-end opponents of the Nazi Third Reich, were thus open and fervent in their support of the war, it may be taken for granted that their less ardent colleagues who did not distinguish themselves by their opposition to Hitler would have shown an at least equally (and possibly more) enthusiastic degree of commitment to the national war effort. This conclusion necessarily follows: among the social controls operative upon the German Catholic must be included the formal directives of his ecclesiastical superiors and the assurance they gave him that it was his inescapable moral obligation to perform whatever services to *Volk, Vaterland,* and *Heimat* might be required of him.

## NOTES

1. *Amtsblatt für die Erzdiözese Freiburg,* No. 8 (August 17, 1945), p. 42. "Trotzdem konnten wir alle uns der Furcht nicht verschliessen, dass schwerste Zeiten sowohl für unsere Jugend als für unser ganzes Volk bevorstehen, wenn nicht die damalige höchst unsichere, zu einem sozialen Umsturz drängende innenpolitische Lage durch eine kräftige Hand gemeistert werde.

"Und nun zu Beginn des Jahres 1933 hatte es nach der Meinung mancher den Anschein, als ob in das zerissene und gärende deutsche Gemeinwesen die ersehnte Beruhigung und Ordnung komme. . . ."

". . . Es erhoben sich dennoch gewichtige Stimmen, dass der neue Staat samt seinen zahlreichen und lauten Versprechungen, und gerade ihretwegen, mit grösstem Misstrauen betrachtet werden müsse. Aber da überraschte uns um die Osterzeit 1933 die erste Kunde, dass sich Herr v. Papen, der Vizekanzler des jungen Dritten Reiches, in der Ewigen Stadt aufhalte, um den Heiligen Stuhl zur Abschliessung eines Konkordates zu vermögen. Tatsächlich kam dieser Vertrag auch im Verlaufe des Sommers ohne wesentliche Schwierigkeiten vonseiten der deutschen Regierung zustande."

2. *Ibid.*, No. 3 (February 5, 1942), p. 22.

3. *Rayrische Katholische Kirchenzeitung*, Vol. 10, No. 16 (April 8, 1934), pp. 127-128.

"Ich sage als Bischof: das deutsche Volk wird seine künftige Grösse nicht erreichen dadurch, dass man die christliche Vergangenheit vergisst, sondern dadurch dass wir herauswachsen aus den Fundamenten des Christentums. Ich rufe euch deshalb auf, treue katholische Männer, und treue katholische Frauen zu sein und zu bleiben, mag kommen was da will. Der grosse Führer unseres Volkes will keinen Kulturkampf, und ich denke, dass er alles tun wird, um einen Kulturkampf zu verhindern. Aber das wollen wir andern gegenüber, die mit dem Kulturkampf spielen, aus unserer katholischen Ueberzeugung heraus sagen: sie sollen uns gewappnet finden, wenn sie es wagen sollten, das Kreuz aus unserer Kirche und Seele, den Glauben aus unseren Herzen zu reissen."

4. Conrad Gröber, *Handbuch der Religiösen Gegenwartsfragen* (Freiburg: Herder, 1937), Preface.

5. *Vom Frohen Leben*, Vol. 11 (1932—exact pagination not noted) reports this November 1931 message.

"Ein wahrer Völkerfriede gründet sich nicht auf den alten Satz: 'Si vis pacem, para bellum', sondern auf der allgemeinen, ehrlichen Absicht, einen neuen, mörderischen Krieg um jeden Preis zu verhindern. Kriegsrüstung ist ein Explosivstoff, der nur eines einzigen Funkens bedarf, um furchtbare Verheerungen anzurichten. Dazu kann es weder vor Gott noch vor der Menscheit verantwortet werden, Milliarden auf Kriegsrüstungen zu verwenden während Millionen von Menschen in fast allen Ländern der Erde der Arbeitslosigkeit und dem Hunger körperlich und seelisch erliegen. Dabei verkenne ich nicht, dass die Abrüstungsidee schon dadurch wirkungslos wird, dass auch nur einer der Grossstaaten sie öffentlich oder heimlich umgeht. Es muss deswegen eine zwingende Völkerüberzeugung angebahnt werden, die den Krieg als eine Kulturschande, einen Massenbrudermord und eine Quelle unsäglichen Elends betrachtet und jegliche Durchlöcherung der allgemeinen Abrüstung verhindert."

6. Conrad Gröber, *Kirche, Vaterland und Vaterlandsliebe* (Freiburg: Herder, 1935), p. 108.

"Die Kirche hat sodann in ihrem fast zweitausendjährigen Bestand noch nie wie einzelne Sekten, z.B. die Manichäer und Wiclifiten, ihre Gläubigen von der Heerespflicht entbunden. Sie hat vielmehr den übertriebenen und kraftlosen Pazifisnus abgelehnt, der im Kriege als etwas Unerlaubtes und

Widerchristliches erblickt und dem Unrecht die Herrschaft überlässt. . . . Die katholischen Theologen haben immer den gerechten vom ungerechten Krieg unterschieden und es niemals in den Urteilsbereich des Einzelnen mit all seinen Kurzsichtigkeit und Gefühlsstimmungen gelegt, im Kriegsfalle die Erlaubtheit oder das Unerlaubtsein zu erörtern, sondern die letzte Entscheidung der rechtmässigen Autorität überlassen."

7. *Bayrische Katholische Kirchenzeitung*, Vol. 10, No. 43 (October 21, 1934), p. 312.

8. *Amtsblatt für die Erzdiözese Freiburg*, No. 26 (September 5, 1939), p. 123.

"Mit Gottes Kraft und Christi Trost wollen wir den Krieg ertragen und unsere Pflicht in Ehrenhaftigkeit, Geschlossenheit und Treue erfüllen, ob wir nun im Felde stehen oder in der Heimat verbleiben. Freilich, das Eine brauchen wir jetzt noch weit mehr als zuvor: Die Freiheit für Gott und seine heilige katholische Kirche, damit aus dieser Freiheit und Gerechtigkeit auch die Freiheit und die gerechte Sache unseres Volkes den Segen des Allmächtigen empfange!"

9. Conrad Gröber, "Arbeite als ein guter Kriegsmann Christi," *Hirtenwort an die Soldaten im Felde* (Freiburg: Herder, 1939), pp. 5-6.

"Zum grossen deutschen Volk gehört ihr als seine Wache und seine Wehr. Blut, Sprache, Kultur, naturhafte Liebe und andere Beziehungen tiefsinnigster Art verbinden euch mit ihm.

"So lebt ihr aus dem Volk.

"Das Volk lebt hinwiederum aus euch. Denn ihr seid der machtvolle Schutzwall, der in schwerster Bedrängnis unser Volk und Vaterland umschirmt. Alle andern Wälle sind tot. Sie leben und kämpfen, sie donnern und sprühen erst durch euch.

"Ihr schenkt mit eurem Soldatentum dem Volk das Wertvollste das ihr besitzt: Zeit, Schweiss, Willenskraft, Gehorsam, Liebe und Geist. Und wenn es das Schicksal will: Eure Gesundheit, euer Blut, und euer Leben.

"Mehr könnt ihr dem Volk und Vaterland kaum geben. Und ihr leistet diesen alles umfassenden Dienst als Pflicht vor Gott, übernommen durch einen Eid! Aus Pflicht, die aber keine leidig erzwungene Haltung sein soll, sondern soldatischer Charakter, d.h. ein überlegtes und mannhaftes: Ich will!

"Fällt der eine oder andere von euch, so ist das weit mehr als nur die Entrichtung der menschlichen Schuld an den Allbezwinger Tod. Es ist letzte Hingabe an das Vaterland und Volk. Soldatentod ist damit Opfertod. Opfertod ist Heldentod. Heldentod ist ehrenvoller Tod, ein Ruhmeskranz, der auch das Grab des unbekannten Soldaten aus der Dankbarkeit des Volksgenossen schmückt.

"Damit werdet ihr mit dem deutschen Volk quitt. Es gab euch sein ruhmreiches Blut, und ihr gebt ihm das kostbare eure. Ihr lebt aus dem Volk, das Volk aber lebt weiter durch euch. Und ihr selber lebt weiter in ihm."

10. *Amtsblatt für die Erzdiözese Freiburg*, No. 17 (June 26, 1940), p. 282.

11. *Münchener Katholische Kirchenzeitung*, Vol. 33, No. 2 (January 14, 1940), p. 8.

12. *Amtsblatt für die Erzdiözese Freiburg*, No. 12 (May 8, 1940), p. 264.

13. *Ibid.*, No. 5 (February 12, 1941), p. 355.

"Wer überhaupt als deutscher Mann denkt oder fühlt, wird einen ehrenvollen Weltfrieden ersehnen, einen Frieden, der unser Volk und Land für eine lange Dauer beruhigt und ihm, mit der ungeschmälerten Freiheit in der Heimat, den notwendigen Lebensraum und den gebührenden Einfluss im Weltganzen verbürgt. . . ."

14. Neuhäusler, *op. cit.*, Vol. I, pp. 304-305.

15. *Amtsblatt für die Erzdiözese Freiburg*, No. 1 (January 16, 1942), pp. 1-5.

"Zum Gotteslob und zur Seelenerhebung bestimmt, bezwingt und entfremdet sie erbarmungslos unser furchtbarer Krieg. So fahret wohl! Wir trauern euch nach und verschmerzen euren Verlust nur mit dem beruhigenden Gedanken, dass ihr auch in anderer Form Christus, dem König, dienen werdet, weil euer Einsatz der Bezwingung des gottlosen und christuswidrigen Bolschewismus gelten soll. . . ."

16. *Ibid.*, No. 3 (February 5, 1942), p. 21.

"Staatsfeinde waren wir so wenig als Petrus und Paulus und die ersten Christen von Rom. Allerdings erkannten und erkennen wir im Staate keine totale und absolute Macht, sondern nur ein Werkzeug des ewigen Ordners, der dem Menschen, wie allem Geschaffenen, sich selbst als letztes und höchstes Ziel gab. Vaterlandsliebe war und ist für uns, obgleich wir durch die Gunst der Grossen alles eher als verwöhnt sind, unabänderliche Naturpflicht und christliches im Gewissen bindendes Gebot. . . ."

17. *Ibid.*, No. 34 (December 22, 1942), pp. 156, 157.

"Das ist freilich nicht wörtlich zu nehmen, sondern nur in dem Sinn, dass fast jede Wehr eine oft gefährliche oder gar tödliche Gegenwehr zur Folge haben kann, was namentlich auch auf den leichtfertig erklärten und ungerechten Krieg zutrifft, durch den schon ganze Stämme und Völkerschaften vom Erdboden verschwunden sind. . . . Möge es endlich—wer will uns diesen frommen, wohl in allen deutschen Herzen brennenden Wunsch verargen oder falsch deuten!—die allerletzte, noch nicht vom gerechten Endsieg gekrönte Weihnacht sein, die unsere Krieger von uns und der Heimat mit ihrem beglückenden Gehalt durch ungeheure Entfernungen und mörderische Gefahren trennt!"

18. *Ibid.*, No. 5 (March 5, 1942), pp. 33, 34.

"Lasst mich zuerst von ihrem Ruhm mit eindringlichen Worten sprechen. Sie starben für unser deutsches Vaterland. Also für etwas überaus Herrliches und ganz Grosses, wenn es auch nicht das Allerhöchste und Allerletzte auf der Stufenleiter der Werte ist, die ein an Gott glaubender Mensch besteigt. . . .

". . . Ja, Gottlob! Unsere toten Helden starben als Sieger. Nur selten in der ganzen Weltgeschichte waren Armeen so sieggewohnt und ruhmgekrönt, wie jene, in deren Reihen sie bis zur triumphierenden Fahnenhissung auf stürmisch eroberten Gebieten kämpften und fielen. . . ."

19. Mother Mary Alice Gallin, O.S.U., *Ethical and Religious Factors in the German Resistance to Hitler* (Washington: The Catholic University of America Press, 1955), p. 184.

20. *Amtsblatt für die Erzdiözese Freiburg*, No. 6 (May 18, 1945), p. 27. "Ich halte dieses Gebet sogar für verpflichtend für uns alle. Auf den Erfolg der Waffen kommt es dabei nicht an. Auch wenn die Kämpfenden den Sieg nicht an ihre Fahnen heften konnten, gaben sie dem Vaterland doch alles, was sie besassen und geben konnten. Und sie gaben es für uns als Väter, Söhne oder Verwandte. Ob man je einmal in den Gemeinden Kriegerge-denksteine zu ihrer Ehrung errichtet, weiss ich nicht: aber das eine ist uns allen bekannt: Stein ist Stein und bleibt Stein, er ist kalt und verwittert und zerbröckelt; das Herz dagegen ist Leben, und sein Gebet ist Gruss an die Toten und Liebeskraft, um ihnen die ewige Seligkeit zu bewirken, sofern sie dieselbe noch nicht besitzen oder sie nicht durch eigene Schuld für immer verscherzten. . . ."

21. *Ibid.*, No. 10 (October 3, 1945), p. 63. "Zweite Anklage: *Warum meuterten denn die christlichen deutschen Soldaten nicht?* Es lag doch in ihrer Macht, damit den Krieg in kürzester Frist zu beendigen und ihr eigenes Leben und das zahlreicher anderer zu retten.

"Demgegenüber ist vielleicht die andere Frage erlaubt, die Frage, ob sich das Meutern mit dem geleisteten Fahneneid und den übrigen Eiden vertrug, mit denen man das deutsche Volk bis in die Schuljugend hinein belastete, um es im tiefsten Gewissen ans Dritte Reich zu binden. Man vergesse weiterhin auch nicht, welches entsetzliche Schicksal alle, bis hinauf zu den höchsten Generälen, traf, die von Kriegsschluss und Frieden zu reden wagten oder es unternahmen, die treibenden Kräfte des Krieges durch ein Attentat zu beseitigen. Dazu kennen wir deutsche Katholiken das Urteil unserer Kirche über den Tyrannenmord, den sie geradeso verbietet, wie den Mord in allgemeinen. . . ."

22. A copy of this letter is in the files of the Freiburg Archdiocesan chancery and was inspected by the writer with the kind permission and co-operation of Msgr. Simon Hirt, Vicar-General. "Metzger ist ein hochveranlagter Mensch, Idealist, dem die Wirklichkeit immer fremder geworden ist. Die Seelsorge in der Diözese genügt ihm nicht, sondern er wollte sozial und charitativ wirken und hat ein Unternehmen in Graz gegründet mit Zielen und Verwirklichungsplänen, wie sie nur ein weltfremder Idealist verfolgen kann.

. . . Zum Idealisten, der von falscher Voraussetzung ausging, in seinem

Volk und Vaterland helfen wollte. Leider hatte ich keine Gelegenheit in den letzten Monaten mit ihm zu sprechen. Als er letztesmal bei mir war, beschränkte ich mich darauf ihm seine Vorträge für die Vereinigung der beiden Kirchen innerhalb meiner Erzdiözese zu untersagen, was er mir übelgenommen hat. . . . Ich bitte Sie, sehr geehrter Herr Rechtsanwalt, alles für ihn zu tun. Wenn Sie ihn retten entziehen Sie nicht einen Verbrecher seiner verdienten Strafe, sondern einen Idealisten und Hyperphilantropen einem Schicksal, das ihm schon mit Rücksicht auf seinen Namen im Ausland und in den weitesten Kreisen der Bevölkerung erspart bleiben sollte. . . ."

# CHAPTER 10

# Franz Josef Rarkowski

*Deo et Militi**

THE OFFICIAL Catholic support for Hitler's wars reaches a peak of dedication and enthusiasm in the writings of the Catholic Military Bishop, Franz Josef Rarkowski. Here we find all of the ultra-nationalistic clichés and symbols that constitute "the myths men kill by" in their fullest expression. Of even greater significance, perhaps, it is in the Rarkowski *Hirtenbriefe* that one finds clear and open expression of continuing support for and even *approval* of the Hitler regime itself.

This is a challenging and crucial point, since it contradicts the widely accepted assumption that the pattern of Catholic behavior at all levels—but most definitely at the level of episcopal authority and responsibility—was one of inflexible opposition to National Socialism. As we have seen, there was general support for the Hitler regime as the embodiment of legitimate authority, but this was usually distinguishable from support for Nazism *per se*—if only in that the former was frequently coupled with open protests or implied reservations concerning specific programs or policies of the Third Reich.

* For God and the Soldier.

With *Feldbischof* Rarkowski the problem is less involved. One finds no open criticism of any aspect of the Hitler regime in his writings. Occasionally there are fervent appeals to Catholic soldiers to make a special effort to remain loyal to their Faith, and special instructions to the chaplains under his command to give themselves in total sacrifice to the task of ministering to the spiritual needs of the soldiers and sharing their every peril. Perhaps these could be read as implicit criticism of anti-Catholic charges circulated by leading Nazi sources; but such an inference would be somewhat strained, for even these moral and religious appeals are all but smothered in their context of nationalistic exhortations. A thorough reading of the text of the Rarkowski messages that are available* leads to the ineluctable conclusion that, in the Bishop's eyes at least, the German Catholic soldier's obligations to serve God and the Third Reich were coextensive if not actually interchangeable.

It would be difficult to overemphasize the importance of Bishop Rarkowski's role in any analysis of Catholic support for Hitler's wars. The other members of the German Catholic hierarchy could and did marshal "home-front" support for the war and, through their reverent acclaim for the soldier and his heroic sacrifices, help to bolster the morale of the German fighting men. Bishop Rarkowski, however, was the spiritual leader most directly involved with those fighting men and their performance of the duties assigned to them. The chaplains serving under his command literally became the immediate pastors of the men in the units to which they were assigned.[1]

It follows that the German Catholic who came to the army troubled by moral misgivings as to the justice of the war or any of the actions involved in that war (or who may have developed such misgivings in the course of his military service) would be expected

* The writer had the privilege of meeting and interviewing Bishop Rarkowski's chief wartime assistant. It was also possible to review the file of Rarkowski *Hirtenbriefe* and other wartime statements. Although this file may not have represented the total production of the Military Bishop, the writer was assured that it did constitute the most complete collection of such documents known to be in existence.

to turn to his chaplain and the Military Bishop for authoritative guidance and direction in solving his problem. The evidence is quite clear that any soldier so troubled who turned to the Military Bishop and his published pronouncements would find his problem swept away in a torrent of nationalistic outpourings. And this would have been just as true at the end of the war as it was in 1939 when the opening of hostilities brought the following statement:

Comrades!

In this serious hour when our German *Volk* must undergo the trials of a test by fire in a struggle for its natural and God-given right to live . . . I turn to you soldiers who stand ready at the front and who bear the great and honorable responsibility of guarding and defending with the sword the life of the German nation.

. . . Each of you knows what is at stake for our *Volk* in these stormy days; and, in whatever is asked of you, each sees before him the shining example of a true warrior, our *Führer* and Supreme Commander, the first and most valiant soldier of the Greater German *Reich,* who is even now with you at the battlefront. We will never forget that first day of September when he issued his formal call to arms to the entire *Volk.* You, too, were somewhere out there—on the borders of the *Reich* or in the barracks or already marching forward on that memorable morning. Your ears and hearts were witness to that historic moment when the *Führer* stepped before the whole *Volk* in his old military cloak of army gray. You heard his words and sensed in them that your Supreme Commander's love and concern—though devoted as always to the entire *Volk*—is in a special sense with you soldiers of the German army in these trying hours. Thus, the example of the *Führer* stands before you in brilliant glory.[2]

Comparing this with the sentiments expressed in the 1944 Lenten pastoral issued when the grim outlines of Germany's total defeat were already becoming clear, we find in the latter an even greater, perhaps more desperate, intensity of nationalistic fervor:

One must be clear about what this phrase means: to serve God. It would be completely wrong to interpret it as a turning away from the world. In order to serve God and to be able to do everything for God, there is certainly no need to flee from the world. Service to God is performed there, wherever one stands, wherever one has his job to do. It is a matter of seeing God's will and a God-given task in whatever burden is placed upon one and the mastering of that task. In that all of us today, on the battlefront and in the *Heimat,* do our very best in this hour of critical need in the service of our *Volk;* that each of us serving his *Vaterland* dedicates his heart, his thoughts, his every power to the service of his *Volk;* that the soldier loyally and bravely follows the path set before him—therein lies the realization of the principle: "I wish to serve God."

* * * * * *

. . . The memory of all that the word *Heimat* means to the German man—the magic of a beloved landscape, family, a home built piece-by-piece—quickens his heart in the quiet hours, though he may be on duty in the vastness of the East or some other place in Europe; though his wife and children may have been separated from house and hearth; though enemy bombs may have destroyed and laid waste that *Heimat.* If you see your soldierly service as a task which God Himself has set before you, this yearning for home on the part of the soul and the spirit will not drain your energy and make you tired of it all; instead, it will serve as a creative force which will ever be a reminder to you of why and for what you are stationed out there. . . .

* * * * * *

Under the sign of sacrifice, the present will give birth to new and great things. There can be no doubt that out there on the battlefronts and at home in the areas visited by the terror of enemy air raids the many veils, cloaks, and masks behind which people were able to hide their true selves in the security of more peaceful times have now been torn away. Now we can distinguish the great from the small, the heroes from the opportunists, the people upon whom one can rely from those by whom he would be abandoned.

In keeping with the occasion, he then turned to a statement of the more specific directives for observing the Lenten season and assured the Catholic servicemen that chaplains assisted by the priests of the locality in which they were stationed would be available to furnish them with all the necessary spiritual ministrations. But

even this leads back to the major theme as he describes the greatest
of these pastoral functions:

They will distribute the Bread of Life among you, and I am certain
that the power of the Lord will come over you and will give you the
strength to give your best as soldiers of the German army for *Führer*,
*Volk*, and *Vaterland*.[3]

The ordinary Catholic soldier who may have been bothered by
doubts would almost surely have found his doubts quieted or removed altogether by such a message. By the same token, we may
conclude that a Catholic conscript who was already convinced of
the war's injustice and who might have sought to refuse to perform
the service required of him by the military authorities would have
found no support whatsoever in these words of the Military
Bishop.*

Even before the Nazi invasion of Poland, the future Bishop's
dedication to the military calling was clearly in evidence. In 1937,
for example, he discussed the relationship between Christianity and

* The controversial Josef Fleischer case may be introduced here as an
illustration of this latter conclusion. Fleischer may be the only German
Catholic "conscientious objector" to Hitler's wars to live to tell the tale,
having been spared the customary death sentence by a commitment to a
military mental hospital. As he tells his story, he was still awaiting disposi-
tion of his case when he was visited by a clergyman who identified himself
as the Military Bishop's chief assistant. This visitor reportedly advanced
every possible argument to induce Fleischer to abandon his refusal to serve
in the armed forces. These efforts failing, he burst into a furious display of
temper and declared that people like Fleischer must be exterminated, that
they should be "shortened by a head." The priest in question was appointed
to a position of comparably high authority in the present German army's
corps of chaplains, and it was a source of great embarrassment to him
when Fleischer publicly denounced his appointment and told the story to
the press. The priest firmly denies ever having met or visited Fleischer or
having any contact at all with the case. In the course of the research interview, however, he did make the rather significant suggestion that the Military Bishop himself may have made such a visit, that the events described
by Fleischer would not have been out of keeping with the Rarkowski
temperament. It is impossible to evaluate here the validity of either the
Fleischer charges or the denials; but the fact that a close associate of the
Military Bishop would even entertain the possibility that he may have been
the clergyman involved is of some significance.

the military life, giving particular emphasis to his denial that a loyal observance of the obligations imposed by the one was at all incompatible with those imposed by the other.

In its thousand years of strife-filled history, the profession of arms has become something of a second nature to the German *Volk*. For this reason the question of whether or not the Christian Faith and the bearing of arms are incompatible is by no means a matter of indifference to the German soldier who, as a young Catholic, is called to service in the army. Were Christianity to exclude the spirit of military preparedness, a true Christian could not be a true soldier. It would not be possible for him to do his part in the military defense of Germany with the help of his Christian commitment; on the contrary, he could only do so in spite of that commitment. He would always have to be wary lest his Christianity present an obstacle to the performance of his military duty to his *Vaterland*. Fortunately, the German soldier need not fear any inner conflict of this nature. If a Christian orientation constituted a weakening of the striking power of the German military forces, it would not have been possible for Germany to hold her own through the four years of World War I in the face of overwhelming [enemy] superiority in men and matériel and still be able to win mighty victories on all fronts. The Christian Faith—and this was demonstrated thousands of times—spiritually strengthened and continually renewed the simple and death-consecrated fighting man of the World War. The sacrificial dedication and the tenacious endurance of the front soldiers, whose memory is brought before you young men in so stirring a fashion every year on Memorial Day so that it may be a spiritual inspiration to you, were in most cases sprung from the soil of the Christian Faith and nourished by the sacrifices of war.[4]

A 1938 message to the chaplains and Catholic servicemen—again, be it noted, prior to the start of the war—set forth a simple command: "Be good soldiers of your *Volk!*" To specify further what being a good soldier implied, he proceeded to enunciate a principle that furnishes a valuable insight into why the German army and its responsible leaders delayed so long their attempt to bring about the downfall of Hitler and the Nazi regime and why they were even then not able to win the full support of their military colleagues. It is, in essence, the same principle advanced by Gröber when he sought to explain the failure of Catholics in the armed services to mutiny and bring the war to an earlier conclusion.

The soldierly calling is distinguished from all other professions and tasks in this: that once the oath of allegiance has been sworn, it demands the heroic dedication of body and soul and elevates this dedication to a conscious and inflexible principle. Thus the military training program to which you have been called at the will of the Supreme Commander represents the highest service to *Volk* and *Vaterland*.[5]

The explanation for the militaristic and extremely nationalistic tone of Rarkowski's messages is to be found, in large part, in his family background and career. A close associate during the war years described him as the son of an old-line Prussian officer who had served with Germany's hero-leader Field Marshal von Hindenburg at a time when the latter was still in the earliest stages of his great military career. This led to a lifelong friendship between the two officers, a friendship that caused Hindenburg to take an almost paternal interest in the young priest who was later to become Military Bishop of Nazi Germany. In his formative years, then, Rarkowski was exposed to his father's strict formation according to the values of the Prussian military code; and this formation was sustained and reinforced by the intimate social relationships he maintained with his father's associates. Indeed, the relationship between the then chaplain and the Field Marshal and President of the dying Weimar Republic was reportedly so close that the former was a frequent guest at state dinners and similar functions. And when, under the terms of the Concordat, a Military Bishop was to be chosen, it was reportedly at the insistence of Hindenburg, and over the objections of the majority of the German hierarchy, that the post was given to the man whose writings we are examining here.

Whether the reports of Hindenburg's intervention are true or not,* it is a fact that Rarkowski's advancement, once under way, was quite rapid. In August 1936 the elevation of *Heeresoberpfarrer* Rarkowski to Papal Prothonotary was announced;[6] three months later, the "newly appointed Apostolic Administrator of the military bishopric" was reported as celebrating his first Pontifical Mass;[7] and, finally, in January 1938, on the fortieth anniversary of his ordination, the formal investiture as Military Bishop took place, with Papal Nuncio Orsenigo officiating and Bishops von Galen and von Preysing assisting.[8]

It is not entirely surprising that the influences of the Rarkowski home, supplemented by the experiences of more than thirty years as military chaplain and *Feldbischof,* would produce patterns of thought and expression more proper to a military officer than to a priest or bishop. And so it was: Rarkowski's personal identification with the rise and fall of German military destiny is repeatedly shown in his pastoral letters, and these often contain more than a hint that this identification tended to blind him to the essential nature of the Nazi regime and its relationship with the Catholic Church in Germany. On his seventieth birthday, for instance, he addressed a message to his chaplains in which his personal motto *Deo et militi* served as the uniting theme for his reminiscences. He described his sad memories of World War I and "the tragic time of breakdown and hopelessness in 1918," and spoke of the scenes "of deepest shame and disgrace" that he had to witness as garrison chaplain on the Western Front when it sometimes appeared "as though the end had come for Germany."

But then things changed again for the better. As *Reichswehr* chaplain

---

* These reports—as well as the episcopal opposition to the Rarkowski appointment—are obviously not amenable to empirical validation. However, some degree of support, at least for the latter, may be drawn from the recollections of a former Czech diplomat who reported, in a discussion with the writer, that a gathering of the German bishops at the funeral of a leading member of the Czech hierarchy was marked by an obvious avoidance of Rarkowski on the part of his fellow bishops. This informant attributed much of this avoidance to the fact—extremely significant in the present context—that Bishop Rarkowski was attending the solemn ceremonies in military uniform.

for a military district, I lived to see the young soldiers of the postwar years and found caring for their religious needs an important and gratifying task. The year 1933 came and with it a new era and a new young army which under its *Führer* and Supreme Commander has, since 1939, performed immortal deeds and reached the heights of accomplishment in offense and defense on all the battlefields of the present war. The German soldier of 1914 and his son who, as the young soldier of 1939, is given the task of fighting the great and decisive military struggle of the present may differ in many respects, since they belong to different epochs of our German history. But in the essential things there is no difference between these representatives of two generations of German soldiering. Fathers and sons join hands as one in the same German nature, in their unflinching bravery, in their loyalty to the *Vaterland,* and in their piety. . . .[9]

If the slightest doubt as to the justice of Hitler's wars ever crossed his mind, Bishop Rarkowski gave no indication of it in his pastoral letters. Sometimes the reader will find the conflict treated as the retributive struggle to erase the shame and disgrace of the 1918 defeat—a defeat he, like Galen, traced to a fatal weakening of the home front which permitted revolution to arise even while the soldiers continued to bleed and die on the battlefields. At other times he saw the conflict as the glorious crusade for a "New Europe," a theme that grew in intensity once Hitler's nonaggression pact with the Soviet Union was thrown into the discard. In every instance, however, the issue was one of a victimized Germany forced to fight in defense of its very right to live against conspiring world forces united in a determined effort to eradicate every last vestige of German greatness. In such a context, it is not surprising that Hitler emerges in a highly favorable light as the inspired leader, the harbinger of the "springtime" of the German *Volk,* even as the man of peace who finds himself rebuffed and rejected at every turn. But the hero of the great national drama is the German soldier, the warrior for God—and, in particular, those soldiers who, having made the supreme sacrifice for *Volk* and *Vaterland,* automatically earned a place in heaven.

In 1939 on the Feast of St. Hedwig, patroness of Poland, Rar-

kowski displayed an almost incredible absence of tact by addressing an exultant pastoral to the men in the service commemorating
the Nazi victory over that first victim of blitzkrieg aggression. He
described the joyous scenes at home with the church bells ringing
out a special noonday *Te Deum* and flags waving and fluttering
over all the houses as "you comrades in the East" went on from victory to victory, striking the weapons from the hands of the deluded
opponent while other comrades stood guard at Germany's western
borders. The joy and thanksgiving were mixed with longing and
proud sorrow over those whose death constituted the grim price
of the great victory:

Their sacrifice for Germany's honor and future lacked nothing of
human greatness and glory. And this dying was not only beautiful and
sublime in a human sense but towers beyond into a higher world. It
is a holy death; for those who have fallen had consecrated and sancti-
fied all their war services through their oath of allegiance and have
thus entered their sacrifices in the ledgers of God which are preserved
in the archives of Eternity.

But still, he notes, the war goes on in spite of these overwhelming
successes in Poland, even in spite of Hitler's peace appeal directed
to the conscience of the nations:

. . . Only one who is not human and not a Christian, one who lacks
the profound German spirit, could fail to be impressed when the
*Führer* lifted his voice in solemn entreaty to warn those who wish to
feed the fires of a horrible conflict by their warmongering.

Comrades! You know how that peace offer was repulsed by states-
men who live in delusion and shut their minds against those farsighted
proposals for a just new world order. Thus, *through no fault of Germany's, the war continues.* But now that our opponents have thrust
back the *Führer's* outstretched hand of peace, you at last know for
certain what you are fighting for in this great struggle. At stake is all
that is the holiest, the most honorable, the dearest, and the most
precious things on earth.

Individually, one might not find it too hard to renounce his personal
claims to these great goods which are usually expressed and described

by such words as security, freedom, peace, happiness, prosperity, and justice. But no one of us, however willing he may be to renounce these blessings for himself, may renounce his *Volk*'s claim to the most precious human ideals [italics added]. . . .

Now that Hitler's peace offer had been rejected, there was only one alternative to fighting; and that alternative was nothing other than wilfully permitting the "ruination of the *Reich* at the hands of senseless warmongers," that *Reich* "whose glorious rebirth we have been permitted to witness these past six years." The issue, then, reduced to its simplest terms is this: "Comrades, your *Heimat* and your *Volk* are at stake! Conduct yourselves like men, and be strong!"[10]

The invasion of France and the neutral Low Countries occasioned a special message to the chaplains accompanying the invading troops. The Bishop pointed out that many of them would recall being in the same areas as soldiers during World War I; now as chaplains they had a different task to perform. One thing, however, had not changed: "Your total devotion to duty and your inflexible readiness to serve *Volk* and *Vaterland*." Stressing the importance of setting a manly example for the soldiers, he reminded them that the military decision of the day would go far to determine the form to be taken by the future of the German *Volk*. "This knowledge must burn in us like a holy fire and make us resolute fighters for the honor and freedom of our *Volk*." In a direct echo of the 1937 message already cited, he declared that

For more than a thousand years, German armies have harvested unparalleled fame as warriors. In the mighty language of deeds they have demonstrated that Christianity has a place for and even encourages the development of the heroic and soldierly character. . . .[11]

It is in the messages addressed directly to the Catholic soldiers that Bishop Rarkowski and his outspoken support for the war assume their greatest significance for us. A series of annual messages —Lenten and Easter pastorals, Christmas greetings, statements marking the anniversary of the war's beginning, and so on—carried unmistakable evidence of the intention to boost and preserve the morale of the armed services, to inspire the Catholic fighting man to the fullest possible dedication in the performance of whatever military duties might be required of him. He would have found the issue set in its starkest clarity in Rarkowski's letter marking the first anniversary of the war: Germany was fighting a just war to "defend her existence against the arrogance of well-fed peoples" who had deluded themselves into believing they could "obliterate us and grind us underfoot."

He who knows war cannot desire war. Because our *Führer* and Supreme Commander of the Army became acquainted with the inferno of war when he was a simple soldier at the front, he has tried as no other statesman to spare Europe from armed conflict. But there was no avoiding this war. It had to be fought. . . .

•    •    •    •    •    •    •

. . . The German *Volk* . . . has an untroubled conscience and knows which peoples bear the responsibility before God and before history for this gigantic conflict that is raging today. It knows who maliciously provoked the war. *It knows that it is fighting a just war,* one born of the necessity of a people's self-preservation, out of the impossibility of solving by peaceful means a difficult and demanding question of justice involving the very existence of the state and of correcting by any other means the screaming injustice that had been done to us. They begrudged us our place in the sun and sought to destroy us forever. They sought to make of us a nation of helots. So there is no question in our minds as to where Right is to be found and, with it, God's help in this war. . . .*

* This passage is quoted by Herman and is preceded by the surprising comment to the effect that this Rarkowski pastoral "was quoted with relish for the benefit of American Catholics but not one word from his pen appeared in the home press." Startling as Herman's inaccuracy in this respect may be, it is even less to be understood than the fact that he omits all mention of this and other Rarkowski statements in later chapters bearing such titles as "The Church Does Not Go to War" and "The Church and the Military Machine." In fact, the only other reference to the *Feldbischof* is a passing reference to "Monseigneur Rarkowski's very cautious policy"! See Stewart W. Herman, Jr., *It's Your Souls We Want* (New York: Harper, 1943), pp. 198, 204.

•　•　•　•　•　•

. . . Whether out on the front or at home, one could understand the *Führer* and Supreme Commander when, more than once in this past year, in thanksgiving and petition he implored God's blessings upon *our good and just cause.* It is precisely in this community of prayer which unites front and *Heimat* that it becomes clear that this war is not just a matter for soldiers but, instead, the business of the entire *Volk.* Certainly, the other peoples arrayed against us also pray to God and pray for victory. God is, of course, in the same manner Father of all peoples; but he is not at one and the same time the advocate of Justice and Injustice or of Honesty and Falsehood.

•　•　•　•　•　•

. . . Thus, we, too, have been called upon by God to shoulder the mighty tasks of the present. In memory of our fallen brothers-in-arms and in one spirit with them, we intend to carry on the fight and, with confident trust in God, continue to build up the holy cathedral of our *Vaterland* until the final victory is won and, with it, the freedom and the future of our *Volk* [italics added]. . . .[12]

The Bishop's emphasis on the "just cause" which brought the war into being was matched by his vision of the just aims to be achieved by the victory of German forces. These aims were not to be limited to the present or immediate future well-being of Germany, but actually extended far beyond this, to include all of Western civilization and the generations still to come. This theme has already been implied in some of the Rarkowski statements quoted above, but it received its most direct expression in the letter which greeted the opening of "the great and decisive conflict in the East" in 1941. It is difficult to reconcile the harshness of his attack upon the "barbarism" and "brutal tyranny" of the Soviet Union with the fact that, in the earlier stages of the war, this nation had been a virtual ally of Germany and had even shared in the partition of Poland with its predominantly Catholic population. Needless to say, the Bishop's message included no reference to this previous partnership. Leading into his major theme by eulogizing a chaplain who had been among the first to lose his life in the Russian campaign, he soon reaches full climax:

Comrades! Who will doubt that we Germans have once again become the "Heart *Volk*" of Europe and this in a sense that reaches far beyond merely geographic or geopolitical considerations? As was so often true in the past, the Germany of today has again become Europe's savior and champion. Many European countries which have until now lived under the threatening shadows of the Bolshevist danger and have had to endure repeatedly internal seditions as a consequence of Bolshevist teachings know that the war against Russia is a European crusade. The peoples of Europe would have had to disavow their history and deny their future had they not yearned, deep down in their hearts, for that decision which will extirpate Bolshevism from history once and for all.

It is, therefore, no exaggeration for me to say today that you in the East, like the Teutonic Knights of long ago, have a task to perform that is of singular meaning and importance and whose consequences for our *Volk*—yea, for Europe and all mankind—cannot even yet be fully grasped. . . .

∙  ∙  ∙  ∙  ∙  ∙

Comrades! What I had to say to you in this hour of great decision is, as already noted, the legacy of a divisional chaplain who died on the Eastern front. Take up your gigantic task in earnest! Be aware of your mission! Live in the strength of your Faith! Then will the victory be yours, a victory that will permit Europe to breathe freely again and will be to all peoples the promise of a new future.[13]

From the first jubilant days of victory in Poland and France, continuing through the serious setbacks in the Russian campaign, and finally down to the bitter days of military collapse and the cruel devastation of the German *Heimat,* a steady stream of episcopal messages poured from the Rarkowski pen. The changing fortunes of war may have brought some difference in tone, but the content remained essentially unchanged. This is clearly shown by a comparison of the 1943 Christmas message with that marking the first wartime celebration of that holy feast. The earlier letter all but claimed Christmas as a purely German affair:

Wherever German soldiers keep watch at the front and fight, there will the night of divine peace be celebrated, even though the alarms of war refuse to be stilled.

Christmas is a festival of the German soul. In every language there are words which work a special magic upon us in their very sound. To these blessed words belongs the word *Weihnacht*. Long forgotten times come alive again when we but speak this word. Though one may search through all the languages of earth, he will find no more deeply mysterious and moving impression of the feast of the birth of the Lord than that given by our German word *Weihnacht*. No other people on earth knows a Christmas celebration like ours. It is a special mark of honor for the German *Volk* to have given the Christmas celebration spiritual value beyond measure. Just as our cathedrals and churches in city and village rise far above the level of the ordinary and radiate a thoroughly unique spirituality and piety, so has the German Christmas, too, come to have a special meaning throughout the world. It is the German song, the German spirit, that has found its loveliest expression in the Christmas festival. And wherever one sings the old Christian German Christmas songs, there sounds the essence of the German soul, there lives the individuality of German folk culture. Ours is the Christmas tree, our German pine which expresses our German nature in its deep shadows that almost make one think of melancholia, just as surely as does its bright tip stretching heavenward. Only one who has spent Christmas in a foreign land will understand this in its fullest depth and truth. What do the French know—or the English—of our German Christmas? We are German and, as such, a *Volk* of particularly deep spirituality. Others will never understand this in us. Nevertheless, we are proud of it, and it is precisely at Christmas that we are made properly aware that, as Germans, we have a mission which the Lord God, the Ruler of societies and peoples, has given us. No one understands these thoughts better than the German soldier. He wields the weapons to defend the *Vaterland*, to keep the shield of honor of our German nation shining and unsmirched; and he will be especially conscious of this, his great responsibility, precisely at Christmas time when all the depths of the German soul are made manifest. . . .[14]

The next to last Christmas of the war brought renewed reference to the holy magic and joy associated with the word *Weihnacht;* but the emphasis was now placed on the Christian's capacity for suffering and the manner in which that capacity is enhanced by the dedication to otherworldly values and ends. There was really only one brief passage giving a direct boost to war morale, and even that carried unmistakable overtones of the impending tragedy:

And may your Christmas joy be especially intensified by the proud knowledge that, true to your oath to the flag, you have made it possible for the German *Heimat* to enjoy the happiness and joys of Christmas through your brave and tenacious fighting in the war year of 1943 that now lies behind us. One dare not think of what would have happened had you weakened in your loyalty, resoluteness, and tenacity and had you not at every moment defended the *Heimat*, even unto the sacrifice of blood and life. Therefore, let no one among you be sorrowful at Christmas time. . . .[15]

The Bishop's Lenten pastoral of February 1944 already quoted[16] is his last available wartime message. It was perhaps fitting that the lesson to be drawn from the total sacrifice of Christ on the Cross should have served as the central theme for this letter and its appeal for the loyal performance of the soldiers' duty to the bitter end. Issued in the face of the total disaster already facing the German forces on all fronts, this statement became a desperate plea to the Catholics in his spiritual charge to "give your best as soldiers of the German army for *Führer, Volk,* and *Vaterland.*"

Cry of desperation or not, the message is extremely significant because it is further evidence of the official religious controls exerted upon the individual Catholic to assure his conformity with the demands of the Nazi war effort even at so late a date and in so hopeless a situation. In addition to the extensive quotation already cited, the following sentences illustrate the directness of the *spiritual* appeal for such conformity. Recalling Christ's rejection of Satan's temptations in the desert and His declaration that He would serve only God, Rarkowski applied this to the difficult test being faced by the German soldier:

We gaze with wonder upon Christ, who so bravely and with such firm decision spoke this emancipating and redeeming Word, and immediately threw off the temptations of the Powers of Darkness. If we are honest with ourselves, we must confess that it is not always easy for us to show the same decisiveness toward the everyday temptations of evil forces we encounter. How hard it often is to carry on against enervating weariness and inner distress! How much strength it takes to perform one's daily service over and over in a spirit of obedience and devotion to duty. How much inner discipline and self-denial are required to counter the dangerous designs of the Lower One! Thus, the brave and decisive word of the Lord, "It is written, God alone shall you serve!" has a binding meaning for us all. . . .[17]

The survey of Bishop Rarkowski's writings, overdetailed and extended though it may seem, does not come close to exhausting the available evidence that the activity of the Military Bishop constituted a significant and direct exercise of social control over the behavior of individual Catholic soldiers. His efforts were clearly designed to induce a pattern of obedient compliance, whatever the burdens or duties placed upon them, and to keep them firmly committed to that behavior pattern despite all the personal trials encountered in a steadily worsening military situation.

Men like Galen may have rationalized their position by appealing to a logical distinction between the war as conducted under Nazi authority for the attainment of Nazi goals and purposes (which they would oppose) and the war as "a defense of *Volk* and *Vaterland*" (which they could encourage the faithful to support). But there is no evidence that such a distinction was ever employed, or even sought, by the Military Bishop. Indeed, the constantly recurring reference to Hitler as "our *Führer* and Supreme Commander," whether it be as model soldier or inspired leader of the German *Volk,* would indicate that he would have had difficulty in understanding any such distinction. In this connection, an article by Bishop Rarkowski published in a soldiers' newspaper under the title "Springtime of our *Volk*" deserves some attention. The article opened with fervent praise for the German past and an acknowledgment that God had blessed the German people with special gifts. It then proceeded to summarize how the war had been forced upon Germany and mentioned the many sacrifices to be made in order that these gifts might be defended. Among the goods to be protected was "what the *Führer* created during the seven years of gigantic constructive effort since 1933." The article was written primarily to mark the first wartime celebration of Hitler's birthday and may be taken as a reliable indication of Rarkowski's evaluation of the man being honored.

Today it is an already incontestable fact that Adolf Hitler has taken on a fateful meaning for our *Volk* and for the entire world. No other German statesman before him had brought about such mighty changes in the most widely different areas of the *Volk*'s existence as he has. Our enemies, against whom we must even now defend the German living space, first viewed his great accomplishments as a major riddle. They felt obliged to criticize; concern and anxiety mounted ever higher; and finally the wildfire of a hatred that would not even stop short of attempted murder burst forth. The success they could not attain in quiet days of peace they hope to achieve now that war has been enkindled: the destruction and annihilation of all that our *Führer* has created. Christianity demands obedience and respect for authority and loyal co-operation in all great undertakings for *Volk* and nation. So let our gift to our *Führer* be the inner readiness for sacrifice and devotion to the *Volk*. If today we know in the depths of our soul that loyalty to the *Volk* is an obligation demanded by God, we thank the *Führer* for the deepening of this awareness. He has brought the big change; through his contributions we have learned to see new values in words like *Heimat* and *Volk,* in national honor and national history. He has awakened us to a recognition of our task as Germans. In the light of our *Volk* heritage, he has discovered the life principle of the German *Volk* and by his acts has made it effective. All of this comes to our mind in these days; and we do not forget that there was once a time for our *Volk* when we beat with powerless fists against a wall of fog that threatened us and seemed to dissipate the last residues of our strength. May our thanksgiving and our readiness to repay loyalty with loyalty find expression in the prayer that means more to us in these days than it did in the quiet days of peace: "Bless, O God, our *Führer* and Supreme Commander in all the tasks placed upon him. . . ." [18]

Perhaps one could dismiss Bishop Rarkowski as the exception to the rule and, therefore, not representative of responsible Catholic opinion. In a published and somewhat indignant reply to an earlier report by the writer on the support given to Hitler's wars by the German Catholic press,[19] a critic stressed the fact that the rest of the German episcopate had avoided the excesses of commitment shown by the Military Bishop. Significantly, however, the same critic questioned whether any violation of Catholic faith and morals could be found in the Rarkowski letters (with which he claimed some familiarity) and went on to reject the present writer's description of them as "classic expressions of nationalistic and militaristic ideology." The first objection is, of course, quite irrelevant in view of the sociological limits set for the present study; the reader is invited to judge for himself whether the description offered for the Rarkowski tone is valid or not.[20]

In a letter to the writer, another critic of the writer's earlier paper also rejected as "historically false" any attempt to use Rarkowski as a basis for judging the position on the war taken by the German hierarchy. This correspondent, now editor of a German diocesan paper, dismissed the *Feldbischof* as a "creature" of one Monsignor Benigni who had been disciplined for his aberrant views by Pope Benedict XV; and he insisted that Rarkowski had been disavowed by the German bishops even before 1914 and had been forbidden to perform any religious functions for a time. It is clear, the letter continued, that such a man would throw himself into the arms of the National Socialists, and the fact that such a "Nazi" could later be made bishop of the armies was a source of great annoyance to the discerning Catholic. He concluded, "Under no circumstances can a man with such a questionable background be compared with the other honorable Catholic bishops."[21]

In all candor, it must be said that these attempts to purge the record clean of the Rarkowski contributions are not entirely convincing. The fact already noted that Churchmen of the stature of Bishops von Galen and von Preysing assisted at his consecration certainly does not support the claim that he was a pariah among his fellow bishops. Nor is there any specific evidence brought forth to show that the other German bishops ever made the slightest move truly to disavow the Military Bishop so that his influence upon the Catholic men in military service could be eliminated or neutralized. On the contrary, religious papers published in other dioceses occasionally reprinted all or parts of the texts of Rarkowski *Hirtenbriefe,* thereby furnishing grounds for assuming that these more responsible bishops approved of their contents. Furthermore, the informant who provided access to the Rarkowski file was quite explicit on this point. In an obvious effort to prepare the researcher for the effect these documents would have, he prefaced the loan of them with the caution that one must make certain allowances for the emotionalism and directness of Rarkowski's temperament. But, as far as the support of the war was concerned, he could assure the researcher that all the German bishops took essentially the same position as that taken by the Military Bishop. The only difference, he insisted, would lie in the fact that Rarkowski tended to be more blunt in his statement of that common position.

But in the last analysis, this too is an irrelevant issue. Regardless of whether or not he was the exception some would claim, Rarkowski was a Catholic bishop. Moreover, *he was the Catholic bishop to whom direct responsibility for the moral guidance and spiritual care of German Catholics in the armed forces had been entrusted.* No more directly operative or official religious social control existed than that represented by the chaplains and their superior, the *Feldbischof.* For this reason alone, Rarkowski's acts and writings would assume critical significance for this analysis. Even if he were absolutely alone in his stand, his pastoral exhortations would be sufficient to justify the basic conclusions advanced earlier.

Of course he was not alone. The preceding sections have furnished ample evidence which clearly substantiates the opinion voiced by Rarkowski's former associate. Under all the extremism and emotionalism of his writings, one finds the same basic themes emphasized by Galen, Faulhaber, Gröber, and the German bishops in general: the stress on the war service as a defense of *Volk, Vaterland,* and *Heimat;* the idealization of the fighting man as the model Christian, the self-sacrificing hero to whom wholehearted gratitude and emulation are owed; the moral obligation of the individual Catholic to perform whatever service is asked of him by legitimate authority. Even Rarkowski's admittedly extreme view of the sacredness of the military oath found explicit echo in the writings of Gröber and at least implicit expression in the writings of some of his other colleagues. Certainly no one can deny that the pro-Hitler overtones of the Rarkowski messages went far beyond the level of commitment to the national cause displayed by most, if not all, of his fellow bishops. Nevertheless, the essential commitment was there; and this is enough to validate the finding that the war support represented by and reflected in that commitment did constitute a social control inducing Catholic conformity to the requirements of the Nazi military effort.

## NOTES

1. See Artikel 27, Konkordat zwischen dem Hl. Stuhl und dem Deutschen Reiche vom 20. Juli 1933, ratifiziert am 10. September 1933. (Neuhäusler, *op cit.*, pp. 412-419.)

2. *Verordnungsblatt des Katholischen Feldbischofs der Wehrmacht,* Vol. 3, No. 2 (September 1, 1939), p. 5.
Kameraden!
"In ernster Stunde, da unser deutsches Volk die Feuerprobe der Bewährung zu bestehen hat und zum Kampfe um seine natürlichen und gottgewollten Lebensrechte angetreten ist, wende ich mich . . . an euch Soldaten, die ihr in diesem Kampf in der vordersten Front steht und die grosse und ehrenvolle Aufgabe habt, die Sicherheit und das Leben der deutschen Nation mit dem Schwerte zu schützen und zu verteidigen.
". . . Jeder von euch weiss, worum es in diesen Sturmestagen unseres Volkes geht, und jeder sieht bei diesem Einsatz vor sich das leuchtende Vorbild eines wahrhaften Kämpfers, unseres Führers und Obersten Befehlshabers, des ersten und tapfersten Soldaten des Grossdeutschen Reiches, der sich nunmehr bei euch an der Kampffront befindet. Unvergesslich wird uns allen jener 1. September bleiben, da das ganze Volk vor ihm zum feierlichen Appell antrat. Auch ihr seid an jenem denkwürdigen Morgen irgendwo draussen an den Grenzen des Reiches oder in der Kaserne oder auf dem Vormarsch mit dem Ohr und mit dem Herzen Zeugen jener geschichtlichen Stunde gewesen, da der Führer im feldgrauen Rock vor die ganze Nation

trat. Ihr habt seine Worte gehört und aus allem, was er sagte, gespürt, dass eures Obersten Befehlshabers Liebe und Sorge zwar wie immer dem ganzen Volke, aber in diesen ernsten Stunden vor allem euch Soldaten der deutschen Wehrmacht gilt. So steht vor euch in hellem Glanze das Beispiel des Führers."

3. *Ibid.*, Vol. 8, No. 2 (February 1, 1944), pp. 6, 7.

". . . Man muss sich nur darüber klar sein, was es heisst: Gott dienen. Ganz falsch wäre es, wenn man sich darunter die Abwendung von der Welt vorstellen wollte. Um Gott dienen und alles für Gott tun zu können, bedarf es wahrhaftig nicht der Weltflucht. Gott dienen heisst, dort, wo man steht, wo man seine Aufgabe zu erfüllen hat, Gottes Willen zu sehen und alles was, einem aufgetragen wird als eine von Gott gestellte Aufgabe zu meistern. Dass wir heute in schwerer Notzeit alle, Front und Heimat, im Dienste unseres Volkes unser Bestmögliches leisten, dass ein jeder von uns in der Gegenwart seinem Vaterland dienend sein Herz, seine Gedanken, seine Kräfte in den Dienst seines Volkes stellt, dass der Soldat in Treue und Tapferkeit den Weg geht, der ihm vorgezeichnet ist, das ist die Verwirklichung des Grundsatzes: 'Ich will Gott dienen.'

⁕　⁕　⁕　⁕　⁕　⁕

". . . Die Erinnerung an das, was für den deutschen Mann die Heimat ausmacht, der Zauber einer geliebten Landschaft, Familie und Heim, die Stück um Stück aufgebaut wurden, rüttelt in stillen Stunden an seinem Herzen, mag er in der Weite des Ostens oder sonstwo in Europa stehen, auf See oder als Flieger die Wacht halten, mag die Frau mit den Kindern von Haus und Herd getrennt sein, mögen feindliche Bomben das Bild der Heimat zerstört und verwüstet haben. Dieses Heimverlangen der Seele und des Gemütes wird Dich nicht entnerven und müde machen, sondern eine schöpferische Kraft sein, welche Dich immer mehr erkennen lässt, warum und wofür Du draussen stehst, wenn Du in Deinem soldatischen Dienste eine Aufgabe siehst, die Gott selbst Dir gestellt hat.

⁕　⁕　⁕　⁕　⁕　⁕

"Unter dem Zeichen des Opfers wird unsere Gegenwart Neues und Grosses gebären. Es besteht kein Zweifel darüber, dass draussen an den Fronten des Krieges und daheim in den vom feindlichen Luftterror heimgesuchten Gebieten viele Schleier, Hüllen und Masken weggezogen werden, hinter denen der Mensch in der Geborgenheit friedlicher Zeiten sein wahres Wesen verstecken konnte. Jetzt vollzieht sich die Scheidung zwischen grossen und kleinen Menschen, zwischen Helden- und Krämerseelen, zwischen Menschen, auf die man sich stützen kann und Menschen, bei denen man verlassen ist. . . .

⁕　⁕　⁕　⁕　⁕　⁕

". . . Sie werden euch das Brot des Lebens reichen und ich bin gewiss, dass die Kraft des Herrn über euch kommen und euch befähigen wird, als Soldaten der deutschen Wehrmacht das Beste zu geben für Führer, Volk und Vaterland."

4. *Bayrische Katholische Kirchenzeitung*, Vol. 13, No. 25 (June 13, 1937), p. 192.

"Dem deutschen Volke ist die Wehrhaftigkeit durch eine seit Jahrtausenden kampferfüllte Geschichte zur zweiten Natur geworden. Es kann deshalb dem deutschen Soldaten, der als junger Katholik in der Wehrmacht seinen Ehrendienst leistet, durchaus nicht gleichgültig sein, ob Christenglauben und Wehrhaftigkeit Widersprüche sind oder nicht. Würde das Christentum den Geist der Wehrhaftigkeit ausschliessen, dann könnte ein ganzer Christ nicht voll und ganz Soldat sein. Es wäre ihm nicht möglich, sich im Dienst deutscher Wehrhaftigkeit zu bewähren mit Hilfe seiner christlichen Haltung, sondern nur trotz derselben. Immer hätte er darauf achtzugeben, dass ihm das Christentum bei der Erfüllung seiner vaterländischen Wehrpflicht nicht als Hindernis im Wege stünde. Glücklicherweise braucht der deutsche Soldat eine derartige innere Disharmonie durchaus nicht zu befürchten. Wenn christliche Orientierung die Schlagkraft des deutschen Volksheeres lähmen würde, dann hätte Deutschland unmöglich während des Weltkrieges vier Jahre hindurch einer gewaltigen Uebermacht an Menschen und Material standhalten und auf allen Fronten Siege grössten Ausmasses erringen können. Der Christenglauben hat—das ist tausendfach erwiesen—die schlichten und todgeweihten Kämpfer des Weltkrieges seelisch gestärkt und immer wieder aufgerichtet. Opferbereitschaft und zähes Durchhalten der Frontsoldaten, die euch jungen Menschen in erschütternder Form jedes Jahr am Heldengedenktag wie ein Mahnmal vor die Seele gestellt werden, wuchsen in den meisten Fällen auf dem Boden christlichen Glaubens und wurden genährt vom Opfer des Krieges."

5. Rarkowski letter to all chaplains and Catholic men in the Army. Issued February 27, 1938. The text of this letter was read in a separate folder made available to the researcher.

". . . Dadurch unterscheidet sich das Soldatentum von allen anderen Berufen und Aufgaben, dass es, wenn einmal der Fahneneid geschworen ist, den heroischen Einsatz des Leibes und der Seele fordert und diesen Einsatz zum bewussten und unbeugsamen Prinzip erhebt. So ist die Schule des Soldatentums, in die euch der Wille des Obersten Befehlshabers der Wehrmacht hineingestellt hat, höchster Dienst an Volk und Vaterland."

6. *Bayrische Katholische Kirchenzeitung*, Vol. 12 (August 16, 1936), p. 264.

7. *Ibid.*, November 22, 1936, p. 376.

8. *Ibid.*, Vol. 14 (January 30, 1938), pp. 32, 56.

9. *Verordnungsblatt des Katholischen Feldbischofs der Wehrmacht*, Vol. 7, No. 5 (June 20, 1943), pp. 20-21.

"Das Jahr 1933 kam und mit ihm eine neue Zeit und eine neue junge Wehrmacht, die unter ihrem Führer und Obersten Befehlshaber seit 1939 Unvergängliches geleistet und Höchstes vollbracht hat in Angriff und Abwehr auf allen Schlachtfeldern des gegenwärtigen Krieges. Der deutsche Soldat von 1914 und sein Sohn, der als junger Soldat von 1939 den grossen und entscheidender Waffengang der Gegenwart auszufechten hat, mögen in vielem voneinander verschieden sein, da sie ja verschiedenen Epochen unserer deutschen Geschichte angehören. Aber in wesentlichen Dingen besteht kein Unterschied zwischen diesen Vertretern von zwei Generationen deutschen Soldatentums. Väter und Söhne reichen sich die Hände und sind von gleicher deutscher Art in ihrer unerschütterlichen Tapferkeit, in ihrer Treue zum Vaterlande und in ihrer Gottesfurcht. . . ."

10. *Ibid.*, Vol. 3, No. 3 (October 18, 1939), pp. 9; 9-10.

"In Ehrfurcht gedachten wir jener deutschen Männer, deren Herzblut zum Unterpfand des Sieges geworden war und über deren Soldatengräbern in Polens Steppe und Sand das Wort aus der Totenpräfation geschrieben steht: 'Deinen Getreuen, o Herr, wird das Leben nicht weggenommen, sondern erhöht.' Höchstes irdisches Heldentum haben diese Gefallenen errungen. Sie sind würdig geworden des unverwelklichen Lorbeers. Nichts menschlich Grosses und Schönes fehlte ihrer Hingabe für Deutschlands Ehre und Zukunft. Und dieses Sterben war nicht nur menschlich schön und erhaben. Es bleibt nicht im Raume des Irdischen, sondern ragt hinein in eine höhere Region. Es ist ein heiliges Sterben, denn diese Gefallenen hatten ja alle ihren Kriegsdienst geweiht und geheiligt durch den Fahneneid und so ihren Lebenseinsatz eingeschrieben in die Bücher Gottes, welche aufbewahrt werden in den Archiven der Ewigkeit.

". . . Man müsste ja kein Mensch und kein Christ sein, man müsste nicht das tiefe deutsche Gemüt besitzen, wenn es einen nicht ergriffen hätte, als der Führer seine Stimme erhob, um mit ernster Beschwörung jene zu warnen, die das Feuer des Weltbrandes schüren und die Völker in einen grauenvollen Krieg hetzen möchten.

"Kameraden! Ihr wisst, dass jenes Friedensangebot von Staatsmännern zurückgewiesen wurde, die in Verblendung leben und sich verschliessen gegenüber jenen weitblickenden Vorschlägen für eine gerechte neue Weltordnung. So wird ohne Deutschlands Schuld der Krieg weitergehen. Jetzt aber, nachdem unsere Gegner die Friedenshand des Führers zurückgestossen haben, weisst du erst recht, wofür gestritten wird in diesem grossen Kampf. Es geht um das Heiligste und Ehrwürdigste, um das Liebste und Teuerste auf Erden. Diese Tatsache steht unverrückbar fest und gibt dir die Kraft zu jedem, selbst zum grössten Einsatz.

"Dem einzelnen von uns mag es vielleicht nicht allzu schwer fallen, für sich selbst, für seine Person auf die grossen Güter zu verzichten, die ausgesprochen und bezeichnet sind mit den Worten Sicherheit, Freiheit, Friede, Glück, Gedeihen und Gerechtigkeit. Aber niemand von uns, mag er auch für sich persönlich auf diese Güter verzichten können, kann für sein Volk auf diese Höchstwerte menschlicher Ideale verzichten. . . .

• • • • • •

"Kameraden, es geht um eure Heimat und um euer Volk! "Handelt männlich und seid stark!"

11. *Ibid.*, Vol. 4, No. 5 (June 15, 1940), p. 22.

"Wir alle wissen, dass durch die kriegerischen Entscheidungen der Gegenwart die Gestaltung der Zukunft unseres Volkes in stärksten Masse beeinflusst wird. Dieses Wissen muss wie ein heiliges Feuer in uns brennen und uns zu entschlossenen Kämpfern für unseres Volkes Ehre und Freiheit machen. In mehr als tausend Jahren haben deutsche Heere einen unvergleichlichen Waffenruhm geerntet. Sie haben durch die mächtige Sprache der Tatsachen erwiesen, dass das Christentum der heroischen und soldatischen Haltung Raum lässt und ihre Entfaltung begünstigt. . . ."

12. *Ibid.*, No. 7 (September 1, 1940), pp. 29, 29-30, 31, 32.

"Wer den Krieg kennt, kann ihn nicht wollen. Weil unser Führer und Oberster Befehlshaber der Wehrmacht das Inferno des Krieges als schlichter Frontsoldat kennengelernt hat, hat er sich wie kein zweiter Staatsmann darum bemüht, Europa die Auseinandersetzung mit den Waffen zu ersparen. Aber dieser Krieg war unvermeidlich. . . .

• • • • •

". . . Das deutsche Volk, welches seit einem Jahre den Kampf gegen seine Neider führt, hat ein ruhiges Gewissen und weiss, welche Völker es sind, die sich vor Gott und vor der Geschichte mit der Verantwortung belasten für diesen jetzt tobenden gigantischen Kampf. Es weiss, wer den Krieg freventlich vom Zaune gebrochen hat. Es weiss, dass es selbst einen gerechten Krieg führt, herausgeboren aus der Notwendigkeit völkischer Notwehr, aus der Unmöglichkeit, eine schwere und bedrückende Gerechtigkeitsfrage des staatlichen Daseins friedlich zu lösen und ein schreiendes Unrecht, das man uns angetan hat, mit anderen Mitteln gut zu machen. Sie gönnten uns den Platz an der Sonne nicht und wollten uns für alle Zukunft vernichten. Ein Volk von Heloten wollten sie aus uns machen und so ist es keine Frage für uns, auf welcher Seite das Recht und mit ihm Gottes Hilfe in diesem Kriege steht. . . .

• • • • • •

". . . Man hat es draussen und daheim verstanden, als der Führer und Oberste Befehlshaber mehr als einmal in diesem vergangenen Kriegsjahre in Dank und Bitte den Segen Gottes für unsere gute und gerechte Sache herabflehte. Gerade in dieser Gebetsgemeinschaft, die Front und Heimat umschliesst, zeigt es sich, dass dieser Krieg nicht nur eine Angelegenheit der Soldaten ist, sondern Sache des ganzen Volkes. Gewiss beten auch die anderen Völker, die gegen uns stehen, zu Gott und bitten um den Sieg. Gott ist zwar in gleicher Weise der Vater aller Völker, aber er ist nicht in gleicher Weise Anwalt von Recht und Unrecht, von Ehrlichkeit und Verlogenheit.

•     •     •     •     •     •

". . . So sind auch wir von Gott gerufen zu den grossen Aufgaben der Gegenwart. Wir wollen im Gedenken an unsere gefallenen Brüder und in der gleichen Gesinnung wie sie weiterkämpfen und im gläubigen Vertrauen auf Gott weiterbauen am heiligen Dome unseres Vaterlandes, bis der Endsieg errungen ist und mit ihm Freiheit und Zukunft unseres Volkes. . . ."

13. Rarkowski letter to the Catholics in the army on the subject of "dem grossen Entscheidungskampf im Osten." Dated July 29, 1941; separate folder copy.

"Kameraden! Wer will es bezweifeln, dass wir Deutsche nunmehr das 'Herz-volk Europas' geworden sind und zwar in einem Sinne, der weit über geographische oder geopolitische Erwägungen hinausgreift? Wie schon oft in der Geschichte ist Deutschland in der Gegenwart zum Retter und Vorkämpfer Europas geworden. . . . Viele europäische Staaten, die bisher unter dem drohenden Schatten der bolschewistischen Gefahr gelebt haben und vielfach innerhalb ihrer Staatsgefüge die bittersten Erfahrungen mit den zersetzenden Auswirkungen bolschewistischer Lehre machen mussten, wissen es, dass der Krieg gegen Russland ein europäischer Kreuzzug ist. Die Völker Europas müssten ihre Geschichte verleugnen und ihre Zukunft verneinen, wollten sie nicht von Herzen jene Entscheidung herbeisehnen, die den Bolschewismus für alle Zeiten aus der Geschichte vertilgt.

"So ist es heute keine Uebertreibung, wenn ich sage, dass ihr im Osten gleich den deutschen Ordensrittern einer Zeit, die weit hinter uns liegt, eine Aufgabe zu erfüllen habt, die von einmaliger Bedeutung ist und deren Auswirkung für unser Volk, ja für Europa und die ganze Menschheit, heute noch nicht überblickt werden kann. . . .

•     •     •     •     •     •

"Kameraden! Was ich euch in dieser Stunde der grossen Entscheidung zu sagen hatte, ist, wie schon bemerkt, das Vermächtnis eines im Osten gefallenen Divisions-pfarrers. Nehmt es ernst mit eurer gigantischen Aufgabe! Seid euch eurer Sendung bewusst! Lebt aus der Kraft eures Gottesglaubens! Dann wird der Sieg euer sein, ein Sieg, der Europa aufatmen lässt und den Völkern eine neue Zukunft verheisst."

14. *Verordnungsblatt des Katholischen Feldbischofs der Wehrmacht,* Vol. 3, No. 4 (December 1, 1939), pp. 13-14.

"Wo deutsche Soldaten an der Front wachen und kämpfen, wird die Nacht des göttlichen Friedens gefeiert, wenn auch der Kampfeslärm nicht verstummen will.

"Weihnachten ist ein Fest der deutschen Seele. Es gibt in jeder Sprache Worte, die schon durch ihren äusseren Klang einen ganz eigenen Zauber auf uns ausüben. Zu diesen gesegneten Worten gehört auch "Weihnacht." Längst verklungene Zeiten werden wach, wenn wir es aussprechen. Man befrage alle Sprachen der Erde und man wird für das Fest der Geburt des Herrn keinen tieferen, geheimnisreicheren und gemüthafteren Ausdruck finden als unser deutsches Wort Weihnacht. Kein anderes Volk auf Erden kennt ein Weihnachtsfest wie wir. Es ist ein besonderer Ruhmestitel des deutschen Volkes, dem Weihnachtsfest seelische Werte von letzter Tiefe verliehen zu haben. Wie unsere Dome und Kirchen in Stadt und Land über den Alltag hinausweisen und eine ganz eigene Innigkeit und Frömmigkeit ausstrahlen, so ist auch die deutsche Weihnacht zu einem besonderen Begriff in der Welt geworden. Es ist das deutsche Lied, das deutsche Empfinden, das im Weihnachtsfeste seinen schönsten Ausdruck gefunden hat. Und wo immer man die alten christlichen deutschen Weihnachtslieder singt, dort klingt das Wesen der deutschen Seele an, dort wird die beste Eigenart deutschen Volkstums lebendig. Nur wir haben unseren Lichterbaum, unsere deutsche Tanne, die mit ihren tiefen, fast an Schwermut errinernden Schatten unserer deutschen Art ebenso entspricht wie mit ihrer hellen, gen Himmel strebenden Spitze. Das alles wird nur der in seiner letzten Tiefe und Wirklichkeit verstehen, der das Weihnachtsfest auch einmal im fremden Lande erlebt hat. Was wissen die Franzosen, was wissen die Engländer von unserer deutschen Weihnacht? Wir sind eben Deutsche und als solche ein Volk von besonderer Gemütstiefe. Die anderen werden uns darin niemals verstehen. Wir aber sind stolz darauf und gerade an Weihnacht kommt es uns so recht zu Bewusstsein, dass wir als Deutsche in der Welt eine Aufgabe haben, die uns der Herrgott, der Lenker der Welten und Völker, gegeben hat. Niemand hat für diesen Gedanken mehr Verständnis als der deutsche Soldat. Er führt die Waffe, um das Vaterland zu schützen und um den Ehrenschild unserer deutschen Nation blank und rein zu erhalten und wird sich gerade am Weihnachtsfeste, wo alle Tiefen des deutschen Gemüts aufbrechen, dieser seiner grossen Verantwortung besonders bewusst. . . ."

15. Franz Josef Rarkowski, Advent pastoral, 1943 (exact date not indicated); separate folder copy.
"Und eines möge euch die Freude des Christfestes noch besonders erhöhen: das stolze Bewusstsein, dass ihr, getreu eurem Fahneneid, durch den tapferen und zähen Kampf des hinter uns liegenden Kriegsjahres 1943 der deutschen Heimat das Weihnachtsglück und die Weihnachtsfreude ermöglicht habt. Es is nicht auszudenken, was geworden wäre, wenn ihr in eurer Treue, Standhaftigkeit und Zähigkeit nachgelassen und nicht allzeit mit Hingabe von Blut und Leben die Heimat verteidigt hättet. So darf keiner von euch an Weihnacht traurig sein. . . ."

16. See above, pp. 145 ff.

17. *Verordnungsblatt des Katholischen Feldbischofs der Wehrmacht*, Vol. 8, No. 2 (February 1, 1944), p. 5.
"Bewundernd blicken wir auf Christus, der so mutig und mit so grosser

Entschiedenheit dieses befreiende und erlösende Wort sprach und sich damit augenblicklich den Lockungen finsterer Mächte entzog. Wenn wir uns selbst gegenüber ehrlich sind, werden wir gestehen müssen, dass es uns nicht immer leicht fällt, den Lockungen dunkler Gewalten gegenüber die gleiche Entschiedenheit an den Tag zu legen. Wie schwer ist es oft, sich gegenüber lähmender Müdigkeit und innerer Bedrücktheit durchzusetzen! Wieviel Kraft kostet es, seinen täglichen Dienst immer wieder in Pflichttreue und Gehorsam auszuüben! Wieviel innere Zucht und Selbstverleugnung ist nötig, um gefährlichen Umtrieben des Niederen in uns die Stirne zu bieten! So hat das tapfere und entscheidende Herrenwort: *"Es steht geschrieben: Du sollst Gott allein dienen!"* für uns alle verpflichtende Bedeutung. . . ."

18. "Frühling unseres Volkes," *Kampf und Glaube* (April 7, 1940), pp. 1-2.

"Am 20. April wird zum ersten Male während des Krieges in ganz Grossdeutschland, an der Front und in der Heimat, des Geburtstages des Führers gedacht. Schon heute steht es als unbestrittene Tatsache fest, dass Adolf Hitler für unser Volk und für die ganze Welt von säkularer Bedeutung geworden ist. Kein anderer deutscher Staatsmann vor ihm verursachte so gewaltige Umwälzungen auf den verschiedensten Gebieten des völkischen Daseins wie er. Unsere Feinde, gegen die wir nunmehr den deutschen Lebensraum zu verteidigen haben, standen zuerst angesichts seiner Leistungen vor einem grossen Rätsel. Sie fühlten sich herausgefordert zur Kritik, Sorge und Angst steigerten sich immer mehr, und zuletzt loderte das wilde Feuer des Hasses empor, das auch vor Mordanschlägen nicht zurückschreckte. Was nicht in ruhigen Friedenstagen gelingen konnte, hofft man jetzt, nachdem der Krieg entbrannt ist, zu erreichen: die Zerstörung und Vernichtung all dessen, was unser Führer geschaffen hat. Das Christentum fordert Gehorsam und Ehrfurcht gegenüber der Obrigkeit und treue Mitarbeit an allen grossen Werken für Volk und Reich. So sei unser aller Geschenk an unseren Führer und Obersten Befehlshaber die innere Bereitschaft zu Opfer und Hingabe an das Volk. Wenn es uns heute so klar vor der Seele steht, dass die Treue zum Volke eine gottgewollte Aufgabe ist, so verdanken wir die Vertiefung dieser Erkenntnis unserem Führer. Er hat uns die grosse Wende, in der Werte wie Heimat und Volk, nationale Ehre und nationale Geschichte neue Wertschätzung erfahren, durch seinen Einsatz geschenkt. Er hat uns zum Bewusstsein unserer Aufgabe als Deutsche erweckt. Ausgehend vom Erlebnis des Volkstums hat er das Lebensgesetz des deutschen Volkes gefunden und durch seine Tat verwirklicht. All das kommt uns zum Bewusstsein in diesen Tagen, und wir vergessen nicht, dass es eine Zeit in unserem Volke gab, da wir mit ohnmächtigen Fäusten gegen eine Nebelwand [—lugen, a word is obscured in the published text by a punched hole] die uns bedrohte und unsere letzte Kraft zu verderben schien. Unser Dank und unsere Bereitschaft, Treue mit Treue zu vergelten, möge Ausdruck finden in dem Gebet, das uns in diesen Tagen mehr bedeutet als in ruhiger Friedenzeit: 'Segne, o Gott, unseren Führer und Obersten Befehlshaber in allen Aufgaben, die ihm gestellt sind. . . .' "

19. The paper in question was presented at the 1959 convention of the American Catholic Sociological Society and bore the title, "The Catholic Press and the National Cause in Nazi Germany." Almost immediately it stirred a strongly adverse reaction in German Catholic circles, a fact which led to its temporary withdrawal from scheduled publication in *The American Catholic Sociological Review*. A somewhat revised and expanded version was later published in the Fall 1960 issue of *Cross Currents* (Vol. X, No. 4), pp. 337-351, under the title, "The German Catholic Press and Hitler's Wars." Before this, however, while publication of the original paper was still being suppressed, attacks upon it and the present author were being published in Germany. See especially: "Die katholische Presse und der Nationalismus in Nazi-Deutschland," *Kirchenblatt für das Bistum Aachen*, Vol. 15, Nos. 17 and 18 (April 24 and May 1, 1960); Karl Al. Altmeyer, "Der Episkopat und die katholische Presse im Dritten Reich," *Herder Korrespondenz*, Vol. 14, No. 8 (May 1960); the same author's "Versagten die deutschen Katholiken im Dritten Reich?" *Deutsches Volksblatt*, Vol. 95, Nos. 213 and 214 (September 15 and 16, 1960); the present writer's rejoinder and Altmeyer's reply, *ibid.*, Nos. 254 and 255 (November 3 and 4, 1960).

20. Altmeyer, "Versagten die deutschen Katholiken im Dritten Reich?" *op. cit.* September 16, 1960.

"Wahr ist . . . dass Militärbischof Rarkowski tatsächlich eine auffallende "Ausnahme von dieser Regel" bildet. Der für die Ideologie des Nationalsozialismus schwärmende "Neue Wille" wurde von ihm in seinen Rundschreiben an die deutschen Soldaten angelegentlich auch dann empfohlen, als die deutschen Ordinariate sich eindeutig von dieser pseudokatholischen Zeitschrift distanziert hatten. Das aber beweist das Gegenteil der Zahnschen Behauptungen, nämlich dass die Bischöfe klar zwischen Staat und Ideologie unterschieden und nicht gewillt waren, dem Nationalisozialismus irgendwelche Opfer zu bringen.

"Da bekanntlich der Militärbischof nicht zum deutschen Episkopat zu zählen ist und er darüber hinaus trotz seiner sonst gemässigten und orthodoxen Hirtenbriefe eine Ausnahme von der Haltung der Diözesanbischöfe darstellt, weil er pronazistische Komplimente nicht unterdrücken wollte, müsste er eigentlich auch als eine solche, allerdings gegen Zahn sprechende, Ausnahme behandelt werden. Ob Zahn allerdings bei der Untersuchung aller Militärhirtenbriefe auch nur irgendeinen Satz fände, der gegen die katholische Glaubens- und Sittenlehre verstösst, muss nach der Durchsicht der meisten Hirtenbriefe Rarkowskis als ausserordentlich fraglich bezeichnet werden. Es scheint vielmehr, als habe Rarkowski nicht dogmatisch, sondern nur persönlich über die Stränge geschlagen durch eine zu grosse "Leutseligkeit" dem NS-Regime gegenüber. Seine Botschaften als einen "klassischen

Ausdruck militaristischer und nationalistischer Ideologie" zu bezeichnen, wird der Wahrheit nicht gerecht und berücksichtigt weder das neu gewordene deutsche Sprachfeld noch die tatsächlichen christlichen Pflichten eines Soldaten im Kriege."

21. Personal letter, dated June 1, 1960.

"Es ist aber geschichtlich falsch, sich zur Beurteilung des deutschen Episkopats auf den Feldbischof Rarkowski berufen zu wollen. Rarkowski gehörte zu den Extremisten der integralen Richtung, die hernach von Papst Benedikt XV, verworfen wurde. Prälat Benigni, welcher der Drahtzieher der Integralen war, ist von Papst Benedixt XV auf das Ungnädigste aus dem kirchlichen Dienst entlassen worden. Pfarrer Rarkowski war seine Kreatur und ist von den deutschen Bischöfen schon vor 1914 desavuiert worden. Er durfte keine kirchliche Funktion mehr ausüben. Es ist natürlich klar, dass ein solcher Mann sich dem Nationalsozialismus völlig in die Arme warf. Dass er von den Nationalsozialisten zum Feldbischof des Heeres gemacht wurde, war einsichtigen Katholiken ein grosses Ärgernis. Ein Mann mit dieser zweideutigen Vergangenheit kann unter keinen Umständen mit den ehrenhaft denkenden übrigen katholischen Bischöfen verglichen worden."

**Part 3**

Part 3

# CHAPTER 11

# Analysis and Interpretation

THE BASIC CONCLUSIONS to be drawn from the documentation presented in the preceding chapters can be simply stated. Indeed, one need only say that this study has provided an empirical validation of Watkin's generalization concerning "the historical fact that Bishops have consistently supported all wars waged by the government of their country."[1] But the purposes of this research analysis extend beyond this; and it is, therefore, necessary that we bring our findings into sharper focus by recapitulating them in terms of the social-control and value-selection dimensions stated in the first chapters.

To do this, it is useful to attempt a reconstruction of the situation faced by the Catholic in wartime Nazi Germany. We are limited to this approach since there is no way to recapture and measure the actual impact of the controls inducing conformity to the totalitarian state; nor is it possible for us to create an experimental situation in which the actual selection between the value systems made at that time could be duplicated and recorded. Even were someone to declare that he had supported Hitler's wars as a direct result of hearing or reading the patriotic exhortations of his bishop, such seemingly conclusive evidence would have to be discounted to the extent that the imperfections of human memory, compounded by the intense emotional stress of the situation being recalled, must be presumed to distort the remembered event. In the same fashion, assurances that the respondent was never aware of the possibility that there could be a divergence between his duty to the national community and the moral obligations arising from his commitment to the Catholic religious community would have to be treated with a good deal of caution; for, certainly, the individual's ego-involvement would make it quite natural for him to repress the memory of an actual value choice in favor of the secular community over that of the religious community or, what could amount to the same thing, an avoidance on his part of the value-selection problem presented by the wartime situation. This would be nothing more than an acknowledgment of the psychological fact that the influences forming or directing human behavior are so complex and often so subtle that any attempt to prove their operation in any given instance with any degree of precision would be quite futile.

Logical reconstruction, as an analytical tool, is an effort on the part of the researcher to structure the situation under study in terms of both the controls known to be present and the postulated value commitments and to infer from these the behavioral consequences. Thus, if we assume a German Catholic were in doubt as to the moral licitness of serving in Hitler's wars, one source to which he would be expected to turn for guidance would be the pastoral directives and other official statements issued by his own and the other German bishops; in such event, it is thoroughly legitimate to hold, the values promoted there would influence him to resolve his doubts in favor of full support of the war. And, given the role of bishop in the institutional structure, this same influence would be encountered in the religious press, in the advice the individual would receive from pastors and confessors, and other subsidiary sources of moral guidance and direction. It should be obvious, too, that the individual who was not troubled by such doubts would also be influenced or "controlled" in his behavior, since the fact that his respected and responsible spiritual leaders issued such war-supporting appeals would serve to reinforce his personal commitment.

But the logical reconstruction of the situation faced by the individual Catholic who was also a citizen of Hitler's Third Reich is not as simple or one-sided as this might indicate. *As a German citizen,* he was subject to the full range of secular social controls organized to induce him to conform to the demands of the war effort. The Nazi totalitarian state formally required such behavior and enforced its requirements by exercising (or threatening to exercise) its power to inflict the penalties of imprisonment and even death for any overt refusal to conform. His fellow citizens likewise demanded such conformist behavior of him and supported their demands by according him the positive rewards of approval and honor for effective compliance, or by subjecting him to the negative sanctions of scorn, dishonor, and even ostracism for any refusal or failure to do his share. Within himself, he felt the stirrings of his own emotional attachments to *Volk, Vaterland,* and *Heimat;* and these would carry with them the satisfactions and pride associated with proper performance of duty as a loyal son of Germany (if he conformed) or the uneasy sense of guilt and shame arising from an unmanly failure to pay his debt to the *Volk* that gave him birth and blood (if he refused). At another level, the emotional attachments to friends and relatives who were stationed at posts of danger and were depending upon his contribution, his personal reactions to news of the death of friends or loved ones in battle or in air raids suffered at home or to reports of the merciless destruction visited upon beloved cities and historical shrines—all of these would similarly serve to stimulate deep and powerful psychological drives toward conformity or the equally deep and powerful sense of self-punishing guilt for non-conformity. Finally, no matter where he turned, he would encounter the external controls and war- and duty-supporting symbols, the inescapable evidences of the total identification of his fellow citizens with the massive common effort involving their, his, and the nation's continued existence.

To stand alone against this flood, to reject the demands of this organized totality of social controls, would have required an extra-ordinary degree of heroic self-determination—and more. It would have required a sense of total commitment to some alternative system of values which, to one so committed, could claim precedence over those values of personal and national survival inducing support for the war.

Such an alternative system of values might perhaps have been found in the stirring challenge voiced by Bishop von Galen: "It is better to die than to sin!" If the German citizen who was Christian, and particularly if he were Catholic, had been convinced that Hitler's wars were unjust wars and that participation in them would be, at the very least, materially sinful, it would have been possible for him to find in the teachings of the Church the inspiration upon which such a refusal to serve could have been based and maintained. For him, the injunction to serve God rather than man would have implied a firm prescription of duty differing sharply from and superseding the call to duty issued by his nation's leaders.

But it is clear that German Catholics were not so convinced. Their actual behavior, on the contrary, exhibited a near unanimity of support for Hitler's wars. This does not mean, however, that the secular controls were so effective that the contest between these alternative systems was decided in favor of the secular. For any contest of this nature that may have taken place within the individual was, in a very real sense, unauthorized and unapproved. Even if the secular controls described above had not been operative or effective, German Catholic behavior, to the extent that it was responsive to the controls exerted by the leadership of the Catholic Church in Germany, would have evidenced the same pattern of full conformity to the demands of the national war effort.

*As a German Catholic,* our hypothetical individual was now subject to the full range of religious social controls directed toward this end. The formal controls of the Church represented by episcopal directives and example have been sufficiently demonstrated here. His local parish community, the Church organizations in which he participated, the content of the religious services he attended—all encouraged him to give his wholehearted support to the war and to show a ready willingness to sacrifice his material well-being to assure its success. His own inner piety would be stirred by the repeated assurances that death in battle was the *Heldentod* (hero death) that ranked with the death of a martyr as a sure means of gaining entry into eternal blessedness; his devotion to his God would be converted into an awareness of the moral obligation to obey the commands of the secular *Obrigkeit* (authorities); his filial attachment to his bishop, perhaps much stronger in Germany than in many other lands, would make him all the more susceptible to the formal controls already mentioned. Finally, all the symbols of a dedicated religious unity behind the war effort that surrounded him, including the patriotic fervor of the appeals to which he was exposed in the pages of his Catholic periodical, would have tightly closed the circle of conformity about him.

To stand alone against *this* flood, to reject the demands of this totality of religious controls inducing conformity to the war effort, would have required both clarity of judgment and an extraordinary degree of heroic sanctity. It may well have required what Franz Jägerstätter's[2] bishop set as the condition for his conscientious objection: a truly personal revelation in which the conscience was directly instructed from above to ignore or reject the instructions and examples set by those responsible for the spiritual guidance of Germany's Catholics.

A note of caution must be introduced here so that the reader will not be tempted to exaggerate the responsibility of Germany's religious leaders. Had the individual German Catholic been presented with a clear and demanding choice between conflicting value systems—that is, had he been encouraged or even directed *not* to give his support to the Nazi government's wars—there is no certainty that the outcome would have been significantly different.* It is en-

* Some might be inclined to regard the findings of this study and the facts upon which they rest as an indictment of the spiritual leadership of Germany's Catholics. This is certainly not the function of this study which is, instead, primarily concerned with explaining German Catholic behavior with respect to Hitler's wars, not with passing judgment upon that be-

tirely possible (one theologian insisted that it would have been highly probable, even certain) that the conformity-inducing pressures involved in the appeals and threats of the totalitarian state would have had greater ultimate influence upon the individual Catholic's behavior than would Church pronouncements, no matter how explicit and official, calling for a contrary course of action. The almost certain penalty of execution might well have had more immediate effect upon individual behavior than could fear of the sanctions associated with mortal sin or the threat of formal excommunication. And nationalistic emotions and sentiments in a time of emergency and stress might have outweighed the inner imperatives of piety and devotion to episcopal authority—especially where the former would be reinforced by general community pressures and the total organization of external secular controls.

The reader is again reminded, too, that this analysis presupposes that the writer and many German informants who gave him their personal evaluations of the attitude of German Catholics, then and now, are correct in regarding Hitler's wars of aggression as unjust wars according to the traditional morality of war, and in assuming that German Catholics, or at least their bishops, had sufficient opportunity to become certainly aware of this injustice. The question of limited access to facts which could lead to such a judgment is, of course, important here. It should not be permitted, however,

---

havior. In the final analysis, any moral judgment of the wartime activities of German Catholics must be left to the moral theologian in his role as specialist in evaluating actual human behavior according to the immutable moral principles of the Church. It is possible—or so one would hope at least—that the present study might inspire such a theologically oriented analysis, preferably by the German theologians, who have thus far tended to ignore the problem; but this would be just an incidental or supplemental good and not an objective of this analysis.

By the same token, any criticism of Germany's spiritual leadership to be drawn from the material presented here should be framed in terms of the value-selection dimension of the problem: namely, their *failure to try* to inspire Catholic noncompliance with an unjust war, rather than their *failure to assure* such noncompliance. To say this does not, of course, lessen whatever degree of personal responsibility may be associated with the active endorsement and support given the war effort by those spiritual leaders.

to serve as the magic key releasing the individual from all responsibility to judge the war and the service demanded of him. If the conditions of the just war were so flexible and so obscure that they defy all application to any actual war-in-progress, then the individual might indeed be trapped into the pattern of blind faith in the cause of his nation prescribed by Laros[3]; and all wars would have to be fought (on all sides) under a suspension of moral judgment until such time as postwar availability of all the facts made it possible to determine which fighters had been guilty of a material sin against the Fifth Commandment. But these conditions cannot be quite as flexible and obscure as all that. One need only review the conditions as they are presented earlier in this study[4] to see that some of them (e.g., the prohibitions against aggressive war, the use of extreme reprisals, direct action against noncombatants and merchant shipping, and so on) were clearly not being observed. We have the testimony of so eminent a spokesman as West Germany's President Lübke; in a most moving memorial address he declared, "No one who was not completely blinded or wholly naïve could be completely free of the pressing awareness that this war was not a just war."[5] It cannot be maintained that such complete blindness and naïveté affected all the members of the German hierarchy—especially since their contact with the outside world through their ties to the Vatican would have freed them from the more stringent restrictions placed upon the information available to the ordinary Catholic citizen of Nazi Germany.

The objection might be raised that too great an emphasis is being placed upon the role of the German bishops throughout this analysis. But this emphasis is justified by the definition of their role as stated by the bishops themselves and by the German Catholic press. Certainly, such emphasis would be quite excessive if one were to accept the extremely limited range of activity and authority described by Reichsminister Kerrl on the occasion of the formal investiture of Preysing as Bishop of Berlin in 1935:

Although your office as a bishop of the Catholic Church restricts your activity to the area of spiritual care and direction, the people entrusted to your religious leadership are at the same time members of the German *Volk* and citizens of the National Socialist state. The relationship which arises from this duality need not, must not, and should not be one of opposition.

. . . Herr Bishop, if, in full awareness of the demands of the time, you promote loyalty to the new state and leader and respect for his authority on the part of your clergy and your followers, then you may be assured that the national administration will undertake to vouchsafe the unhindered practice of religion and will demonstrate a complete understanding of religious needs. . . .[6]

But the opposition of interests which, in Kerrl's opinion, should not arise did arise; and the bishops did avail themselves of many opportunities to define these areas of opposition and to clarify moral teachings that had direct social and even political implications. In doing so, they made it quite clear, too, that they laid claim to a far broader range of activity and authority than Kerrl was willing to grant. One of the more outspoken in this respect was Cardinal Faulhaber; and it is no accident that Bishop Jakobus von Hauck of Bamberg should turn to the topic of the love and care required of a bishop in fulfilling his role as shepherd for his Catholic flock when, in 1936, he delivered the sermon marking a Faulhaber jubilee.

Foremost among the shepherd's activities . . . belongs the execution of the teaching office of the Church. The bishop is the *real teacher* of his flock. He should reveal to them the sacred and sanctifying truths the Savior preached. He should lead them to an ever broader knowledge and ever deeper understanding of the truths of Salvation [italics in published text]. . . .

In the course of this eulogy, the speaker noted the Munich Cardinal's dedication to his chosen motto, *Vox temporis, vox Dei,* and called upon his listeners to do homage to the leadership they had received from him and to acknowledge

How, with his far-seeing intellect he always addresses himself to precisely those questions that trouble the times and for which the Catholic *Volk* desires a solution! How he is always able to expose the essential fallacy in the foolish errors of the times which assail the Faith, and to refute them clearly and decisively and thus prevent them from creating confusion in the hearts of the faithful. Be grateful to your shepherd for being so zealous and accomplished a teacher and preacher of the Truth! [7]

With these words as a background, it is difficult to overemphasize the importance of the fact that Faulhaber's signature was to head the statement of the Bavarian bishops which, only three years later, would exhort the faithful "to devote your full efforts to the service of the *Vaterland* and the precious *Heimat* in conscientious fulfillment of duty and serious awareness of your mission."

An even more explicit description of the role and responsibility of a Catholic bishop is furnished by the 1933 pastoral letter issued by the newly consecrated Bishop von Galen:

Never think that your bishops issue irresponsible exhortations or admonitions without regard for circumstances, that your bishops recklessly shut their eyes to dangers if they do not [*sic*] keep silent while you call for leadership. Be assured instead that every day the knowledge of the responsibility for your souls weighs heavily upon them and that they know they could not save their own souls if they were to keep silence or to speak out at the wrong time. I will gladly accept from others—including the laity and even well-meaning adherents of other confessions—information concerning the state of the times, their good wishes, and also their good advice. But I know that the duty to make the decision about necessary instructions and warnings for my flock rests upon me alone and weighs upon my conscience and that no one can relieve me of them. "Neither human respect nor fear of men" [*Nec laudibus, nec timore,* the Bishop's motto] will ever keep me from fulfilling this duty.

To make the application sharp and clear, the Bishop continued:

And if, in certain instances, the bishop should make a mistake in his assessment of the necessity or propriety of an instruction he decides to issue; should his subjects in a given instance have a better insight into

the circumstances of the times and their requirements than does the
bishop who bears the responsibility and, therefore, believe themselves
justified in bringing their opinions before the bishop in proper fashion
—we must never forget this fact: Just as the Pope in the universal
Church and the bishop in his diocese are entrusted with the administration of and the responsibility for the Church, so is it the place and
responsibility of the faithful placed in their pastoral charge to render
obedience to the Church. And, as it is for every Catholic bishop, it is
my clearly revealed duty to go before you, at all times setting the good
example, in unbounded, childlike obedience to the Supreme Shepherd,
the Father.[8]

Bierbaum, the Bishop's biographer, in discussing Galen's attitude
toward Germany's involvement in World War II, anticipates a
question we must consider later: If the Germany hierarchy did fail
in not opposing Hitler's wars of aggression, how can we account
for this failure? His argument is important at this point because it
sets forth the limitations upon the Bishop's behavior imposed by
considerations of episcopal prudence. At the same time, Bierbaum
extended his analysis to include the question of the justice of the
war itself, and in doing so he made the following analysis of
Galen's position:

The Bishop did not investigate whether this war was just or unjust, but
merely described it as unchristian because it was conducted in an un-
chivalrous fashion. To such and similar criticisms of the conduct of
Clement August, one must reply that the Bishop did not take a specific
and express public stand with regard to every violation of justice of
the time. Does this mean that he failed—in the theological formulation,
*per defectum?* Could a bishop, for example, openly designate the war
as unjust as early as 1939 without placing himself and the Church in
Germany in even greater danger—even prescinding for the moment
from the fact that a decision concerning the justice of a war in
progress is one of the most difficult problems to challenge the human
intellect? On the other hand, it must not be overlooked in this connection that Clement August frequently, even in wartime, issued reminders of the provisions of international law and divine morality and,
whenever possible, sought to gain a hearing for the voice of reason in
the midst of the passions of war. One may personally choose death in

preference to even the appearance of weakness; but as a leader one has the obligation to question whether such valor is compatible with the prudence that should go with that virtue. One must consider, too, whether one might not, through such behavior, expose unnumbered believers and the Church in his own country to the gravest danger.[9]

These are effective arguments and certainly deserve most careful consideration, but they do not completely satisfy the objection they seek to answer. For in the light of their own self-definition of the role and responsibility of the episcopal authority, the statements and actions of the German bishops must be viewed as a major source of influence and control inducing German Catholics to support the Hitler war effort. As the "real teachers" of the Catholic faithful, the bishops would seem to have a distinct obligation to "take a specific and express public stand" on so vital a moral issue as participation in a war of such highly questionable justice. And Bierbaum's defense contains one fatal flaw in that he completely ignores the fact that the German bishops, including Galen, did take a specific and express public stand by placing their followers under a moral obligation to support Hitler's wars. The ordinary Catholic, the man-in-the-pew who went to war, dropped the bombs, and sank the ships, could do so partly because his bishops told him he not only had a right to do so but was actually duty-bound to do so. If these wars were unjust, the charge Bierbaum seeks to refute has real substance.

But the issue should not be left at this. Some further consideration must be given to possible explanations of the position taken by the bishops. One is offered by Bierbaum and was advanced by many of this researcher's informants: under the dictates of prudence, the bishops had no alternative. And this explanation cannot be dismissed lightly. It is certainly true that a bishop has the responsibility to consider the physical and material, as well as the spiritual, well-being of the flock placed in his charge and to avoid exposing it to unnecessary peril. One must also recognize that any effort to rally Catholics in opposition to Hitler's wars would have evoked a response of merciless reprisal. Add to this the practical consideration that any such effort on the part of the bishops would most likely have been unsuccessful, that the flocks which enthusiastically followed the episcopal encouragement to support the war would have been far less willing to follow them in a course that would have involved serious immediate risks for themselves and those dear to them. All of these considerations taken together are a strong argument against a policy of episcopal opposition to Catholic participation in Hitler's wars.

But, again in terms of the Catholic value system, another equally serious consideration must be taken into account. It is the scriptural injunction to preach the Word "in season and out of season." The cardinal virtue of prudence governs the choice of the proper means to accomplish a legitimate end; it is not to be confused with a decision to abandon the legitimate end altogether because its attainment would entail serious risks and hardships.

A second explanation, which is really an extension of the first, would take account of the consequences of Catholic support for the war. In its crudest restatement, the defense advanced by Bierbaum could be reduced to a kind of implied and unworthy "deal" whereby the German bishops permitted their followers to fight in an unjust war (with Catholic populations numbered among their victims) in order that the Church might be spared the reprisals that would greet a contrary course. It is, of course, unthinkable that dedicated and heroic leaders like Faulhaber, Galen, and others of their stature would knowingly participate in or even silently condone such an exchange.

Episcopal prudence, then, is not a sufficient explanation. Even granting Bierbaum's thesis in every detail, it would at most explain a policy of episcopal silence with respect to the war and service in it. But there was no policy of silence; it was, instead, an active, concerted and continued effort on the part of the German hierarchy to encourage, maintain, and intensify the Catholic contribution. In this connection, too, one must discount explanations which posit an episcopal unwillingness to require martyrdom of their followers by counseling or directing them to refuse military service in these wars of aggression. For the bishops did call for martyrdom on the part of German Catholics—but it was a "martyrdom" for *Volk* and *Vaterland* and not for the religious values represented by the traditional Catholic morality of war. Even in the midst of total military collapse, with the Third Reich tottering to its death, bishops were raising their voices to inspire men to offer their last drop of blood for the national cause. Shils and Janowitz, in their study of *Wehrmacht* desertions, found that ethical-religious scruples played a small role in such desertions and went on to note that, "Although there were a few interesting cases of Roman Catholic deserters, Roman Catholics (except Austrians, Czechs, and Polish nationals) do not seem to have deserted disproportionately."[10] The episcopal appeals, considered in the social-control and value-selection framework employed here, may throw some light upon this sociological finding.

Perhaps a better explanation of the episcopal position is inadvertently suggested in a letter written to the present author by a priest who had published an autobiographical account of life in a Nazi concentration camp. Responding to what he felt was an implied criticism of the hierarchy in a reference to the support they had given the war effort, he somewhat indignantly declared that "of course" the bishops had given such support, that bishops, too, had their duty to perform and should not be blamed if the faithful performance of that duty was perverted by the Nazis for their own evil purposes.

*Bishops, too, have their duty to perform.* Up to this point in the analysis we have concentrated upon their duty to provide spiritual guidance and direction to the faithful assigned to their charge. Now some consideration must be given to the extent to which they may have felt obligated to support the nation's cause as good and loyal Germans. One theologian—not a pacifist, incidentally—discoursed at some length over what he felt was too uncritical a stress upon the virtue of obedience in German theological thought. He maintained that there had long been a tendency to reduce the concept of

*Gehorsam* to a pattern of unquestioning and virtually unlimited compliance with every demand of the secular authority. He traced this tendency to the success achieved by Bismarck in his program of welding a number of minor states and principalities into one powerful empire. This success, he continued, imposed upon all Germans the legacy of Prussian militarism with its rigid discipline and dedication to a strict code of military honor. The German bishops of World War II were men who had known the Empire in its days of glory, and who had been formed under these influences; it was, therefore, only natural, he felt, that their thinking and behavior would be shaped by this background and experience.

This view is strikingly similar to that part of Meinecke's explanation of "the German catastrophe" in which he touches upon the content and influence of that same legacy. As Meinecke puts it,

As long as the synthesis of intellect and power seemed to look hopeful in the nineteenth century, we regarded even militarism with a more benevolent eye; we emphasized the undoubtedly high moral qualities which were evident in it: the iron sense of duty, the ascetic strictness in service, the disciplining of the character in general. Easily overlooked, however, was the fact that this disciplining developed a levelling habit of conformity of mind which narrowed the vision and also often led to a thoughtless subserviency toward all higher authorities. . . .

However, in the era when the Empire was founded, the aspects of Prussian militarism which were bad and dangerous for the general well-being were obscured by the imposing proof of its power and discipline in its service for national unity and in the construction of Bismarck's Empire. The military man now seemed to be a consecrated spirit—the lieutenant moved through the world as a young god and the civilian reserve lieutenant at least as a demigod. He had to rise to be reserve officer in order to exert his full influence in the upper-middle-class world and above all in the state administration. Thus militarism penetrated civilian life. Thus there developed a conventional Prussianism *(Borussismus)*, a naïve self-admiration in Prussian character, and together with it a serious narrowing of intellectual and political outlook. Everything was turned into a rigid conventionalism. One must have observed this type in countless examples with one's own eyes in the course of a long life, one must have felt in one's own self, struggled with it, and gradually liberated one's self from it, in order to understand its power over men's minds—in order to understand finally the effect of the touching comedy in the Potsdam church on March 21, 1933, which Hitler played with Hindenburg beside the tomb of Frederick the Great. For here National Socialism was expected to appear as the heir and propagator of all the great and beautiful Prussian traditions.[11]

In the light of the analysis offered by the author's informant, it is not too much to say that Hindenburg was not the only leader in Germany who could be moved by Nazi appeals to Prussian traditions and virtues. Many of the episcopal messages quoted in the body of the present study contain unmistakable echoes of the social context described by Meinecke.

But the Bismarck era left an even more significant legacy as far as German Catholicism was concerned. The intensity of his *Kulturkampf* against the Church burdened it with something of an inferiority complex which continued long afterward to manifest itself in a compulsive drive to prove that Catholics *could be* good and loyal Germans, that they *were* good and loyal Germans, that, in fact, their religious formation made it certain that they would be the *best* and *most loyal* Germans of all. This legacy, too, is evidenced throughout the wartime pastorals of the hierarchy.*

This turn in the analysis has shifted the focus of attention from the external controls to the internal controls as an explanation of the position the German bishops took on the war. In this perspective, they supported Hitler's wars because, as citizens, they felt they

* It should be noted that this interpretation was abruptly rejected as absurd by a prominent German Jesuit in the course of an interview in Rome. This noted theologian denied that there had been any need since the end of the *Kulturkampf* to "prove" German loyalty and patriotism. No one, he declared, even questioned these; and he referred to the fact that Catholics had held important civil posts as evidence to support his point of view. However, it is extremely difficult, if not impossible, to reconcile this point of view with the many documented instances reported in Neuhäusler's *Kreuz und Hakenkreuz* and elsewhere in which the loyalty of German Catholics was challenged by Nazi spokesmen and publications, and was most energetically defended by Catholic spokesmen.

had a duty to obey the legitimate secular authority represented by the Nazi regime and to see to it that their followers did the same. Despite their firm and continuing public opposition to euthanasia, the new heathenism, and the concerted Nazi assaults upon the Church, they were now able to demonstrate that they and the other Catholics of Germany were loyal and devoted members of the *Volk*.

These internal controls may well provide the ultimate key to the explanation we have been seeking in this study. One need only recall the reminder given by a Berlin informant that bishops are men and, as men, are subject to all the weaknesses and limitations of human nature. In applying this reminder, he limited himself to the probability that the bishops had not been fully cognizant of the true nature of Hitler's wars. But it is possible now to go beyond this to other and more significant applications. Bishops, too, are men who can be and undoubtedly are susceptible to the lure of nationalistic sentiments and pride; bishops, like other men, are emotionally involved in the "myths" of *Volk, Vaterland,* and *Heimat,* and all their lesser derivatives. The operation of these internal social controls was most clearly evident in the writings of Bishop Rarkowski, but one may say that the other episcopal documents furnished strong evidence that they affected the behavior of the other bishops as well.

Indeed, in an interview with one of his theologian-informants, the writer suggested that nationalistic identification and sentiments would best explain the support given the Hitler war effort by the German hierarchy. To emphasize the point, it was suggested that this would hold true "even for Faulhaber and Galen." Instead of the mild indignation the writer expected this observation to stir, he was surprised to find it received with a nod of agreement and the friendly suggestion that it might be best to amend the statement to apply the finding *especially* to Faulhaber and Galen.

From time to time Catholic writers have referred to nationalism as "the heresy of our day," and the German experience might well be taken as a justification of this charge. Nationalism as a term is subject to a wide variety of definitions ranging from a set of common recognitions and aspirations on the part of the inhabitants of a definable territory to the "my country, right or wrong" model of chauvinistic extremism. Boehm's use of the term incorporates something of this range of meanings. In his words, nationalism

in its broader meaning refers to the attitude which ascribes to national individuality a high place in the hierarchy of values. In this sense it is a natural and indispensible condition and accompanying phenomenon of all national movements. Insofar as the political life of the national state is governed by national forces there is hardly ever any sharp distinction between patriotism and nationalism. On the other hand, the term nationalism also connotes a tendency to place a particularly excessive, exaggerated and exclusive emphasis on the value of the nation at the expense of other values, which leads to a vain and importunate overestimation of one's own nation and thus to a detraction of others.[12]

It is not difficult to see that the latter usage, in which love for and attachment to the nation and its interests are given priority over all other competing values, justifies use of the term "heresy." Yet it was precisely this kind of nationalism that was a fundamental of Nazi ideology. It would be too much to say that the same kind of nationalism was a factor motivating the episcopal activity cited here; but it is permissible to suggest that, to the extent that this activity approached its maximum intensity of commitment to the prosecution of the war, it did tend to duplicate the excessive nationalism described above. This would apply, too, perhaps with even greater force, to the motivations affecting the behavior of the ordinary Catholic called into actual military service.*

* As Shafer points out, "A short, scholarly definition of a sentence or two, a precise definition which includes everything nationalism contains and excludes all that is irrelevant, may be impossible." After an extensive exposition of ten beliefs and conditions commonly present in the myth of nationalism, he offers a summary paragraph in which, like Boehm, he includes the notes of common historical experience, aspirations, culture, economic and social institutions; loyalty to the nation-state whatever its government; and ethnocentric preference for one's fellow nationals. "In its most modern form it requires, as Rousseau advocated as early as the eighteenth century, almost absolute devotion to and conformity with the will of the nation-state as this is expressed by the ruler or rulers (autocratic or democratic), and it demands the supremacy (in watchmaking or military might)

Such nationalism appears to have influenced German Catholic behavior in two ways. First, it distorted moral judgment by giving priority to the nation's interests and needs, sometimes even over the demands of traditional theological considerations; the Laros pamphlet cited earlier[13] may be taken as an example of this. Its influence was more subtle—and perhaps far more effective—because it operated to forestall the likelihood of troubling doubts ever arising as to the justice or injustice of the war. In this way, the individual simply did not have the terrible problem of having to choose between conflicting value systems; it was possible for him to proceed upon the unstated, and hence irrefutable, assumption that the national cause must be right merely because it involved the nation's security and honor.

Something of this may be found in the frequently made distinction between fighting for Hitler, his aims, and his evil regime, and fighting for *Volk* and *Vaterland*. This distinction was given expression in the 1941 sermons of Bishop von Galen, and one may assume that it helped many other earnest and sincere opponents of Hitler to free themselves from the horns of a terrible moral dilemma. And it was a distinction honestly made and deeply held. Archbishop Gröber's 1945 statements reveal how it held its force even after the dilemma was resolved by the elimination of Hitler and his Nazi regime; in May he addressed the following message to the Freiburg Catholics:

Anyone who has more than the barest passing acquaintance with me

---

of the nation to which the nationalist belongs." Boyd C. Shafer, *Nationalism: Myth and Reality* (New York: Harcourt, Brace & Co., 1955), Chapter I. Kohn similarly opens his valuable short work on the topic with a definition even better suited to this discussion: "Nationalism is a state of mind, in which the supreme loyalty of the individual is felt to be due the national state." Hans Kohn, *Nationalism: Its Meaning and History* (Princeton: D. Van Nostrand, 1955), p. 9. Other important works bearing upon this discussion and even more directly concerned with the relationship between religion and national loyalties and obligations are John J. Wright, *National Patriotism in Papal Teachings* (Westminster, Md.: Newman, 1943), and Carlton J. H. Hayes, *Nationalism: a Religion* (New York: Macmillan, 1960).

will know my state of mind as I write this pastoral message. Despite all the hidden and public assaults upon me and all the soul-rending sufferings of the past few years, despite the repeated and severest threats on the part of the previous rulers about their postwar intentions, as a German man I have always remained sincerely "German" in my feelings. . . .[14]

This same sadness over the final defeat of Nazi Germany was echoed by Galen. In a special public denial of the "widely circulated lie and libel" that he had re-entered his cathedral city in the company of advancing enemy troops and had attached himself to them, he spoke of the "shattering experience for me as for every German" which "will always remain a bad memory." The experience to which he referred was "the sight of these advancing enemy troops, here in our *Heimat,* on German soil. Today is not the time, nor is this the place to speak of these things, how bitter this event is to us, and how our hearts bleed over the *Volk* in its hour of need. . . ."[15]

That most, if not all, of the responsible Catholic leaders made such a distinction between fighting for the *Vaterland* and fighting for the Third Reich may be taken for granted. It is not at all so certain that the bulk of the Catholics engaged in actual combat took the occasion or, indeed, felt any need to make such a distinction. However widespread its application may or may not have been, it is quite clear that the distinction can be fatal to any effort to apply responsibly the "just war" formula to any war in progress, even to wars of such obviously questionable justice as Hitler's wars are generally conceded to have been. For all the crucial injustices— the manner in which they were begun, the world order they were to bring into being, even the manner in which they were conducted —all of these could easily be associated with the "fighting for Hitler" which was ostensibly not intended; whereas the "defense of the *Vaterland*" against the enemy which threatened to destroy it takes on a far more justifiable cast *once the distinction is granted*.

Not everyone made the distinction. Mention has already been made of the Austrian farmer who was beheaded for refusing to serve. In his trial he is reported to have stated his refusal in simple and direct terms: as a Catholic he could not take up arms because he would at the same time be fighting for National Socialism, something he could not in good conscience do. But such an exception only serves to prove the rule in an unusually dramatic and tragic fashion. Those responsible for his moral guidance—his bishop, the priest who had replaced his pastor, the prison chaplain—made every effort to induce him to abandon his position. Nor was this done entirely out of concern for his life and the security of his wife and infant daughters; even after the war his bishop intervened to block the publication of an article praising his action because he, the bishop, considered those who did fight to be "the greater heroes" when compared to a man who "in erroneous conscience" had refused to bear arms in Hitler's wars.

In the compilation of resistance documents cited earlier, Strobel states the problem in terms which reveal what may be a critical weakness of the traditional "just war" formulation. After pointing out that the German bishops had called upon the faithful to fulfill their "soldierly duty," he stated:

The Catholic Church will always speak thus in all times and all situations of this kind. For she will comply with Christ's commandment to give unto the state what belongs to the state and to resist only those orders which are immoral. But, one may ask, how could the German bishops have strengthened in this fashion the German power to resist in an admittedly criminal war? Did they not thereby work hand-in-hand with the regime? The following must be considered in this connection:

1. Because of the one-sided Nazi propaganda line and the concurrent suppression of all the publication resources of the Church, it was impossible for the bishops to organize and conduct any real countermeasures. Any unsuccessful attempt to do so would have been exploited by the Nazi propaganda to greatly increase the spiritual confusion and the conflicts of conscience among the faithful. Similarly, the Church could not permit itself to stir even the suggestion of a political sabotage which she did not wish to encourage either through silent participation or active leadership.

2. Bishops and Catholics acted in the war they considered just out

of the same Christian sense of duty evidenced by the Catholics of the opposing states;

3. But theirs were mixed feelings: they fulfilled their duty to the *Vaterland*, of course, but continued to fight as before against the regime. It is significant that the bishops and faithful never prayed for the victory of the Third Reich but, instead, always for a just *peace*. It is well known how much this annoyed the Party—an annoyance which is documented in the Gestapo reports for the war years published by Steward. One could formulate the position of German Catholicism in wartime somewhat in these terms: "We fulfill our Christian and patriotic duty; beyond this: deliver us, O Lord, from the Nazi regime!" (italics in published text).[16]

The present study contradicts Strobel's analysis in two respects. For a time at least, some Catholic publications did continue to appear, and they gave no evidence of any intent to depart from the "one-sided Nazi propaganda" line. Secondly, the prayer for victory did occasionally creep into episcopal pastorals; in some cases these prayers may indeed have included mental reservations, but in others —most particularly, but not exclusively, those of *Feldbischof* Rarkowski—there is every reason to believe these prayers were sincere. The broader discussion of the critical observation he makes, namely, that the Catholic Church will always and everywhere conduct itself as it did in Germany with respect to Hitler's wars, will be considered below in the discussion of the sociotheological implications of the present study.

One can understand the genuine sorrow the bishops felt in the face of the great disaster their country had undergone; one must truly honor the bishops in their sincere identification with the tragic sufferings already borne and still to be faced by the defeated nation. But this crucial distinction must also be put to the test of critical analysis. Germany's war was a war for the defense of *Volk* and *Vaterland* only to the extent that the enemy nations had taken to arms in an effort to repulse the aggressions of Hitler's totalitarian state. Even if it were true that most or all of these enemy nations had benefitted from unjust provisions in the agreements ending

World War I, this would not mask the fact that each new move of the Hitler armies involved a violation of these and other solemn agreements between the German nation and its neighbors. And if these enemy nations did come to employ unjust means and proclaim unjust war aims, such moral wrongs would not make the original Nazi aggressions morally right, nor would they justify a continuation of an unjust war. It is, of course, a logical impossibility that a war could be just for all participants, but it is entirely possible that none of the participants would be fighting a just war. The distinction fades before the reality: Germany's wars were Hitler's wars; the *Endsieg* he sought would have brought all of Europe, perhaps even the whole world, within the same political and social system Germany had suffered since his rise to power in 1933.*

There was, as we can see, a real problem of alternatives. In Catholic political philosophy, the maintenance of social and political order is an important component of the common good; and Hitler's Third Reich *as order* might have seemed preferable to the chaos that was likely to follow upon its defeat. Furthermore, Bolshevism, that archenemy of the Church, would certainly have been strengthened by a Hitler defeat. The advantage of distance and historical hindsight makes it easy for us to say that this only meant that Germany's Catholics were faced with a choice between a chaos of terror and a chaos of disorder, between a native-bred, antireligious totalitarianism and one of foreign origin. At the time, the matter was not as clear as that; therefore, it is possible to defend a preference for the Nazi order as a choice between alternatives with inescapable evils. But this would not explain actions which identified the interests of the Catholic Church with those of

* Hitler certainly recognized no validity to such a distinction between Germany and his Third Reich. The rejection of Pastor Niemöller's offer to resume his World War I submarine service makes it quite clear that, as far as the Nazis were concerned, an enemy of the Third Reich could not be entrusted with any role in what Galen and his fellow bishops saw as the defense of *Volk* and *Vaterland* as distinguished from the crusade for a new world order the Nazis intended it to be.

the Nazi regime. To call for support for Hitler's wars not as a thoroughly distasteful lesser evil but, instead, as a Christian duty, as a means of protecting Germany's and Western civilization's most cherished values, can only be viewed as a tragic distortion of traditional Catholic teachings—a distortion that must be traced, at least in part, to the emotional coloration engendered by excessively nationalistic leanings.*

Should it ever be established that World War II was an unjust war for all participants, this interpretation would of course have wider application. For the injustice pursued or protected by the enemy could not justify a pattern of behavior in which the Catholic bishops of all participating nations would call upon their followers to war with one another—and all in the name of a defense of the values most precious to men.

It follows, then, that focusing attention upon German Catholics and Hitler's wars, as this study has done, could easily lead to unfair interpretations if it did not call attention to parallel behavior exhibited by the Catholics of the other warring nations. If nationalism is or tends to become a heresy, it would be an error to restrict its influence to the Catholics of Nazi Germany. American Catholics and their bishops failed to take open issue with the officially proclaimed and morally questionable war aim of "unconditional surrender" despite the fact that Pius XII made no secret of his desire that an early and just peace be negotiated. Similarly, neither the spiritual leaders of American Catholicism nor their British counter-

* At this point a clarifying statement is in order. One must respect and give due honor to the men—Catholic or non-Catholic—who endured the dangers and hardships of military service and, in so many instances, sacrificed their lives in what they believed to be the performance of a moral obligation. If they were misled, if their sincere dedication to duty was in sad truth a contribution to an unjust war effort, the responsibility is not theirs. Some men, it is true, did violate their consciences by knowingly participating in what they believed to be an unjust war; but the intricately involved processes of human psychology are such that it is wiser to accord these men, if not the respect we give the others, at least the sobering recognition that whoever would presume to judge their actions can never be at all certain that he would not have done the same under the terror and oppression of Hitler's Third Reich.

parts distinguished themselves by protesting the inhuman strategic and terror bombings of civilian areas, a rather obvious violation of the conditions of the just war that destroyed most of Germany's major cities and culminated in the atrocities of Hiroshima and Nagasaki.

Even had the religious leaders of the nations ranged in combat against Hitler's Germany spoken out against these morally questionable acts, there is little reason to believe that the Catholics under their spiritual jurisdiction would have paid them much heed. The Catholic man-in-the-pew in New York or London was probably as little concerned about the morality of the means being employed by his nation's military leaders as was the Catholic man-in-the-pew in Berlin or Munich. For all of them, the question of the legitimacy of service in the armed forces—and, in most cases, of the acts such service might require them to perform—was largely settled by nothing more than the fact that their respective nations were at war. "Praise the Lord, and pass the ammunition"—so went the words of an American popular song. It is not too much to say that, had a situation ever developed in which one or the other activity had to be suspended, Americans, including American Catholics, would have kept the ammunition moving.

This extended discussion of nationalism and its effect upon the moral judgments of Catholics, both in Germany and in the other nations involved in World War II, may seem to have led us rather far afield. But such is not the case. For we have been probing into what is probably the heart of the whole research problem, the point of full convergence of the social-control and value-selection dimensions. Nationalism itself is, of course, merely another way of referring to what can be termed "the myths men kill by." Here, however, the reference is not so much to the specific myths and their contents as to their fusion into a more insistent unity. A mental cast results which governs how the individual addresses himself to the ranking of the competing values from which his choice must be made. Perhaps more important, it also determines whether or not the individual will recognize that other values exist or are relevant to the immediate situation in which he finds himself.

If we are justified at all in focusing attention upon German Catholics and their particular solution to the value-selection problem presented by Hitler's wars, the justification would lie in the assumption that, in their case, the value conflict was sharper and the opportunities for confusion fewer than was true for Catholics of other nations. American Catholics, too, may have been serving in an unjust war, but the circumstances were such that they could find stronger and more objectively demonstrable evidence to support their choice. Had the Pearl Harbor attack which brought formal involvement been the intentionally provoked "back door to war" some writers have claimed; had the American actions in support of one of the European belligerents and even overt acts against the other been as much a technical violation of the neutral and nonbelligerent status as were some of the violations of neutrality perpetrated by Nazi Germany—none of these could equal the clearly aggressive character of the Nazi assaults upon Poland, the Low Countries, and the Soviet Union, to cite only the more obvious instances. And if the issue was more clear-cut, if Hitler's wars did constitute the classic example of the unjust war, the fact that German Catholics supported those wars is startling testimony of the crucial importance of nationalism as a force controlling human behavior.

This reintroduces the question of the access to facts upon which the value selection would have to be based. If we consider merely the aspect referred to earlier, the Nazi control of propaganda and information channels and the restriction of *availability* of facts made possible by that control, one can argue that the German Catholic actually had less opportunity to doubt the justice of his nation's cause than did his American counterpart. In the United States, right up to the very beginning of the war, there was a strong and highly organized opposition to the "war-provoking" acts and policies of the Roosevelt administration; and the debate flourished in public meetings, in the press, on the radio, even in the halls of Congress. Such was not the case in Nazi Germany. There the citizen found nothing in his controlled press and radio but one-sided accounts of the provocations, insults, and indignities suffered by the

Third Reich at the hands of her jealous and vindictive neighbors. The other side of the story was available to them only in foreign broadcasts, and listening to these involved serious risks and penalties.*

But nationalism limits the access to facts in still another way by blocking the individual's *receptivity* to facts which might otherwise cause him to question the justice of his nation's cause. This takes the form of a selective perception in which one sees the atrocities perpetrated by the enemy but is blind to the same acts performed by the military forces of his own nation. It is manifested, too, in a refusal to accept purported facts which reflect adversely upon the nation and its cause. Thus, many who did listen to foreign broadcasts might have done so out of curiosity to see what kind of lies the enemy propagandist was circulating; even the listener disposed to believe or hope for the worst as far as the Nazi regime was concerned would perhaps be inclined to discount much of what he heard as being an exaggerated or otherwise distorted version of the facts. In either form, however, the limitation of the access to relevant facts associated with nationalistic commitment will certainly affect the solution the individual will reach in any value-selection problem involving his role as citizen of the national community.**

* In terms of individual moral responsibility—an issue excluded from the scope of this study—it could be argued that the German soldier who fought in support of Hitler's wars could claim innocence of any wrongdoing by virtue of the fact that he had little or no access to the true facts of the situation. But this, too, would be an effect of the social controls which were successful in blocking such access.

** Just as a bishop held an advantage over the ordinary Catholic, since his contacts through the Vatican to the outside world meant greater access to the facts in the sense of their availability, so the status he held in the supranational institution of the Church furnished him with the opportunity to free himself from the nationalistic limitations upon receptivity to those facts. His extensive training and "professional outlook"—to say nothing of the special graces associated with his sacramental consecration—might be expected to produce a more binding allegiance to such universalistic concepts as "the brotherhood of man under the common Fatherhood of God" and the Mystical Body of Christ, and a greater immunity against the more particularistic attitudes and responses associated with nationalism. One may hold, therefore, that the greater availability of information and the freer receptivity made possible by his responsible post in a higher institu-

It is the essence of a totalitarian sociopolitical order that all lesser groups and institutions, as well as the individual citizen, be reduced so far as is possible to mere agencies or tools of the monolithic nation-state. Family, school, youth groups, trade associations, labor unions—all find their responsibilities and their privileges spelled out for them entirely in terms of the part they can play in producing and forming the members of society according to whatever pattern may best suit the current needs or objectives of the ruling authority. Total regimentation of thought and action is made possible by the nation-state's mastery over the channels of information and communication to such degree that even the innermost sanctity and integrity of the human personality is denied and contravened. The totalitarian state brooks no competition; it admits of no limits to its own prerogatives.

This means that in such a sociopolitical order all the lesser organizations and institutions are forced to become channels through which the state can control their members in such a way as to assure the attainment of its ends and the extension and perpetuation of its hegemony. The family, the school, the youth group, the trade association, the labor union, and all similar agencies continue to exercise discipline and control over their members—but only to the extent that such discipline and control are permitted or delegated to it by the nation-state in furthering what it defines as its own paramount interests. In this formulation, the religious institution, too, finds itself forced to act as an agency of social control exerted on behalf of the totalitarian secular power.

What can be described so simply in theoretical statement is not

tion than the national state should have made it easier for him to encounter and recognize the evidence that Hitler's wars were unjust wars of aggression. And this, in turn, would have made it all the more imperative that this evidence be translated by him into pastoral instructions designed to give the faithful the spiritual guidance and support the situation demanded. Thus, we come back to the role and responsibility of the bishop as defined by Bishops von Hauck and von Galen; but their primarily theological formulation has been expanded to include some sociological consideration of the special advantages and responsibilities relating to the particular behavioral problem with which this study is concerned.

so easily established in the real order. Even Nazi Germany, which came close to the "ideal" described above, fell short of it. Certainly the continuing opposition of the Catholic Church, selective and restricted though the areas of opposition may have been, was an "imperfection"; for the mere idea that the Church, or any other institution of society, could claim a body of rights against the authority of the state is clearly contrary to the sociopolitical order fashioned according to the totalitarian ideal. But we should neither minimize nor exaggerate the degree of imperfection; for, even though it did hold its own against Hitler in some respects (or, at least, tried to do so), the Catholic Church did at least inadvertently serve the purposes of the Nazi regime to the extent that it formally recognized that regime as Germany's legitimate authority and placed its members under a moral obligation to render civil obedience to that regime. And when war came in 1939, this obligation to obey was given such repeated and fervent emphasis that we may justly conclude that, to all intents and purposes, the Church did become an agency of social control operating in behalf of the Nazi state insofar as insuring wholehearted Catholic support of the war was concerned.

The effect may certainly have exceeded the intention behind it. One must remember that when a bishop spoke, or when the editor of one of the few remaining Catholic periodicals selected some episcopal statement for prominent quotation, they necessarily had two audiences in mind. Most obvious, of course, was the listening or reading Catholic public; but at least equal importance had to be given to the Nazi censor or the Gestapo official who was also listening and reading. To have offended the latter audience would have meant (and often did mean) seriously endangering communication with the former. Thus the framers of Catholic opinion faced a true dilemma: either they could meet the standards set by the Nazis (which involved supporting the war and studiously avoiding all open criticism of the regime and its policies) or face the almost certain prospect of being silenced. That the former course was chosen is clearly demonstrated by the content and tone of the

Catholic publications during the war* and by the patriotic or morale-boosting appeals contained in the episcopal statements quoted in this study. Even if one were to grant that this was a pattern imposed by the circumstances of the time (and to ignore the strong internal evidence that these appeals also represented their authors' personal commitment), this would not lessen the validity of the principal conclusion that has been drawn: that, in World War II, the leading spokesmen of the Catholic Church in Germany did become channels of Nazi control over their followers, whether by their general exhortations to loyal obedience to legitimate authority or by their even more direct efforts to rally these followers to the defense of *Volk, Vaterland,* and *Heimat* as a Christian duty.

In this we have what is perhaps the most crucial element in the explanation of the "how" and the "why" of German Catholic support of Hitler's wars. It can be seen in terms of a massive pyramiding of formal and external social controls, supported and enhanced by the informal and internal controls. At the apex of the pyramid we find the power and authority of the Third Reich and its *Führer* operating upon all individuals and the lesser social institutions, now through exercise of legitimate police power, now through suppression by means of violence and terror or the threat of these. The ordinary Catholic German, at the base of this pyramid, was the object of these combined secular controls; and it may be assumed that these accounted for much, probably most, of his war-supporting behavior. But not all. For these formal, informal, external, and internal controls of the secular order were reinforced and supplemented by a parallel set of social controls operating within the religious community of which he was a part. Together these controls virtually produced an acceptance of conformity with

* The sensitive reader can often uncover evidence of between-the-lines opposition to Hitler and his policies (but not to Hitler's wars) in these periodicals, but to do this he must subject their content to intensive and systematic scrutiny. Only those already set in their opposition to Nazism would have been likely to seek or to find these subtle messages.

the demands of the war effort as, almost literally, the only course open.

And in the process the value-selection dimension of the problem all but disappeared, or so it would seem from the degree of conformity that did obtain. Actually, it is more reasonable to assume that individual Catholics may have faced the problem, that they may have been troubled from time to time with the suspicion that the war was not the "just war" of the theology handbooks; but neither the suspicion nor the behavior alternatives it might suggest were ever presented in such a way that there would be the likelihood of any substantial number choosing to follow the example of St. Martin of Tours. Certainly there was no institutional encouragement for such a choice or, for that matter, any support for those few who did make it. Some informants voiced the opinion that few Catholics gave any thought to the over-all justice of the war; for them, the value-selection problem did not exist except, perhaps, at the level of a subconscious avoidance of a responsibility to make some kind of an evaluation. Those who did think about the matter were usually described as recognizing the injustice of Hitler's wars but serving anyway—again the kind of surrender to social controls described in the preceding paragraph whether they were the formal controls acting upon the individual from without or the nationalistic sentiments operating as an inner imperative. The case of the officer who went off to war complaining because his duty required him to lead his men in an unjust cause would fit into this category. Few informants were willing to grant the possibility, but one may allow the possibility that some Catholics did consider the matter and conclude that the war was a just war; for them, too, there would be no selection problem, for the values of the secular and religious communities would then converge into a common support for something resembling a crusade. Finally, there were the very few who, after thinking about the problem, recognized the conflict of values arising from the injustice of the nation's cause and then chose what they regarded as obedience to God in preference to obedience to the unjust demands of the Nazi Caesar.

## NOTES

1. Watkin, *op. cit.*, p. 57.
2. See above, p. 78 n.
3. See above, pp. 56-57.
4. See above, pp. 28 ff.
5. *Volkstrauertag* address, November 13, 1960.
"Wer nicht völlig verblendet oder gänzlich unerfahren war, konnte nicht gänz frei sein von dem drückenden Bewusstsein, dass dieser Krieg kein gerechter Krieg war."
6. *Bayrische Kathölische Kirchenzeitung*, Vol. 11, No. 37 (September 15, 1935), p. 296.
"Verweist nun Ihr Amt als Bischof der katholischen Kirche Ihre Tätigkeit auf das Gebiet der Seelsorge, so sind doch die Ihrer geistlichen Führung anvertrauten Menschen zugleich deutsche Volksgenossen und Bürger des national-sozialistischen Staates. Die Beziehungen, die sich aus dieser Verbundenheit ergeben, brauchen, dürfen und sollen nicht im Gegensatz zueinanderstehen.
"Wir wollen es ruhig eingestehen, dass trotzdem gewisse Trübungen im Verhältnis zwischen Staat und Kirche zur Zeit bestehen. Eine Untersuchung darüber, wodurch sie entstanden sind, ist hier nicht am Platze, wohl aber möchte ich betonen, dass ich gerade darin die Aufgabe der verantwortlichen Männer in Staat und Kirche erblicke, diese Trübungen durch Achtung vor der gegenseitigen Ueberzeugung, durch das Vermeiden jeder unnötigen Schärfe und durch klares Erfassen der tatsächlichen Gegebenheiten zu überwinden. Wenn Sie, Herr Bischof, mit voller Aufgeschlossenheit für die Erfordernisse der Gegenwart die Treue zum neuen Staat und Führer und die Achtung vor seiner Obrigkeit unter Ihrem Klerus und Ihren Diözesanen pflegen, dann dürfen Sie versichert sein, dass die Reichs- und Staatsregierung jede Gewähr für die ungehinderte Religionsausübung übernimmt und volles Verständnis für die kirchlichen Bedürfnisse beweisen wird. . . ."
7. *Ibid.*, Vol. 12, No. 8 (February 23, 1936), pp. 60-61.
"Zum Hirtenwirken, Geliebteste, gehört vor allem die Ausübung des kirchlichen Lehramtes. Der Bischof ist der *eigentliche Lehrer* seiner Diözesanen. Er soll ihnen die heiligen und beseligenden Wahrheiten verkünden, die der Heiland einst gepredigt hat. Er soll sie zu immer grösserer Kenntnis und immer tieferem Verständnis der Heilswahrheiten führen. . . . Wie greift er weitschauenden Geistes gerade die Fragen auf, die die Zeit bewegen, nach deren Lösung das katholische Volk verlangt! Wie weiss er die törichten Zeitirrtümer, die gegen den Glauben anstürmen, in ihrer inneren Unwahrheit aufzuzeigen und wie klar und überzeugend sie zu widerlegen, auf

dass sie nicht Verwirrung stiften können in den Herzen des gläubigen Volkes. Danket eurem Oberhirten, dass er euch ein so eifriger, wirksamer Lehrer und Prediger der Wahrheit ist!"

8. *Ibid.,* Vol. 9, No. 48 (November 19, 1933), p. 380.

"Glaubt nicht, dass eure Bischöfe leichtfertig Mahnungen oder Warnungen aussprechen, ohne Erkenntnis der Verhältnisse, dass eure Bischöfe sorglos Gefahren übersehen, wenn sie nicht schweigen, während ihr nach Wegführung verlangt! Seid versichert: zentnerschwer lastet jeden Tag das Bewusstsein der Verantwortung für eure Seelen auf ihnen, und sie wissen, dass sie ihre eigenen Seelen nicht retten können, wenn sie zur Unzeit schweigen oder sprechen. Gern werde ich von anderen, auch von Laien, auch von wohlmeinenden Andersgläubigen Informationen über die Zeiterscheinungen, Wünsche und auch guten Rat annehmen. Aber ich weiss, dass die Pflicht zur Entscheidung über erforderliche Weisungen und Warnungen für meine Diözesanen auf mir allein und auf meinem Gewissen lastet und von niemand mir abgenommen werden kann. "Nicht Menschenlob, nicht Menschenfurcht" (*Nec laudibus, nec timore,* des Bischofs Wahlspruch) soll mich jemals hindern, diese Pflicht zu erfüllen! . . . Mag auch in einem Einzelfall der Bischof sich irren über die Notwendigkeit oder Zweckmässigkeit einer Anordnung, die zu erlassen er sich entscheidet, mag auch der Untergebene in einem Einzelfall eine bessere Einsicht in die Zeitlage und ihre Erfordernisse zu haben glauben als der für die Führung verantwortliche Bischof und darum berechtigt sein, in geziemender Weise sein Bedenken dem Bischof vorzutragen—, dennoch wollen wir niemals vergessen: wie der Papst in der Gesamtkirche und der Bischof in seiner Diözese für die Regierung der Kirche bestellt und verantwortlich ist, so sind ihrer Hirtensorge anvertrauten Gläubigen bestellt und verantwortlich für den Gehorsam in der Kirche. Euch in unbedingtem kindlichem Gehorsam gegen den obersten Hirten, den Vater, jederzeit mit gutem Beispiel voranzugehen, ist meine wie jedes katholischen Bischofs selbstverständliche Pflicht!"

9. Bierbaum, *op. cit.,* pp. 305-306.

"Der Bischof habe nicht untersucht, ob dieser Krieg gerecht oder ungerecht sei, und ihn, weil er unritterlich geführt worden sei, nur als unchristlich bezeichnet. Zu solchen und ähnlichen Kritiken an der Haltung von Clemens August ist zu sagen, dass der Bischof nicht ausdrücklich und namentlich zu allen Verletzungen der Gerechtigkeit seiner Zeit Stellung genommen hat. Hat er dadurch—nach theologischer Formulierung—per defectum gefehlt? Durfte ein Oberhirt z. B. auch schon 1939 den Krieg ausdrücklich als ungerecht brandmarken, ohne sich und die Kirche in Deutschland noch mehr zu gefährden, ganz abgesehen davon, dass ein Urteil über die Gerechtigkeit eines ausgebrochenen Krieges zu den schwierigsten Aufgaben des menschlichen Geistes gehört? Andrerseits darf in diesem Zusammenhang nicht übersehen werden, dass Clemens August öfter, auch während der Kriegszeit, an die Satzungen des Völkerrechts und an das göttliche Sittengesetz erinnerte und nach Möglichkeit sich bemühte, in der Leidenschaft des Kampfes der Stimme der Vernunft Gehör zu verschaffen. Man kann für sich selbst den Tod sogar dem Schein der Schwäche vorziehen, aber als Führer hat man die Pflicht zu fragen: ob solche Tapferkeit sich auch mit Klugheit vereinbaren lässt, die zu jeder Tugend gehört, und ob man nicht durch solches Verhalten zahllose Gläubige und die Kirche in eigenen Lande grösster Gefahr aussetzt."

10. E. Shils and M. Janowitz, "Cohesion and Disintegration in the Wehrmacht in World War II," *Public Opinion Quarterly*, Vol. XII (1948), pp. 280-315.

11. Friedrich Meinecke, *The German Catastrophe*, trans. by Sidney B. Fay (Cambridge: Harvard University Press, 1950), pp. 11-12.

12. Max H. Boehm, "Nationalism," in Edwin R. A. Seligman and Alvin Johnson, eds., *Encyclopedia of the Social Sciences*, rev. ed. (New York: Macmillan, 1933), Vol. 11, pp. 231-240.

13. See above, pp. 56-57.

14. *Amtsblatt für die Erzdiözese Freiburg*, No. 4 (May 12, 1945), p. 13. "In welcher Stimmung ich dieses Hirtenwort verfasse, kann wohl ein jeder sich denken, der mich mehr als nur oberflächlich kennt. Ich habe als deutscher Mann, trotz aller versteckten und öffentlichen Angriffe auf mich und aller seelisch zermürbenden Leiden der vergangenen Jahre, trotz wiederholter schwerster Drohungen der früheren Machthaber für die Zeit nach dem Krieg immer *ehrlich deutsch* empfunden. . . ."

15. Bierbaum, *op. cit.*, p. 256. "Gestern haben die ersten Truppen unserer Kriegsgegner unseren Ort durchzogen. Wir wollen Gott danken, dass diese Stadt auch dabei noch, wie in der bisherigen langen Kriegszeit, keinen grösseren Schaden erlitten hat. Aber wie mir, so wird es auch allen, jedem Deutschen, ein erschütterndes Erlebnis gewesen sein und eine traurige Erinnerung bleiben, was der gestrige Karsamstag uns gebracht hat: der Anblick der durchziehenden Truppen unserer Kriegsgegner hier in unserer Heimat, im deutschen Land. Es ist heute nicht der Zeitpunkt, und es ist hier nicht der Ort, darüber zu sprechen, wie bitter uns dies Geschehen ist und wie unsere Herzen bluten bei der Not unseres Volkes."

16. Strobel, *op. cit.*, pp. 59-60.

# CHAPTER 12

# Sociotheological Implications

IT COULD BE SAID that, as a sociologist, the author has reached the goal set at the beginning of the study. As a Catholic, however, he finds himself impelled to turn, however briefly, to some of the more demanding sociotheological implications of these findings. For one thing, it should not be a matter of indifference that a value-selection problem which should have arisen did not arise or, if it did, was so easily and decisively resolved in favor of the values of the secular order. Nor can we be content merely to present the obvious fact that the copybook cases and abstract formulae which form so significant a part of the just-war teachings proved to be of little or no value to the Church in Germany (and the world, for that matter) when it was suddenly faced with the challenge of history's most total and most brutal war.

If there is a legitimate distinction to be made between the just war and the unjust war, it should be possible to recognize the one or the other, so that the individual may govern his behavior accordingly. If the definition or the application of the just-unjust distinction is so flexible or obscure that such recognition must be reserved for a post-factum analysis, there is a real danger that this most crucial area of moral theology may lose all relevance to the actuality of modern warfare and become little more than a useless academic exercise. By the same token, if this distinction does not give rise to a moral obligation on the part of the Christian to refuse all participation in the unjust war, there is very little point in bothering to make the distinction in the first place.

In its more sociological formulation, the issue may be summarized as follows: (a) the institution of the Roman Catholic Church incorporates a system of values which it claims are supernatural, supranational, and unchangeable; (b) the individual Catholic, through Baptism and Confirmation, assumes a responsibility to live and act according to those values, whatever his nationality, whatever the price such adherence might entail; (c) since that value system includes provision for a just war defined according to a set of specific and rigorous conditions, it would necessarily imply the possibility of an unjust war which does not meet these conditions; (d) the existence of these dichotomous categories would seem to require that actual wars, and especially modern total war, are to be put to the test of the conditions of the just war; (e) if modern total war in general, or any given war in particular, fails to meet this test, the individual Catholic is to be expected to refuse to co-operate with the evil of an unjust war; and (f) in such event, the Church must marshal whatever social controls it has at its command to assure conformity to its value system on the part of its members, even though such conformity may conflict with the behavior required by other value systems, including those associated with the preservation of national or personal survival.

Cardinal Faulhaber's stirring call for a new ethic of war, to which attention was called in an earlier chapter, is relevant here. As he saw it, moral theology would develop a new language which would take important new facts into account while remaining true to its unchanging and unchangeable principles. In retrospect, we can see that the Cardinal was wrong in placing too much confidence in advances in communications technology as a means of guaranteeing continued peace; instead, the shrinking globe has learned that the reverse is more often true, that these advances have made it possible for any nation to develop dangerous and immediate enmities with other nations formerly far removed from its network of associations and to subject them (or be subjected by them) to total destruction and devastation in a matter of hours or even less.

If he was over-optimistic here, the experiences of World War II more than vindicated his prediction that the advance in war technology would produce a situation in which war consumed itself, destroying victor and vanquished alike. Unfortunately, this new fact, too, did not then bring about (and still has not brought about) the absolute renunciation of war he thought it would. And since the end of that war, the even newer facts of atomic and hydrogen war have given further emphasis to his position by raising serious doubts as to whether, even in terms of abstract theoretical possibility, any future general or world war can be expected to meet the strict conditions of the theologian's just war.

Should it develop that they cannot be met, serious consideration must be given to the possibility that the new language of theology must now address itself to the task of preparing Catholics to assume their most likely obligation, that of refusing to participate in the unjust war. This clearly would involve a reversal of emphasis and direction from those prevailing until now—in Nazi Germany as we have seen in some detail and in all other nations as well—under which Catholics have been prepared and counseled to give the benefit of every doubt to the secular authority and, in effect, presume that any war in which they were called to take part was a just war.

For it may well be that the most crucial new fact of all is one that the Cardinal failed to see: the rise of the modern secular state with its own demanding system of values often antithetical in content to those of the Church, and its own and highly effective social controls to enforce compliance with those values. Traditional Catholic thinking on war has usually tended to favor the state and its interests; this has often led to the *Gehorsam* mentality, an automatic and unquestioning submission to legitimate authority, which, in the opinion of one informant, was a factor contributing to German Catholic support for Hitler's unjust wars. This tendency receives formal expression in the granting of the presumption of justice to the state and its rulers in cases where the individual Catholic citizen is in doubt as to the legitimacy of a war—a teaching which, in effect, directs the citizen to resolve or suspend any moral doubts in favor of the state and its interests. An American theologian has recently given this teaching renewed expression in an article in which he declares that "in the practical order, for the ordinary citizen, it seems to me that Catholic theology demands obedience to legitimate civil authority unless the command is certainly unjust; that in doubtful matters the presumption favors legitimate authority."[1] Such a principle might conceivably hold some validity in the ideal state ruled by the "Christian prince" as he appears in the abstractions of political philosophy; but the history of war reveals that it is not really much help in the practical order when the secular ruler happens to be a Hitler, a Stalin, or even a political pragmatist of the Roosevelt-Churchill-Truman variety. It is significant, perhaps, that those who so freely promulgate this principle never seem inclined to spell out its obvious implications: that Catholics will forever be "obligated" to fight and kill fellow members of the Mystical Body just so long as the warring governments on both sides of every conflict are accorded this presumption of justice.

One of the most important sociotheological implications of the present study, then, is the need for reassessment of the relationship of the religious institution to the institution of the modern secular state—a reassessment in which the long-dominant tone of almost automatic support for the legitimate authority and its programs would be replaced by a tone of cautious reserve and, in case of war, even suspicion. It cannot be denied that the German Catholic experience in Hitler's Third Reich clearly demonstrates that a too eager or too close indentification of the Church with the authority of the state and its interests has tragic consequences. Although Pius XI was later to speak of the serious misgivings he had at the time, the Vatican's haste in extending recognition to the newly established Nazi regime offers further evidence of a sometimes uncritical effort to create a Church-state relationship of mutual support leading to a virtually complete interpenetration of the religious and civil obligations of the individual. That co-operation and some degree of mutual support between these two great social institutions are highly desirable and even essential to the proper functioning of both is beyond question; but it is also to be recognized that attempts to formalize such relationships often create a situation which benefits the secular authority at the expense of the religious community and the purity of its value system. Such was the case in Nazi Germany, it is maintained here, during and to some extent even before the years of World War II.*

* The issue of the Concordat and its effect upon subsequent events is a subject of much controversy. Franz von Papen in his *Memoirs* (London: Deutsch, 1952) reports that Pius XII felt as late as 1945 that the Concordat had spared the Church in Germany from greater persecutions than those it actually suffered under Hitler. Robert Leiber, S.J., in a significant article ("Reichskonkordat und Ende der Zentrumspartei," *Stimmen der Zeit,* Vol. 86, No. 3 [December 1960], pp. 213-223), takes issue with recently published analyses which interpret the dissolution of the Catholic Center Party as something of a price exacted by Hitler for the willingness to conclude a concordat. In rejecting these interpretations, Leiber declares that the Concordat negotiations were initiated by the Nazi regime and that the Vatican had little choice but to acccept this as a request in good faith, especially since it coincided with its own intention of putting the welfare of the Church in Germany under the protection of an internationally recognized formal treaty. There is no desire here to enter into this controversy, but the present author would insist that the effects favorable to the Nazi regime were much more certain and much more immediate than those hoped for by the Vatican parties to the agreement. The August 20, 1935 Fulda statement of the combined German hierarchy mentions some of these in quite specific terms. Protesting the campaign being directed against the Papacy by some Nazi organizations, the bishops reminded Hitler of the fact that Pius XI had been "the first foreign sovereign to extend to you the handclasp of trust." Furthermore, the bishops noted, the Pope in open consistory on March 13, 1933—that is, before the Concordat negotiations were opened—had praised Hitler in the presence of representatives of other nations as the first statesman to join him in open disavowal of Bolshevism. As the bishops put it, "Millions of foreigners, Catholics and non-Catholics, found it possible to overcome through this evidence of the Pope's trust their original mistrust of your regime" (Neuhäusler, *op. cit.,* pp. 83-84). If such effect were produced outside of Germany, one must assume that the papal actions had at least equal impact as far as the German Catholics themselves and their attitudes toward the National Socialist regime were concerned.

The problem, of course, is larger than that of the Church in the Third Reich. The idea that the Church as a temporal social institution can accommodate itself to any regime which affirms its willingness to respect Church property and prerogatives seems almost to have become an unchallengeable truism in Catholic political philosophy. Even the modern papal encyclicals, especially those of Leo XIII dealing with the then emergent democratic and republican regimes, make much of the distinction between the *form* of government (a matter of little or no moral concern) and the divine source of the government's *authority* (by which the Christian is committed to its support, whatever form it may take). The tragic history of the rise and reign of modern totalitarianism, of which Hitler's Third Reich was only one version, suggests that the time has come to subject this truism to more careful consideration.

Certainly, from the standpoint of the temporal needs of the Church as a social institution, the truism has proved highly functional. The accommodation pattern enables the highly bureaucratized social institution to preserve its authority within the scope defined by the accommodation agreement; to protect its property and continue those services and functions it considers most essential; and, perhaps most important, to spare its members the difficult conflict of conscience which would arise from the Church's refusal to accommodate itself to the secular power and also spare them persecution that might be directed against them as reprisal against any such refusal. The latter gain can be stated, too, in another way, in terms which might be even more meaningful to the bureaucratized social institution: accommodation is functional because it safeguards the religious institution against the probable defection of great numbers of Church members who would most likely choose to resolve such a conscience conflict in favor of the secular power.

As a point of fact, this reasoning was frequently encountered in the course of interviews as an explanation of and justification for the failure of the Catholic Church in Germany to make a total break with the Nazi regime. The speedy conclusion of the Concordat and the failure on the part of Rome to abrogate that Concordat even after the full extent of Nazi excesses became known or suspected were also explained in those terms. The opinion attributed to Pius XII—that the Concordat, however personally distasteful it may have been to him, had spared the Church in Germany a far greater measure of hardship and persecution than that actually suffered by it during the Nazi years—was undoubtedly true.

However, there is another side to the question which must be considered: the possibility that certain regimes—including present-day totalitarian states—may be intrinsically evil or that the evils they perpetrate may so outweigh the legitimate acts they perform that accommodation of any kind could be, at the very least, a matter of scandal and might even constitute an active, however incidental, collaboration with evil. In such a case, it might be held that such accommodation would be proscribed by the very nature of the Church as a divinely instituted guardian and dispenser of spiritual good. This writer is fully aware that anyone who would question the prudence of the Concordat with Hitler, or the maintenance of the formal official niceties on the part of the German hierarchy with a regime that was quite obviously dedicated to the ultimate destruction of the Church and its values, is usually accused of being over-superficial and naïve (or, what is apparently the most serious of all possible charges, "too idealistic").

The question, nevertheless, must be posed. Is it enough for the leadership of any national segment of the *Catholic* Church to limit its concern to its own institutional interests or the personal welfare of its own membership? In Nazi Germany the areas of open Catholic resistance were almost exclusively those directly affecting such interests and concerns: the secularization of religious schools; the closing of convents and the confiscation of their properties; suppression of Catholic organizations and arrests of their leaders and members; interferences with pastoral functions and activities; the official promulgation of a consciously anti-Christian neopaganism, and associated pressures upon those who aspired to civil service to renounce their membership in the Church. All of these may be viewed as self-centered concerns of the Church as a bureaucratized

social institution; only the heroic resistance to the infamous euthanasia program and the more direct Nazi assaults upon traditional
family values went beyond these self-centered interests to a more
general level of moral concern.

But let us, for the moment, consider a hypothetical situation. Assuming that the Nazis had faithfully adhered to the letter and the
spirit of the Concordat and had respected all the defined areas of
Church responsibility and prerogative, would it then have been altogether proper for the Church to accommodate itself to the Nazi
regime? Had these issues around which resistance centered not been
present, would it have been permissible for German Catholics and
their spiritual leaders to support the Third Reich despite its aggressions against other groups and against some of the most vital rights
of the human person? Or did the Church have broader responsibilities than the preservation of some measure of material well-being
and security for itself and its members? It is difficult to imagine that
the Church leadership could ever have taken much satisfaction in
knowing that Catholic churches and services were unmolested at
the same time that synagogues were being burned and Jews de-
ported. Nor would there be much merit in an accommodation which
found Catholics actually granted a full measure of civil liberty
under the terms of a protecting Concordat, while men of other
faiths and even unbelievers were filling the concentration camps and
suffering all the insecurities of a "form of government" which
placed complete and arbitrary power in the hands of a tyrant-dicta-
tor, supported by the total mobilization and control of all informa-
tional and educational media, and enforced by a nationwide
network of secret police who were freed from all the recognized
judicial and procedural restraints by which the basic rights of the
human person are preserved. Indeed, the counteraccusation might
well be directed against those who would still maintain that the
Church as a social institution can or should accommodate itself to
such a form of government that *they* are too superficial, too naïve,
too uncritically dedicated to the standards of "practical reality."

An example more directly pertinent to the social-control framework of the present study may be offered here. A German bishop, speaking in justification of the stand taken by the wartime hierarchy, described a conversation he had relatively early in the Nazi period with a priest who had emigrated to Switzerland because he could not bring himself to begin his sermons with the Nazi salute.* The Bishop went on to say that he had posed the question to this priest: What would he have done had he known that refusal to give the salute would have jeopardized the Christian education of five million Catholic children? The question is of course extremely pertinent; but the answer is perhaps a bit more involved than the narrator realized, either at the time he posed it to the priest or later when he described the exchange to the present writer. The sociologist would hold that the mere act of giving a Nazi salute must also be regarded as a form of education; and, to the extent that it symbolized an accommodation to the Hitler regime, it represented a part of a broader educational context which in itself could serve to jeopardize the "Christian education" of the children who received that education within that context of accommodation to an essentially unchristian regime. For—and this is the crucial sociological fact that is all too often ignored but which is fully documented by the present study—*to the extent that the Church does accommodate itself to a secular regime, it becomes, in effect, an agent of that regime, supplementing the secular controls with those of the spiritual order.*

The great stress placed in the Catholic value system upon obedience to the legitimate secular authority has already been discussed in Chapter 3, as has its ideological link to the scriptural instruction to "give back to Caesar what is Caesar's." But, in the context of role analysis, it is altogether proper to raise the question whether, even in the light of this scriptural source, this obedience should become the major concern of religious leaders and teachers, or whether these roles should require a more primary concern for the

---

* It should be noted here, however, that this practice was not at all general, although it was customary, even for priests, to comply with the required "German greeting" in ordinary social interaction.

need to prepare the members of the religious community so that they are always ready to reject any excessive demands Caesar might make. Certainly such a responsibility is imposed by the remainder of the Gospel instruction to "give back to God what is God's." One might insist that the present study has revealed a pressing need for any "new ethic" of war to develop and incorporate some safeguards that will make it less likely that Catholic spiritual leaders and spokesmen, whatever their nationality, will ever again be forced into a moral dilemma which finds them assuming the role of a recruiting agent rallying the Catholic faithful to serve in an objectively unjust war as a fulfillment of their moral obligations.

This crucial problem demands much more study and careful analysis before the lessons of the tragic past are fully learned. In this connection, a postwar statement by the bishops of the state of North Rhine-Westphalia assumes a disturbing significance when viewed in the context of Catholic support for Hitler's wars; for it reveals a tragic failure to read the lessons of recent history. Addressing themselves to a political controversy over a proposed nuclear arming of West Germany, the bishops are reported to have issued a formal statement declaring, "No Catholic is bound in conscience, on the basis of Catholic teaching, to reject defensive measures that the majority of responsible politicians consider necessary to the present situation."[2] The statement itself, couched as it is in negative terms, is not as disturbing as are its underlying premises. For, while it does not go to the extreme position held by Gröber when he virtually denied the Catholic any right to oppose such measures on the grounds of moral teachings, this statement does imply a surrender of what is essentially a moral judgment to "the majority of responsible politicians." All the atrocities of World War II—whether visited upon Hiroshima and Hamburg or upon the populations of nations victimized by the Axis Powers—would have been described as "necessary to the present situation" by the men considered "responsible politicians" by the general public. With specific reference to the situation in Hitler's Third Reich, it would certainly have taken little more than the 1939 *Te Deum* in the Munich cathedral to convince the ordinary German Catholic that the *Führer* was, as his title proclaimed, the responsible political leader empowered to make such decisions. The present study has established the need for a contemporary reformulation of the question of obedience to the secular authority and its limits; the 1958 statement of the bishops cited here may be taken as evidence of the extreme urgency of that need.

Another critical question arising from the study concerns the self-image the individual Catholic might be expected to have in a time of moral crisis of the dimensions presented by the Nazi demands during World War II. Certainly the repudiation of individual responsibility implied in Gröber's statement delegating to the secular authority the ultimate decision as to whether a war is just or unjust deserves to be challenged. It is now clear that the shortsightedness and emotionalism which supposedly rendered the individual incapable of such decision may now be seen as far less serious a hazard than the Machiavellian standards of action subscribed to by the modern state in the game of international power politics. Indeed, one might properly suggest that this decision must, in the final analysis, be left to the informed Christian conscience. To do so would not only remove the responsible judgment from the area of state prerogative, but it would also imply a rather drastic restatement of the role of episcopal authority.

This change would reflect a new awareness and recognition on the part of bishop and flock alike that bishops, too, are men; that they, too, are not immune to the distorting effects of shortsightedness and emotionalism—to say nothing of the additional temptations arising from institutional concerns and needs. Out of this recognition could develop a new assessment of their role vis-à-vis the faithful assigned to their pastoral care. This would not be, of course, a role implying an equality of competence; for it must be recognized that the bishop's more extensive education and training, his greater access to the relevant facts, and the special sacramental gifts and guidance which are his will always give him advantages not available to the ordinary Catholic. He is and must continue to be recognized as the shepherd of his spiritual flock. But his followers are sheep only in a figurative sense and should not be expected to manifest, even to him, a kind of docile and uncritical obedience that would be unworthy of their nature as free, rational, and responsible human beings.* A new note of episcopal restraint could regard the function of the bishop as one in which he, as shepherd, would clearly and openly set forth the moral principles governing a given behavioral situation, and call upon the faithful to make a personal and responsible application of these principles in determining for themselves how they are to act. This does not deny in the least that there are some areas of human behavior in which the application as well as the principle is specifically defined as dogma, and others (such as those relating to the proscription of artificial birth control, for example) in which the relation to dogmatic teachings is quite direct; in such areas, the bishops and other teachers of the Church are obliged to be explicit in requiring or forbidding certain patterns of behavior. However, in other areas—and the morality of war would seem to be one such—care and restraint would be in order, so that explicit episcopal directives are restricted to only

---

* The issue of the nature and extent of the obedience to a religious superior is extremely important; it is, unfortunately, an area of considerable confusion. Much serious thought and writing are being devoted to the subject. An extremely valuable contribution is the article by Karl Rahner, S.J., "Reflections on Obedience," *Cross Currents*, Vol. X, No. 4 Winter 1960), pp. 363-374. Father Rahner writes: "It might here be in place to recognize that morality and spontaneous moral judgment have a greater function than is ordinarily supposed. The command of a superior may be objectively sinful, and if recognized as such by the inferior it should not be put into execution." And again: "Do we avoid talking about such possibilities out of the fear of evils produced by the conscientious objector, and so act as if something of this kind practically never occurs? But is not the consequent evil caused to conscience greater than the utility of a frictionless functioning of external government requiring of subjects a literal obedience to commands? Even the subject has the duty in conscience of examining the moral admissibility of what has been commanded. The just 'presumption' that the command of a superior is not only subjectively but also objectively morally unobjectionable does not constitute a simple dispensation from the essential obligation of every man to attain to moral certitude in regard to the free action he is about to perform. This action is no less his own, and no less one for which he will be responsible, just because it is commanded."

those matters which are clearly established in the doctrinal or dogmatic core of Catholic teachings (such as, perhaps, the condemnation of specific acts of war: the killing of the innocent, reliance upon intentional falsehood or the distortion of truth in propaganda, direct appeals to national or racial hatreds, and so on). And, needless to add, whenever the bishop has access to information necessary to the proper formation of the Christian conscience, he would have a manifest obligation to communicate such information to his flock.

Thus far this discussion of the sociotheological implications of the study has focused upon the determination of the justice or injustice of a given war and the scope of individual competence and responsibility in making such determination. Some attention must now be devoted to the other side of the coin: the behavioral consequences of this determination and the extent to which the social controls of the Church may be required to induce and maintain conformity to them. This discussion up to this point has presupposed a willingness on the part of the individual to assume full moral responsibility for his actions. It has also been assumed that he would be willing and prepared to make any sacrifice in meeting that responsibility. Neither of these assumptions, however, should be taken for granted.

At the behavioral level the value system of the religious community faces a serious challenge, which arises in part from a weakening tendency in its own theological structure. For some time Catholic moral teachings have displayed a tendency to develop and even emphasize "reasonable" applications of seemingly unreasonable demands posed by certain moral principles in their literal statement. This is in rather sharp contrast to the earlier ages of the Church's history, which were marked by an almost crude literalism in the moral evaluation and choice of behavior patterns. More recent eras have seen the direction of moral thought change somewhat, have seen the stringency of the moral imperatives moderated. The *contemptus mundi,* so important a part of earlier Christian thought, has seemed to give way to a "more balanced" or "reasonable" or "practical" approach which places its stress on coming to terms with "the world." This is not to suggest that there has been any compromising change of basic principle; instead, it reflects the coming into prominence of the kind of moral theology which is almost completely concerned with finding the permissive loopholes and charting the outermost limits of sin—this development taking place at the expense of an ascetic theology which would emphasize instead the search for new and more direct routes to the fullness of the Christian experience. Modern Catholics have taken the "principle of the double effect" so much to heart that they are in danger of succumbing completely to the lure of the lesser evil. Their counterparts of the Age of Martyrs were not particularly noted for any comparable facility in making hairsplitting distinctions or for balancing the scope of legitimate Roman authority against the sacrilegious or otherwise immoral demands of the state. Their refusal to cast the pinch of incense upon a pagan altar stone was a simple and unequivocal decision and act. The modern Christian, in contrast, apparently finds it impossible to reach a similarly clear and unequivocating moral judgment about dropping a hydrogen bomb upon a helpless city.

These early Christians became martyrs—or, at least, some of them did. The absence of adequate data on Church membership at that time makes it impossible to estimate the proportion who died for their Faith, but one has the impression that it would have exceeded that of the Nazi period in Germany. Part of the explanation for any such difference would be attributable to the fact that more explicit controls were brought into play by the early religious community. Along with the trend toward a more "reasonable" application of religious requirements and prohibitions, there has been a drastic reduction in the severity of sanctions employed by the Catholic community to enforce moral obligations and to punish deviance. The spiritual direction the early Christians encountered, at least as it is reflected in something like the body of literature associated with the Apostolic Fathers, was more ascetical in tone and leaves the impression of insistent warning against being "conformed" to the world.

In such a context one would expect to find a greater willingness to accept and even welcome martyrdom; for martyrdom would be regarded as the always possible, often probable, price one had to pay for being part of the Christian community. This attitude does not distinguish the Christian of our day. One is often tempted to conclude that the greatest commandment of all in the presently prevailing Christian hierarchy of values is not the love of one's fellow man out of love of God but, rather, the law of self-preservation. The avoidance of martyrdom, not the expectation of martyrdom, has become the rule. Indeed, as we have seen, Father Metzger's sacrifice was dismissed as folly by a theologian who declared that one has no right to follow a course of action certain to lead to his own destruction. Perhaps an even more significant discussion of Catholic attitudes toward the German resistance to Hitler as set in terms of moral virtues is Bierbaum's recollection that

At that time there soon developed a secret resistance in Germany which fought the slowly mounting tyranny, not without bravery but more in the sign of prudence; to avoid bringing the Gestapo down upon himself, one spoke and wrote in imagery and symbols. This went so far in those times that people held—even in religious circles—that "while Prudence is, of course, not the only cardinal virtue, it was viewed as being so cardinal that Fortitude was not given the place it deserved—so much that, not only was there no call for martyrs issued, but martyrs were actually not wanted." [3]

This quotation refers more directly to the question of a political resistance to the totalitarian regime, but it obviously has a meaning which would carry over to such a decision as the willingness or refusal to take part in Hitler's wars of aggression.

But the really important point is not that German Catholicism failed to produce a wave of martyrs refusing such service. A far more important sociotheological implication of this study is that the same failure would have been evidenced by the Catholics of every nation. Taking a cue from the almost total and generally unquestioning support given by Catholics to America in World War

II, despite the questionable means employed and the doubtful justice of unconditional surrender as a war aim, one may grant the probability that, had Hitler, his regime, and his wars been American phenomena, the behavior of Germany's Catholics would have been duplicated here. Perhaps the enthusiasm would have been less evident, for the cultural background of submission to a militaristic code of values would have been lacking; but the essential commitment would have been just as thorough and just as sincere. One need only cite the absence of any concerted Catholic protest against America's atomic bombings of Japan (and, for that matter, to the continuing stress placed on this weapon and its even more terrible successors in postwar military planning) to show that there is little or no compulsion to submit these policies or their implications to the test of a strict application of moral principles. And, be it noted, Americans were not, and are not, in the situation faced by the German Catholic in which opposition to such policies would have been an invitation to martyrdom.

One need not be a pacifist to hold that every war represents a failure of Christianity in the sense that Christians have not converted the world to their gospel of peace. World War II, thus far the most extensive orgy of fratricide and self-destruction in which the peoples of the world have indulged, was certainly such a failure. And if this failure can most clearly be seen in the support given by German Catholics to Hitler's wars, as this study has held, it presents a real challenge to the theologian to analyze that failure and to discover the weaknesses in the traditional formulation and application of the Catholic morality of war that made such a failure possible.

This is not a matter of raking over dead ashes or reopening old wounds. It is an opportunity to learn from the past and to prepare for the future in the hope that, should it ever have to face the challenge of another world conflict, Christianity will not fail again. This is where the theologian and the sociologist can and must find a common area of discourse. For, just as the sociologist who would ignore the moral dimensions of social behavior (or, to put it another way, the influence of religious values in determining the patterns of human social action) would thereby reveal himself ill-equipped even to approach a satisfactory performance of his scholarly task, just so would the theologian who sought to make his applications of moral principles to problems rooted in social reality without first attending to the social scientist's analysis of that reality find himself helpless in the face of the most vital challenges of the day. If this mutual exchange has not yet developed, the fault lies with both parties. It is to be hoped that this study and its findings may offer the occasion for joining forces in attacking a moral and behavioral problem that should rank second to none in its importance to the Catholic in the modern world.

*NOTES*

1. John J. Farraher, S.J., "Notes on Moral Theology," *Theological Studies,* Vol. 21, No. 4 (December 1960), p. 593.

2. *New York Times,* June 30, 1958, 6:8.

3. Bierbaum, *op. cit.,* p. 215.

"Es gab damals schon bald einen geheimen Widerstand in Deutschland, der nicht ohne Tapferkeit, aber mehr im Zeichen der Klugheit gegen die langsam aufsteigende Tyrannis kämpfte; man vermied es, sich dem Zugriff der Gestapo auszusetzen, man redete und schrieb in geschichtlichen Bildern und Symbolen. Das ging so weit, dass man in jener Zeit—auch in kirchlichen Kreisen—'die Klugheit zwar nicht für die einzige Kardinaltugend ansah, aber doch so kardinal, dass sie die Tapferkeit nicht genügend zu ihrem Recht kommen liess—so sehr, das Märtyrer nicht nur nicht aufgerufen, sondern vielen sogar unerwünscht waren.' "

# Bibliographical Note

FOR OBVIOUS REASONS the limited focus of the present study would ordinarily restrict a bibliography to the source materials employed and to references relating to the social-control and value-selection frames of reference. However, in view of the fact that this work will undoubtedly find a place in the growing body of literature dealing with the position of the Catholic Church in Germany vis-à-vis the National Socialist regime, it has been deemed advisable to include a few of the more important books and articles dealing with that broader area of historical concern. Thus, Part I of this bibliographical note will be concerned with the references most directly pertaining to this study, and Part II will expand upon this to include the second type of references.

## Part I

The most important source materials employed in the study were the official diocesan journals, or *Amtsblätter* (published as sources of information and instruction for the clergy of each diocese), and the general diocesan newspapers, or *Kirchenzeitungen* (published for the guidance and instruction of the laity). The former continued to appear—though only at irregular intervals toward the end of the war—throughout the Nazi period. The latter were progressively reduced and controlled by the Nazi authorities until, early in the war years, they were eliminated altogether. All the wartime issues of both categories of periodicals listed here which could be obtained through the interlibrary loan services by the library of the Julius Maximilian Universität in Würzburg were reviewed in this research: *Amtsblatt für die Erzdiözese Freiburg (Br.)*; *Amtsblatt für die Erzdiözese München-Freising; Amtsblatt für die Diözese Münster; Bayrische Katholische Kirchenzeitung; Katholische Kirchenzeitung für die Basilika Skt. Gereon (Köln)*; *Kirchlicher Anzeiger für die Erdiözese Köln; Klerusblatt; Münchener Katholische Kirchenzeitung; Würzburger Diözeseanblatt; Verordnungsblatt des katholischen Feldbischofs der Wehrmacht*. In addition to these, unbound pastoral letters issued by *Feldbischof* Rarkowski, as well as a copy of the *Katholisches Gesangbuch* prepared by Chaplain Felix Gross and published "with the permission of the Catholic Military Bishop" (Berlin, 1939), were made available to the researcher.

A more extensive development of the social control concept may be found in Richard T. LaPiere, *A Theory of Social Control* (New York: McGraw-Hill, 1954). Somewhat less satisfactory textbook presentations are: Morroe Berger and others, *Freedom and Control in Modern Society* (New York: Van Nostrand, 1954); L. L. Bernard, *Social Control in Its Sociological Aspects* (New York: Macmillan, 1939); and Joseph Roucek, *Social Control* (Princeton: Van Nostrand, 1956).

Particularly valuable insights into the internal social controls described in Chapter 3, especially as relating to the "myths" discussed there, can be obtained from Howard Becker, *German Youth: Bond or Free?* (London: Kegan Paul, Trench, Trubner, 1946).

The value-selection frame of reference centers, of course, upon the question of nationalism and the Catholic morality of war, especially as the latter relates to the scope of the obligations of the

Catholic citizen and the legitimacy of Catholic conscientious objection. The following references range from "pacifist" approaches
(Fleischer, Ude) to at least one (Schöllgen) which utterly rejects
that approach. Included, too, are some of the standard works dealing with the subject of nationalism:

Aufhauer, Johann B., and others, *Das Gewissen Ruft!* Munich,
Verlag Josef Mayr, n.d.

Baron, Salo Wittmayer, *Modern Nationalism and Religion*. New
York, Meridian Books, 1960.

Emanuel, Cyprian, O.F.M., *The Morality of Conscientious Objection to War*. Washington, Catholic Association for International
Peace, 1941.

Eppstein, John, *The Catholic Tradition of the Law of Nations*.
London, Burns, Oates & Washbourne, 1935.

Fleischer, Johannes, *Das fünfte Gebot*. Donaueschingen, Katholisches Friedensbüro, 1955.

Gröber, Konrad, *Kirche, Vaterland und Vaterlandsliebe*. Freiburg,
Herder, 1935.

———, *Handbuch der religiösen Gegenwartsfragen*. Freiburg,
Herder, 1937.

Hayes, Carlton J. H., *Nationalism: A Religion*. New York, Macmillan, 1960.

Hirschmann, Johannes B., S.J., "Zur Diskussion um die Wehr-
dienstpflicht," *Stimmen der Zeit*, Vol. 159 (December 1955),
pp. 203-216.

Kohn, Hans, *Nationalism: Its Meaning and History*. New York,
Van Nostrand, 1956.

Laros, M., *Was Ist Zu Tun?* Dülmen, Verlag Laumann, n.d.

———, *Gott und der Krieg,* Dülmen, Verlag Laumann, n.d.

Lorson, Pierre, S.J., *Wehrpflicht und christliches Gewissen*. Frankfurt, Verlag Josef Knecht, 1952.

Meisner-Peuler, *Der junge Mensch und seine Ehre*. Dülmen, Verlag
Laumann, n.d.

Nagle, William J., ed., *Morality and Modern Warfare*. Baltimore,
Helicon, 1960.

Peuler, Wilhelm, *Die Jungen und der Krieg*. Dülmen, Verlag Laumann, n.d.

Schöllgen, Werner, *Ohne Mich, Ohne Dich*. Salzburg, 1951.

Shafer, Boyd C., *Nationalism: Myth and Reality*. New York, Harcourt, Brace, 1955.

Stratmann, Franziskus, O.P., *Weltkirche und Weltfriede*. Augsburg, burg, Haas und Grobherr Verlag, 1924.

————, *Krieg und Christentum Heute*. Trier, Paulinus Verlag, 1950.

Thompson, Charles S., ed., *Morals and Missiles*. London, James Clarke & Co., 1959.

Ude, Johannes, *Du sollst nicht töten!* Dornbirn, H. Mayer, 1948.

Wright, John J., *National Patriotism in Papal Teachings*. Westminster, Newman, 1943.

Evidence that the aspects of the Catholic value system which could have led to widespread German Catholic conscientious objection to Hitler's wars were known and had been widely discussed in German Catholic intellectual circles before the advent of Hitler may be found in such publications as *Vom Frohen Leben,* the monthly magazine published by the *Grossdeutschen Volksgemeinschaft,* and *Friedenskämpfer,* the official journal of the *Friedensbund deutscher Katholiken*. It should be unnecessary to add that both publications were suppressed as soon as Hitler came to power; however, their closing issues contain lively discussions of the pacifist implications of the Catholic morality of war.

*Part 2*

The remaining references constitute a mere sampling of the already extensive and still growing body of literature dealing with the Nazi period in Germany. Some are general histories of the regime and the resistance movements it called forth. Others deal more specifically with the relationships that obtained between the Catholic Church in Germany and the Nazi state. At the present writing, there is a lively series of somewhat controversial exchanges appearing in Germany dealing with such topics as the sudden change on the part of the German Catholic hierarchy from opposition to the Hitler movement to loyal recognition of the Hitler regime; the reasons for and the effects of the Concordat concluded between the Vatican and the Third Reich; the series of policy decisions that led to the end of the Catholic Centre Party; and so on. Included, too, are some references dealing with the sharp controversy stirred by the present writer's earlier paper dealing with the support given by the German Catholic press to Hitler's war effort.

A note of warning must be struck at the very beginning, however. Some of the references listed here have recently been exposed as unreliable in that their authors have actually doctored or distorted the texts of the documents they purport to present. The article by Hans Müller clearly shows that this caution would apply in particular to Neuhäusler's book, which has come to be regarded as something of a "standard" source relating to the Church's resistance to Hitler. It appears, then, that some of the works published in Germany during the years immediately following World War II may have been consciously prepared to present the religious opposition in a somewhat stronger and certainly more consistent light than was actually the case. It is, of course, impossible to check all the documentation presented in the books and articles listed below; nevertheless, they are included here with the warning that some may fall more into the category of "alibi" literature than into that of reliable scholarly historical studies.

Adolph, Walter, *Im Schatten des Galgens*. Berlin, Morus Verlag, 1953.

———, *Erich Klausener*. Berlin, Morus Verlag, 1955.

Bierbaum, Max, *Nicht Lob, Nicht Furcht: Das Leben des Kardinals von Galen*. Münster, Verlag Regensburg, 1957.

Bischöfliches Ordinariat Berlin, *Dokumente aus dem Kampf der katholischen Kirche im Bistum Berlin gegen den Nationalsozialismus*. Berlin, Morus Verlag, 1946.

Böckenförde, Ernst-Wolfgang, "Der deutsche Katholizismus im

230     German Catholics and Hitler's Wars

Jahre 1933," *Hochland,* Vol. 53 (1960/61). Translation in *Cross Currents,* Vol. XI, No. 3 (Summer 1961), pp. 283-304.

Buchheim, Hans, "Der deutsche Katholizismus im Jahre 1933," *Hochland,* Vol. 53 (1960/61). A rejoinder to the Böckenförde article.

Corsten, Wilhelm, *Kölner Aktenstücke zur Lage der katholischen Kirche, 1933-1945.* Cologne, J. P. Bachem, 1949.

Deuerlein, Ernst, "Zur Vergegenwärtigung der Lage des deutschen Katholizismus, 1933," *Stimmen der Zeit,* Vol. 168 (April- June 1961).

Dulles, Allen W., *Germany's Underground.* New York, Macmillan, 1947.

Erb, Alfons, *Bernard Lichtenberg.* Berlin, Morus Verlag, 1949.

Europäische Publikationen, *Die Vollmacht des Gewissens.* Frankfurt, 1960.

Fitzgibbon, Constantine, *20 July.* New York, Norton, 1956.

Fried, Jakob, *Nationalsozialismus und katholische Kirche in Oesterreich.* Vienna, Wiener Dom Verlag, 1947.

Gallin, Mother Mary, O.S.U., *Ethical and Religious Factors in the German Resistance to Hitler.* Washington, Catholic University of America Press, 1955.

Gollwitzer, Helmut, and others, *Dying We Live,* trans. by Reinhard C. Kuhn. New York, Pantheon, 1956.

Harrigan, William M., "Nazi Germany and the Holy See: The Historical Background of *Mit brennender Sorge,*" *The Catholic Historical Review,* Vol. XLVII, No. 2 (July 1961).

Graef, Hilda C., *The Scholar and the Cross: The Life and Work of Edith Stein.* Westminster, Newman, 1955.

Herbermann, Nanda, *Der Gesegnete Abgrund.* Nuremberg, Glock und Lutz Verlag, n.d.

Herman, Steward W., Jr., *It's Your Souls We Want.* New York, Harper, 1943.

————, *The Rebirth of the German Church.* London, S.C.M. Press, 1946.

Hitler, Adolf, *Mein Kampf.* New York, Reynal & Hitchcock, 1939.

Hofer, Walther, ed., *Der Nationalsozialismus: Dokumente 1933-1945*. Frankfurt, Fischer Bücherei, 1957.

Hofmann, Konrad, *Zeugnis und Kampf des deutschen Episkopats*. Freiburg, Herder, 1946.

Kogon, Eugen, *The Theory and Practice of Hell*, trans. from the German by Heinz Norden. New York, Farrar, Straus, 1950.

Kreuzberg, Heinrich, *Franz Reinisch: Ein Martyrer unserer Zeit*. Limburg, Lahn Verlag, 1953.

Kühn, Heinz, *Blutzeugen des Bistums Berlin*. Berlin, Morus, n.d.

Lenz, Johannes Maria, *Christus in Dachau*. Vienna, Buchversand "Libri Catholici," 1957.

Meinecke, Friedrich, *The German Catastrophe*, trans. by Sidney B. Fay. Cambridge, Harvard University Press, 1950.

Metzger, Max Josef, *Gefangenschaftbriefe*, ed. by H. Bäcker. Meitingen, Kyrios Verlag, 1948.

Morsey, Rudolf, "Die deutsche Zentrumspartei," in Matthias, Erich, and Morsey, Rudolf, eds., *Das Ende der Parteien, 1933*. Düsseldorf, 1960. See also the critical discussion by Leiber, R., S.J., "Reichskonkordat und Ende der Zentrumspartei," *Stimmen der Zeit,* Vol. 167 (1960/61).

Müller, Hans, "Zur Behandlung des Kirchenkampfes in der Nachkriegsliteratur," *Politische Studien,* Vol. 12 (July 1961).

Neuhäusler, Johannes, *Kreuz und Hakenkreuz*. Munich, Verlag Katholische Kirche Bayerns, 1946.

Pechel, Rudolf, *Deutscher Widerstand*. Zürich, Eugen Rentsch Verlag, 1947.

Portmann, Heinrich, *Bischof von Galen Spricht*. Freiburg, Herder, 1946.

Ritter, Gerhard, *Vom Sinne des Todesopfers*. Munich, Franz Hanfstaengel, 1947.

———, *Carl Goerdeler und die deutsche Widerstandsbewegung*. Stuttgart, 1955.

Schneider, Reinhold, *Gedenkwort zum 20. Juli*. Stuttgart, Verlag Gerd Hatje, 1945.

Scholl, Inge, *Six Against Tyranny,* trans. by Cyrus Brooks. London, Transatlantic Arts, 1955.

Shirer, William L., *The Rise and Fall of the Third Reich.* New York, Simon and Schuster, 1959.

Stevenson, Lillian, ed. and trans., *Max Josef Metzger, Priest and Martyr.* New York, Macmillan, 1952.

Strobel, Ferdinand, *Christliche Bewährung.* Olten, Switzerland, Verlag Otto Walter, 1946.

Von Papen, Franz, *Memoirs,* trans. by Brian Connell. New York, Dutton, 1953.

Weissthaner, Josef, *Michael Kardinal Faulhaber, 80 Jahre.* Munich, Katholische Kirche Bayerns, 1949.

Zahn, Gordon C., "The German Catholic Press and Hitler's Wars," *Cross Currents,* Vol X, No. 4 (Fall 1960). See also Altmeyer, Karl A., "Der Episkopat und die katholische Presse im Dritten Reich," *Herder Korrespondenz,* Vol. XIV, No. 8 (May 1960); Altmeyer, "Versagten die deutschen Katholiken im Dritten Reich?" *Deutsches Volksblatt,* Vol. 95 (September 15 and 16, 1960); Zahn (rejoinder) in *Deutsches Volksblatt,* Vol. 95 (November 3, 1960); Altmeyer (rejoinder) in *Deutsches Volksblatt,* Vol. 95 (November 4, 1960).